Praise for Ara Lucia Ashburne's
Reconstruction

"*Reconstruction* is an intensely powerful book, the tale of one woman's spiraling path from traumatic, nearly fatal experiences to a new, stronger and radiantly beautiful self." —*Indie Reader,* Four Stars (out of Five)

"A gripping memoir and an exploration of the human will to survive.... A learning experience for doctors and nurses, as well as an informative lesson for any patient facing a potentially risky procedure. Ara's story is an example of motivation, drive, and stamina emerging when weaker individuals would give up and die. An educated winner at her best has evolved from a lethal situation that could have snuffed out her brilliant mind in its prime."
—*Foreword Review,* Five Stars (out of Five)

"Her struggle to fully heal was nothing short of heroic. At times, Ara's story is so horrific it may seem unbelievable. Yet the medical notations, specific drugs and dosages, and other information she includes more than uphold her veracity.... Astonishing and inspirational." —*Kirkus Review*

"I couldn't put it down... Ara Lucia Ashburne writes about love, anticipation, disappointment, pain, depression, anxiety and abuses. She shares her story in a surprisingly straightforward and insightful way, offering a glimpse into the challenges posed by anxiety, depression and pain. Creative expression and art, in particular, can aid significantly in the healing process. That was certainly the case with Ara, who experimented with different forms of creative expression. Ara risks vulnerability to share her story in the hopes of encouraging others. It's a case in which truth is not only stranger, but stronger than fiction." —Lee Anne White, *Her Own Way*

Reconstruction
First a Body
Then a Life

Ara Lucia Ashburne

with Michael J Ashburne

What does it mean to be beloved?

2/2015

Copyright © 2014 Ara Lucia Ashburne and Michael J Ashburne
Cover art Copyright © 2014 Alan Pollack

ISBN: 1-5033-8364-4
ISBN-13: 978-1-5033-8364-7

All rights reserved. In accordance with the U.S. copyright act of 1976, the scanning, uploading, electronic sharing, or any other form of reproduction of any part of this book without explicit written permission constitutes unlawful piracy and theft of the author's intellectual property. If you would like to use any material from the book for purposes beyond those of review, please contact Reconfig Incorporated, P.O. Box 451, Berrien Springs, MI 49103.
Thank you for your support of the authors' rights.

Names of all medical personnel, businesses, facilities, and corporations have been changed and identifying characteristics removed. Names of certain non-medical individuals have been changed to protect their privacy.

Book design by Ara Lucia Ashburne
www.aralucia.org

Cover Art by Alan Pollack
www.alanpollack.com

Printed in the United States of America.
First Edition
www.reconstructionbook.com

For Ginger,
who always said to me,
"You should write that story down."

Acknowledgments

Ara Lucia wishes to thank

I thank you, Michael. We call each other Friend as a term of endearment. I'm continually learning its meaning. My life is blessed by you.

Devon Erickson, Wendy Werpetinski, Yvonne Danjuma, and Diane Newberg, your friendship has shaped me and your support sustains me.

Drs. Joshua Straus, Jefferey Trunsky, Gregory Dumanian, and Robert Moretti, I want to express my deepest gratitude to you, and also to the support people in your life, professional and personal, who make it possible for you to be so dedicated and to give me such remarkable care.

Orion Danjuma, Michael Madill, Marc Sirinsky, Amanda Leat, Vince Smith, Jenn Meyer, Elizabeth Cross, and Ched Bendson, you are especially dear and all of you have repeatedly encouraged, advised, and cajoled me at critical moments when life's challenges felt bigger than I.

There are people that just plain matter for a number of reasons, because they visited me in the hospital, provided some kind of rescue(s) during a crisis or a recovery, or are a significant part of my life story. Only for the sake of a shorter tome were they edited out of the memoir:

Mary Vinette, Elizabeth McAloon, Laura SandEastman, Anne Engle Cummings, Rudy Bauer, Sharon Bauer, Gwen Hurd, Deborah Hanson, Janet Bridgland, Dick Schwartz, Jim Picard, Doug McGoldrick, June Eaton, Christine Eischen, Jillian D., Josh Harris, Kathleen Kustra, Joe Balesteri, Jason Arends, Tami Miller, Nathan Margoni, Susan Johnston, Peyton Brown, Jamie Murphy, Frank and Carrie Hillis, Jeff Kott and Amanda Kaleta-Kott, G.C. Guard, Doug Chamberlin, Sally Eames, Shiva Rea, Tiamo De Vettori, Karla Donnell-Bragg, Faith Newberg, Linda Gardner Phillips, Susan Cahill, Kristin Terry, Molly Isenberg, Rich Logan, Brian Eaves, Deborah Steinkopf, Charleen Madill, Helene Albert, Lisbeth Riis Cooper, Ken Preston, Thomas Jamroz and

Alexandra Krygowska-Jamroz, Cosette Cole, Mai Vu, Michi Rose, Mari Krebs, Candace Onweller, David Carbonell, David Richards, Holly Morrow, Jerry and Drieka Bloom, Kate Fiello, Enisa Krzic Seric, Lori & Donna, Doug Corella, Joan Ganzevoort, Lawrence Suda, Jennifer Van Winkle, Rebecca Liebman, Judy Deam, Scott Sternaman, Mike Huspen, The Late Pastor Freak of Michigan's Safest Riders, Thunder Allee Cycles, the St. Louis Scooter Club, The Harley Riders from Beaver Dam, and Mesa Luna.

It would be remiss not to acknowledge my gratitude to Michael's parents, the late Jack and Pat Phipps, for their encouragement and support of all my endeavors which was steadfast long before Michael and I were a couple. And last but not least, thank you to my family, whose strength and faith were an assurance that I would endure somehow, someway, eventually.

I've created a separate acknowledgements section specifically with respect to the creation of the book, but since by nature it includes spoilers, I have saved it for the end.

Michael wishes to thank

Ara, my Beloved and my Friend, thank you for finding the courage to stick around, through all the changes of our lives.

There were many times and many reasons I was certain this project would never reach completion. I am relieved and grateful that I was wrong—largely because I have believed, from the beginning, not only that you have so much worth sharing with the world, but a wonderfully unique voice with which to share it.

Author's Note and Trigger Warning

A number of primary documents were incorporated into the narrative of this book. Whenever possible, every effort was made to maintain the original content of these documents. When this was not possible, for whatever reason, the utmost consideration was used in an attempt to preserve the spirit or intention of the original.

Medical Records
Ara's medical records for the period detailed herein filled two three-foot file boxes plus an additional cubic-foot file box. These records comprise physicians' notes, nurses' notes, progress notes, surgery reports, pre- and post-operative reports, and so on, the majority of which were handwritten. Frequently, there was chronological overlap between individuals' notes. Often there were inconsistencies in the way the information was recorded, sometimes in the data as well.

Obviously, the excerpts selected were those deemed most important or salient with regard to the story. Nevertheless, tremendous care was taken to duplicate the chosen records in a way that maintained their authenticity. Occasionally records were chosen where it was unclear who had made the original notation. These appear without attribution.

Emails
While Wendy's emails are presented in their entirety, many of the emails between Kelli and Ara have been abridged. In a few cases, grammar has been corrected (and in one of Wendy's emails, a date was changed by a day) to improve flow of the story, but only when the meaning or tone of the content would not be altered by doing so.

Trigger Warnings
This book contains periodic profanity throughout. Although most scenes of violence occur in a hallucinatory state, there are nevertheless multiple scenes of physical violence. A few scenes contain descriptions of sexual assault and/or depictions of nonconsensual sexual domination and slavery.

Introduction

The IVF hadn't gone well. The brief pregnancy hadn't gone well. And the last 48 hours had gone from bad to unconscious. I didn't know it at the time, in fact I didn't know *anything* at the time, but I was on my way to becoming the kind of patient that the best surgeons in the country want to run away from. The kind of patient doctors put in their special "I never should have done it" file hidden in their private desks. There were only eight patients in the country's top abdominal surgeon's file. I was number eight.

Dr. Townsend strode into the ER lobby and seeing my husband Michael headed straight over with wide eyes. "What is going on?"

"You tell me," Michael replied angrily.

A mask came down over Townsend's face. She was in business mode. She ushered my friend Wendy and Michael through the lobby's double doors to just outside the trauma area. Michael could hear my moans coming from behind a curtain pulled around a gurney. There was a flurry of activity behind the curtain and voices talking to me and to each other. He saw four pairs of feet moving around the gurney's legs.

Dr. Townsend explained that the trauma team had inserted a syringe into my vaginal canal and withdrawn a volume of pus, and that as a result I was being prepped for the operating room. She handed Michael my clothes. They were damp and had been cut in order to get them off. Inexplicably, Michael raised them to his face and took a deep breath. He later told me that he'd never smelled anything like the odor in those clothes before or since.

He said they smelled like death.

Beginnings

It all started so much simpler. Like so many married couples, we decided to have a baby and getting pregnant was a happy, hazy plan for the future. These plans took a sharp turn when Michael developed testicular cancer, and we made the choice to store his sperm. That's when Michael's dream of conceiving a child together collided with my age, which in turn caused us to ricochet off our neat plans of financial preparations into the high pressure world of *In Vitro* Fertilization (IVF).

The "Fertility Through *In Vitro* Fertilization" community message board had become my haven, an underground source for truth, my lifeline. We followed each other's protocols, predictions, wisdom, and research. Those who had been through many rounds and the ones who had successfully had children through IVF were considered the wise ones. The women who were trying to conceive (shortened on the board to TTC) were under intense stress and pressure, living with constant anxiety that they might never finally hear they were pregnant. The strain was so great that the experienced travelers, once successful in carrying a child to term, were inevitably asked to leave the IVF board. The perception was that these experienced women would no longer be able to fully identify with the agony the women TTC were in—even though these women had often spent years TTC themselves. It was a tortured and high-drama world, where everyone constantly analyzed and reanalyzed bits of medical data, making calculations and predictions. The board was like Wall Street for the stock market of the body, and everyone was a big investor. Some gambled thousands, some mortgaged homes, only to get negative results cycle after cycle, losing everything. Others won, scoring twins or triplets or more.

I was guarded on the forum. Since the beginning of my web use, I've understood that words I post are public and forever. Even statements believed to have been made "in private" can later be copied and reprinted by others.

I'm careful—very careful—about what I say on the internet. I was also aware that my experience wasn't wholly my own, but an experience I shared with my husband, Michael, and when I posted, I tried to be respectful of him, his thoughts, his experience. Many women used it as a place to rant about their husbands, but I never posted anything I wouldn't want Michael to see.

The most difficult aspect of my experience—what I couldn't write about on the board, what set me apart—was that I hadn't spent my whole life dreaming of being a mother. Likewise, my "maternal clock" had not kicked into overdrive. I didn't have a passion for motherhood. I wasn't even so sure about the word *mother* all by itself. I only wanted to do this, to have a baby *with Michael*, as an expression of our relationship. I wanted to be PARENTS, with an emphasis on the plural. We were going to do this TOGETHER. It was something I was up for only because of him. He inspired it.

We had been friends for over seven years the night the fates took over our friendship, and, for the first time, each of us thought, "Oh my, what about 'us?' You and me, could we be something more?" There was no turning back from that place. Whether we went through with it and became a couple or not, the innocence of being only friends was over.

At the time, I was living in the Bay Area and my marriage had recently ended. I'd heard about a bar in the Marina District where a high percentage of architects and designers hung out, and it was my intention to make that bar my new haunt. I made a list of ten qualities the next person in my life would have, and the list wound up being a balance of creative and technical skills. My previous relationship had lasted seven years, so I hadn't been on the singles' dating scene for some time. I planned to share my list with all of my friends so they could help out.

I was a dance major at Mills College back then, and it was the Wednesday night before Thanksgiving break. My two guy buddies and I were at my new bar having a few beers, and they were teaching me to play pool. I was grilling them on what guys like, and all their answers were a split decision—useless. When I got home I figured I would call my old friend Michael, so he could serve as a tie-breaker. Three time zones east made it late for him, about 1:00 a.m., but I wanted to hear what he would say. I explained my situation to him, and he seemed game, despite the late hour, so I began the inquisition. Many of my questions were about dating in general, but some felt a little weird to ask, such as, "What do guys like in bed?" Like I said, it had been a long time.

This wasn't the first time Michael and I had talked about issues like these. When our friendship started he was only 17, while I was 21. I gave him hours and hours of dating advice and very specific advice about kissing chicks. Now, seven years later, the tables were turned. While he had sought information very plainly, most of my questions were couched in a new vulnerability or uncertainty about being myself and being available. I suppose this insecurity may have contributed to clouding my memory, as I cannot recall a single specific question to this day. All I remember is the nature of his answers. Each one had the same format:

"Well, *most guys* blah-blah-blah, but *I* exactly-what-you-want-to-hear."

This went on long enough that I became uncomfortable, so I decided to change my approach, make it less direct and more playful, something easy, something safe.

"I've made a list of attributes for the next person in my life. I want to read it to you, so you can keep an eye out for me."

"But I live in South Bend, Indiana, and I'm moving to Chicago. How is that going to help you?"

"You never know, people move. Just listen."

Now, dear reader, I so wish I still had a copy of this list. I could make it up, because it wouldn't be too hard, but what is more important is what was happening as I read it. I read the first item on my list and paused briefly. Neither of us said anything, but in that silent space I noted Michael had that attribute.

Item Number two. Pause. *Huh, Michael has that one too.*

Number three. *Yep.*

Number four. *Check.*

Number five. *Oh, shit. Should I start making stuff up that isn't about him?* But I'd had two beers, and for me, on the Starving Student Dancer Diet, that was enough to get fairly drunk, so I couldn't think fast.

I decided to read on, figuring, *The whole list can't be like this. It must be a coincidence, right?*

Number six. *Check again. I better stop, he might think I'm trying to say something to him that I'm not trying to say.*

Looking for a quick way out, I said, "Well, anyway, you get the idea."

"No, I want to hear the rest of this list."

"It pretty much goes on like that." *Oh my God, that isn't helping my case. Why did I say that?*

"No, seriously, why won't you read it to me? I want to hear the rest of the list."

"Okay fine." I read the remainder quickly.

Seven, *Check*. Eight, *Check*.

Nine—*No Check! Oh, thank God, at least there was* one.

Ten, *Check*.

Fuck.

"Hm," he said. "That's interesting, considering what I realize now has been my own history."

"What does that mean?"

"Never mind. I'd rather not say."

"Oh, come on, I read you my list."

"I guess if we were drunk or high or something we could talk about it."

"I'm drunk," I replied. *What? Why did I say that? He gave me a way out and I blew it! You have got to be kidding me!*

"Okay, well, it's just that, when I look back over my dating and girlfriend history, such as it is, I mostly decided whether or not I would see someone based on how they compared to you. Like, you know, you were the yardstick I've been using, unconsciously, my whole life, to measure a partner for myself."

"Huh."

"Because, you know, you, uh, you were never available. Up to now."

We spent the next few hours analyzing our personal relationship and life desires and goals. After five hours on the telephone our seven-year friendship had crossed over into a committed relationship. Only a few things were unknown. I had to live in a city and he didn't want to live on either coast, so we agreed we would live in Chicago.

"What about kids?" he asked.

I wasn't interested, but was open to it.

Later that day he called me to tell me he'd had this flash, a vision of a sort. He pictured us in a kitchen. I was crouched down with two little ones, bundling them up to go out and play in the snow. Then I look up to see him standing there, and we give each other a knowing glance.

That was it: the knowing glance. It signified for both of us our deep understanding, the beauty and expression of the Venn Diagram he and I would make as parents, the parts that we would share, what he would contribute that I could not and what I could contribute that he could not. He would be the stay-at-home dad/musician, I would be the working-professional-mom. I couldn't believe it. I always said I could date anyone, boy or girl, so long as they weren't a red head. Now I was in love with one.

In only a few months we were both living in Chicago.

We knew we were going to get married sooner or later, but sooner came, well, even sooner than we expected. I was working at a job with health benefits. Michael found himself out of work during the summer of 1994 and was about to lose his own health insurance. Michael, always one to play things safe, was concerned about becoming uninsured and knew all of the potential pitfalls that brought. One day he called me at work in a panic, saying, "I'm going to be losing my health insurance here at work. We are going to have to get married by the end of the year."

That was it. It wasn't like the romance was gone from our relationship at that point, it was just a matter-of-fact situation for him.

Every woman's fantasy marriage proposal.

That night we met at a coffee shop called Urbis Orbis in the Wicker Park neighborhood to talk about the ceremony and to consider dates. Michael couldn't handle a large number of people and the anxiety around planning such an event, so we decided to elope. We had a ceremony with witnesses, but no guests. We were married at The Eclipse Theatre in Chicago, back when they had their original space in Bucktown which was two blocks from where we lived. We had seen our first play together there, *Exit the King*, by Jean Cocteau. We lit the space with 150 votive candles and then sent them as belated Christmas presents to the guests we would have invited if we'd had a full-scale affair. It was perfect for us.

* * *

Kids remained an abstraction. I wasn't yearning for them, only for more of what Michael and I could create together. This made me the odd duck on the IVF board. *In vitro* fertilization is often the last stop after years of other less expensive or invasive treatments, which means the majority of women in this situation have already been through a lot and emotions and investments are running hot.

There were several women whose presence on the board touched me. Becca had been around the block the most times and was the most grounded. She was the den mother of the bunch, and she had eventually succeeded in having twins from IVF after several failed rounds. She was eventually ousted by the board, which I thought was nuts because I believed the group needed her to keep everyone's anxieties from dragging them into total despair. Her grounded nature helped her advise the overly optimistic (which included me during my first round) as well as guide women through eternally dark and anguished times when yet another cycle failed. She was both respectful and tender.

In the end, I was there for the same reason as everyone else. I had to go through IVF to get pregnant. I needed information and support and was eager to share whatever information I had and to support others going through the process. It was important to me to be respectful of the journeys of the other women on the board. I tried as much as possible to keep my lack of passion for motherhood to myself.

When I first got to the board, I was certain Michael and I would conceive in the first round. Of course, the doctors couldn't guarantee this, but we weren't there because of a typical fertility issue. There was nothing wrong with my eggs and nothing wrong with his sperm, except that it was frozen.

About a year before, Michael and I were packing to go to my brother John's wedding. It was a Friday evening and a particularly hot one. We were trying to pack lightly. Michael was walking around in his boxer shorts. He said to me, in his typical blunt fashion, "I think I feel something in my nut."

"You what?"

"I think I feel something, something hard, in my nut. Like a combat boot crammed into a pillowcase."

We both knew what this most likely meant: cancer. With the weekend upon us, even if it was a significantly-sized lump, we could go to an ER, but to what end? He wouldn't be able to get in to see anyone who could say or do something about it until Monday, so we agreed to wait. This made the weekend a bit weird.

We didn't tell anybody, so as to not distract from my brother's wedding, but Michael and I were certainly distracted ourselves. All weekend, we kept exchanging fitful glances and not saying anything. I don't know what was going through his head, but all I could think was, *"Our lives haven't even started yet. If you fucking die on me, I'm gonna kill you."* Or, *"I'm gonna find a way to come to the other side of death and do something mean to you."* Or *"OMG, if you are gonna die—we are gonna have to figure out how to save you, because hey, I just landed you, and I want to do this life thing with you now!"* Or *"This can't be happening!"* Or *"What the hell?"*

On Monday we got in to see Michael's internist, who then called in a favor to get us an appointment with a urologist a couple of hours later. An ultrasound was performed promptly, and the urologist told us what we already knew. "There is a mass in there. Whatever it is, we need to get it out."

"If it is cancer, surgery is sufficient in 99% of the cases, but we recommend a round of radiation afterward to be certain you don't have a recurrence. We need to do this immediately, but considering you are so young, we'll give you a couple of weeks to bank sperm, just in case. Your parts should still work to have sex, but you'll have to go through IVF to get pregnant. They've gotten quite good at it now. If you have healthy sperm and you have healthy eggs, the IVF process should be easy for you two."

So, Michael banked sperm before the surgery, heading to a hospital on the south side of Chicago every few days for a little over a week. After each sample was processed, he would receive the data about motility, viability, and so on. And while his first sample was good, each subsequent one returned poorer results than the last. Something was definitely going on down there.

The surgery was successful and easy, and the lump did turn out to be cancer. Unfortunately, the radiation knocked him out. He spent the better part of a month lying on the couch. He was exhausted all of the time and sick to his stomach, so he had very little to no appetite. The few times he felt like eating, all he wanted was what I called the White Foods, things like instant white rice and instant mashed potatoes. Needless to say, he lost weight. As grim and depressing as that time was, we knew his cancer had been eradicated. We believed the hurdle to be behind us.

Not long afterward, we sought out an IVF professional so we would know what we might be in for when the time came for baby-making. The chosen ones are frequently talked about on the board. They're experts; their statistics and their failures are known. Oddly, there was no one else in the Chicago area on the forum, so all the information was about professionals on the coasts. I would have to be in the vanguard for the Midwest, but with the other TTC women as my guide. I did extensive research and determined the Chicago expert was Dr. Matthew Kesson, a reproductive endocrinologist.

When we first met Dr. Kesson in his office I was a bit taken aback. His Armani suit, French cuffs, cocky manner, and excessively familiar charm—delivered with a British accent—plus all the data about the *in vitro* fertilization process, was a lot to take in. This doctor seemed to enjoy the power he had, power to change the lives of desperate people who only wanted one thing: a child. But I was not one of those women. Instead of making me feel like he could solve all my troubles, answer all my prayers, his demeanor seemed odd and disturbing.

Still, he did confirm what the urologist had said. "This will be easy. Ara, you don't have any fertility issues, only Michael's frozen sperm. I think it will be one, two rounds tops."

I was surprised to hear a doctor make a proclamation like that, since they seem to wrap every possibility in different versions of "maybe," because they are both respecting science (which can't be guaranteed) and protecting themselves from expensive lawsuits. So, I figured, if Dr. Kesson said this, he must be sure.

We explained that we wanted to wait. He said he understood, but warned us that there was a cut-off. Once I hit 35, what was termed Advanced Maternal Age, all the stats take a major downturn. It would be harder to get pregnant, with lower egg production and reduced quality of the eggs leading to a significantly increased likelihood of birth defects. We understood, and we assured him that he would see us by the time I was 35 at the latest. This would give us two years to get our lives together.

*

Our life was complicated, as it had a way of being. We were on the right track, but things were taking longer than we had expected to fall into place when the Advanced Maternal Age deadline arrived. Shortly after we married, a whole cascade of unfortunate events began. In hindsight, we refer to this period of our lives simply as when Everything Bad Happened.

Just a couple years before Michael's cancer diagnosis, both of his parents died within ten months of each other. Michael, an only child with no other close family, had no one besides me to help him process the experience, to assist in the final details of their death and sorting out of their estate, or to determine what should become of all his parents' possessions. His parents had moved to Tennessee. After months of struggling down there, it didn't make sense for Michael to stay any longer, going through their entire house *alone*. So he brought all the contents back to Chicago, and we put them in storage. We figured we could go through them over time as we tried to move on with our lives.

We used resources Michael inherited from his parents to buy a typical Chicago three-flat in February of 1998. It was a three-story building in the Roscoe Village neighborhood, with two residential levels and a first floor zoned for business use. We moved into the top floor and rented out the second floor. It was the following summer when Michael felt something hard in his nut.

I was in a low-residency graduate school program, completing a degree in psychology and spirituality through Vermont College. As a resident of Illinois, I was able to provide counseling services under the supervision of a licensed psychologist. Since the building we owned had a commercial space in it, I started my private practice there. Michael was in a band and learning web design. We weren't on our feet financially, but were on the right track—things were taking longer than we had expected to fall into place, but we figured, since my practice was growing at a steady rate, we would be okay. Then, Advanced Maternal Age arrived. I was 35, our agreed upon deadline. So, we made another appointment with Dr. Kesson to tell him we were in for baby-making.

As it turned out, it wasn't so easy for us to get pregnant after all. I was warned by Becca, the elder on the board, not to get my hopes up. I didn't listen. *After all*, I thought, *she's used to people with actual fertility issues. We were different! We didn't have a fertility issue, we only had frozen sperm. Everything else was fine!*

There was so much, though, that I didn't know. I hadn't counted on enduring the episodes of dehumanizing treatment at the clinic or Michael giving me shots for weeks on end. I had daily ultrasounds for however long was required. It was one thing to understand the process intellectually and quite another to actually go through it. Still, all the while, I had the support of the women on the board. We became invested in each others' lives. I knew their histories, what support they did and didn't have from family members and friends. We all read each other's updates of the dramatic roller coaster rides, the minutiae of the journeys we were all braving in order to cross over into parenthood.

Michael and I decided early on that if we were going to be making new life through this scientific process (even before we knew that we would be subjected to a hideous, systematized, dehumanizing industry) that we would have to figure out a way to create our own intimacy and weave in our own sacredness. The first major procedure in IVF is the retrieval—the egg extraction. To celebrate, we made love the night before as a way to put our energetic intention out into the world. Then we hovered for days, waiting for word on the embryo development progress. The lab provides nutrients and enzymes after the eggs are fertilized and watches the resulting embryos' cell division progress very closely. It selects the more robust specimens for the next procedure, the transfer to the patient's uterus. So, in a way, the embryos determine what day we would have the transfer. The embryos are placed in the uterus, and you wait to see if they catch.

We created an altar of a sort on the sidebar in our home. I had asked our closest friends and my two sisters to each send us an object to place upon it. At the end of a session with my therapist, she had given me an abandoned bird's nest; it was in the center. Michael had put two plastic Easter eggs in the nest, one yellow and one orange. The objects came streaming in: a stone, a piece of crystal, a cross, a St. Christopher medal... my sister Melissa made an elaborate collage postcard of all the activities that we might share with our child. There were others.

We were buoyant during the first round, because we believed it was going to be easy. All the doctors said so. It was exciting. They retrieved twelve eggs and ten of them fertilized, a super-high fertilization rate of 83% (doctors are happy with fifty percent). Then we waited a few days for the "embies," as they are affectionately called, to grow in the lab. At this time, most doctors transfer after three days, but if they think they can push it to five days in the lab without compromising them, the embies have an even higher rate of taking. We transferred three embryos after three days.

Then we were in the process the women on the board called the Waiting Room, the period between depositing the embryos and waiting to see if they have found their way into the uterine wall. Everyone is waiting for the "doctor-approved" pregnancy test that comes eleven days after transfer. Some women take home pregnancy tests sooner, despite the fact no one had ever heard of someone getting a positive on a home pregnancy test prior to the more sensitive "beta" tests[*] offered at the doctor's office. They can't bear the suspense and would hope in vain they could get a tiny inkling of a sign.

On the morning of the 11th day post-transfer, we would all go into our respective clinics, and a nurse with no emotion and a fake smile would draw blood. By two in the afternoon, we were allowed to call the clinic and a nurse would give us a number reported by the lab. The lab measures the amount of the beta hCG in the blood in thousandths of International Units[**] per milliliter (mIU/ml). Under 5 mIU/ml is definitely not pregnant; 5 to 25 is unclear; over 25 is pregnant; and over 45 usually means twins.

Our first round was a zero.

We were unlucky. Becca was right: regardless of the reason we were doing IVF, the process was still complicated, and there was no predicting the outcome. We agreed to endure the process again. This time I knew what I was

---

[*] Short for beta human chorionic gonadotropin (hCG), a hormone produced by the embryo.

[**] Just as a frame of reference, 1 International Unit (IU) of hCG is about 6×10^{-8} grams, or 0.00000006 grams. (Canfield RE, Ross GT (1976). "A new reference preparation of human chorionic gonadotropin and its subunits". *Bulletin of the World Health Organization* 54 (4): 463–472. PMC 2366462. PMID 1088359. Retrieved 2012-07-23.)

getting myself into. Again, we were unlucky. I needed the support of the women on the board if I was going to do this a third time.

There were so many different women on the board, young ones, women of advanced maternal age (including two women in their forties), ones with mates that were supportive, ones with mates that were only going along for the ride (it seemed that those marriages didn't usually make it through more than one round of IVF), and one woman who had no mate at all. Many of us were addicted. We spent every available minute there, grasping for a minuscule piece of information that might give us an edge or increase our odds of success. We talked statistics; we kept track of everyone's complex schedules and protocols; and we calculated everything: numbers, wishes, fears, and prayers. Everything added up to a gestalt of hope and terror. These were our daily lives in this online world. Mostly, though, we created a genuine communal gathering. We were huddled together, sharing a rare and horrible experience which could, if one were lucky, bring home the ultimate prize: a child of one's own.

Tracking

The truth was most of the women on the IVF board would not actually get the good news that they were pregnant. This was a fact that we all knew, but we each desperately hoped that sad fate would not come to us. The generally positive tone of the board served to keep everyone from jumping off a cliff. As I quickly learned, even when someone did receive the wonderful news they were pregnant, often after waiting for years and through a second mortgage to hear the good news, the pregnancy could still disappear. Often, it seemed, these women would miscarry within the first few weeks. That wasn't something I had expected or even considered before arriving on the board.

There were many women on the IVF forum, but one of them, Kelli, stood out to me. I felt especially connected to the spiritual outlook she had toward pregnancy. I'd always been very private about my spiritual beliefs, so I hadn't posted any of that on the forum. I had once heard someone say that there are all these spirits waiting to be born, and when the baby takes its first breath, the spirit who has chosen those two parents or this potential trajectory of life will make its way into the infant's body. Although I wasn't attached to this being true per se, I sometimes wondered, *If that were true, which soul would choose Michael and me? Who would want the life we believed we could offer?*

Michael and I jumped into the IVF process determined to beat the plummeting success curve on the graph of Advanced Maternal Age. I was in it because Michael had created a picture of parenting together that made me want to parent with him. Kelli, however, was one of the desperate women on the board: a mother without a child. She and her husband, Andy, had already been through four years of other processes and IVF was their last and final hope to conceive a child. This was the focus of their lives.

I was captivated by her story, but even more by the way she communicated with other members on the board and the way she expressed herself. I felt connected to her. She was ahead of me by a couple weeks, on her third cycle,

Ara Lucia Ashburne

while I was on my second. So, while she was in the Waiting Room, I was in what we called the Stimming Phase prior to retrieval. This is when patients are taking drugs to stimulate the ovarian follicles* to release as many eggs as possible, instead of the usual single egg produced in a woman's natural cycle.

But then it happened. Kelli finally got her good news: she was pregnant. This had happened to her before, but it hadn't held for more than a few weeks, so she was cautious. Everyone on the board was saying over and over "this was the one" and "everything would be okay." She was doing her best to stay positive, but I could tell she didn't believe anyone's encouragement. Soon she was reporting fairly heavy bleeding. Then it stopped. Then it started again. Then stopped. Then started. It was possible this bleeding was part of the pregnancy process, but in her heart she knew she was losing this one too.

Everyone on the board was trying to comfort her, saying, "It's okay, that happens sometimes," but she couldn't be consoled. Based on her comments, it was clear to me she was sobbing uncontrollably. She had been through this before and was convinced the pregnancy was over. I sent her a direct message and asked her if I could call her on the phone. This was beyond the privacy etiquette of the board, but I felt we had a strong connection and she would feel supported rather than encroached upon. She agreed and sent me her number. I called her immediately.

"Oh Kelli, I'm so very, very sorry."

She sobbed—the most deep-down, aching sob. Never in my life had I ever heard the cries of such loss. I knew there would be no soothing her.

"Kelli, I know there is nothing I can do. I thought that maybe you wouldn't want to be alone right now."

"Thank you, Ara. I don't know how I am going to bear this. I can't go on like this. I can't. I don't know what I'm going to do."

Even though she wasn't ready to think about it or talk about it, I knew she would be doing another round. She wasn't ready for adoption or donor eggs or some of the other choices that people make when IVF is exhausted. It takes time to recover from the build-up toward the stages of this high-stakes game, and when the answer comes before the pregnancy test, the pain lasts longer.

My intuition proved true. Kelli and her husband, Andy, decided to do another round of IVF. It would be their fourth. A month later, we were tallying dates and realized that after waiting out the required down month, she and I would be cycling at the same time—most likely only a few days off from each other. This was rare on the board, and we were thrilled.

*   *   *

---

* The functional structure of the ovary, which contains an egg cell as well as cells that release supportive hormones during the ovulatory cycle and pregnancy.

Tuesday, 8/1/00 9:41PM
To: Kelli
From: Ara

Kelli!!!!

I am cycling with you this time girlfriend!!! I'm on Day 2 of my period and will be on BCPs* starting Thursday! I will be on leuprolide** for 7-10 days. Remember that I'm the slowest stimmer ever, with the stim part of the cycle taking me to the absolute cut-off (14 days) in both of my previous rounds...

Today, I found the sacred object I want to send to you and I will do so by the end of the week.

We are on sister!
So much love,
On the journey,
Beside you,
Ara

Friday, 8/04/00 6:03PM
To: Kelli
From: Ara

This whole baby situation is so very weird because I don't have a huge deep longing to be a mom. My life is quite full right now. It is only because of my wanting to do this *with* Michael and his desire to have a biological child. I don't feel like this makes me any less compassionate about you or your full desire to have a family, but at this point with us cycling at the same time and with neither of us being on the board anymore, I worry about you feeling fully supported by me, from this not very normal for IVF place.

Thursday, 8/10/00 3:13PM
To: Kelli
From: Ara

...On Sunday evening we are going to Michigan to hang out on my Dad's sailboat for two nights and a day. Michael spent a month

---

* Birth control pills.

** Synthetic analog for a naturally-occurring hormone produced in the brain, with numerous medicinal applications for both men and women. Here, it is used to suppress the signal that triggers ovulation, so follicles develop without releasing their eggs. This increases the number of eggs which can be collected for fertilization.

every summer on his parent's boat as a kid, so he has been eager to have the chance to relive it, so to speak. We also had a boat growing up and the boat is docked almost exactly where my Dad's boat was when I was a kid. I loved the rocking of the boat at night, the smells, and the sounds of the clanking hardware on the other boats. I expect it to be a peaceful respite from all the stress of commuting out of state to school, building my psychotherapy practice and the craziness that we are getting ready to embark on with this third IVF cycle.

```
Monday, 8/14/00 5:38PM
To:     Kelli
From:   Ara
```

I received your precious gift today as well. I put it on the altar along with the card beside a duplicate of the pen that I sent you. Today I put the water image up. The reaching cherub you sent is placed right in front of the water image.

```
Tuesday, 8/15/00 12:19AM
To:     Ara
From:   Kelli
```

Well, two hours after I pick up the medroxyprogesterone* and take the 1st pill, my stubborn period shows up! So girlfriend, here we go -- IVF #3 FOR US BOTH! This happens to me every time just when I give up on it showing, there she is.

```
Tuesday, 8/15/00 2:12PM
To:     Ara
From:   Kelli
```

I spoke to my nurse coordinator this morning and we have me set-up with a tentative schedule for my cycle. I go in next Tuesday 8/22 for a saline sono** to check uterine lining and my pre-leuprolide sono. Start leuprolide 8/24, baseline sono 8/31 and start urofollitropin† 9/2.

---

* Used to decrease the chance of developing ovarian cysts while on leuprolide. Though the cysts are not dangerous they may delay the start of the stimulation phase of one's IVF cycle.

** Sonogram.

† Purified form of human follicle-stimulating hormone, used, as one might guess, to stimulate growth of the follicles.

My expected egg aspiration is Tuesday 9/12 which would have me doing a beta test 9/26th!

I am out of here soon to run errands and have some time to sit and journal. I have my workout clothes on and I will make a stop at the gym while I am out. But I am also finding I enjoy my evening walks so will do that later as well.

How are you?????

In the middle of jockeying the various stages of daily shots and ultrasounds followed by surgical procedures and excruciating waiting, I began my private therapy practice. I had six regular clients and an occasional one referred to me by Dr. Richard Schwartz, whom I saw whenever Dr. Schwartz was out of town. Dick, as he told us to call him, was the author of *Internal Family Systems Therapy* and the creator of that psycho-therapeutic model. I sought him out when I was trying to determine which graduate program I should attend so I could begin working with the model.

It was an inspiring experience for me to work with clients and witness their lives shifting, changing, and transforming to become more aligned with their purpose. I would climb the three floors to our apartment from my ground-floor office beaming. Entering the apartment I'd see Michael at the computer or the electronic music sampler, and every single time I shouted, "I LOVE MY JOB!" And he would laugh and shake his head.

We felt good. Things were moving forward.

```
Wednesday, 8/16/00 8:07PM
To:    Ara
From:  Kelli
```

...When you and I get pregnant (and we WILL get pregnant my dear friend) we are going to walk around for weeks not believing it. When you go through such struggles to manifest your dreams and they arrive -- ahhh! But you have worked so hard Ara to not only vision your career path, but have put so much heart into it -- I can feel that all these miles away. You care about making a difference in your clients' lives. I was in the healing/medical field for ten years and sadly not everyone who is in the field really cares about the well-being of their clients/patients.

Friend, I have to share that I am still having a hard time gearing up for this IVF. I started to get this sort of detachment defense after the 1st try. I want this with all my heart. I know that I have to own that desire and be open to the manifestation of my dream. I also know all too well that I have no control over the outcome.... There is where I get stuck -- it is my control issues being brought out BIG TIME. This was the same when Andy and I were first dating, before we had made any commitment to each other. It was very very scary for me. Abandonment is a biggie for me.

We are going to go to our favorite café tonight, sit outside and do writing. Journaling all this angst will help me -- it always does.

Wednesday, 8/16/00 9:37PM
To: Kelli
From: Ara

I understand the attachment/detachment issue and I move back and forth on the balance of the two my own self....

So here we go again. On this wild IVF ride. I always have this subtle hopefulness right after the first meeting with the RE,[*] because there are always some adjustments being made to the protocol that make me feel like we are getting a bit closer, increasing our odds just a little.

Friday, 8/18/00 6:03PM
To: Kelli
From: Ara

...I'm in Michigan and I have to leave here on Sunday as we have to transport Michael's cryo-sperm, from the lab the doctor used for our first two rounds, to the lab in the suburbs our doc is using for our third round. It is going to be very weird to be in the passenger seat with Michael driving and me holding a tank that contains all of his biological material in the whole world ever, period. It is completely surreal.

Friday, 8/18/00 6:46PM
To: Ara
From: Kelli

...Much has happened for me emotionally and spiritually since I wrote earlier, sharing my struggle to gear up emotionally.

I shared my struggle with Andy. I asked him to participate in bringing forth the hope and faith we had when we first started this process. This weekend, my darling husband is going to help

---

[*] *Reproductive Endocrinologist.*

me create a vision board with lots of hopeful affirming thoughts to look at each day we do the injections....

...I wish you were here across from me, sharing a cup of tea, and I could give you a big hug. I am teary thinking of you and cannot wait to meet face to face. I always wanted a sister that I could be this close with. Thank you, thank you God for bringing Ara, my soul sister, to me.

You are loved.

Kelli

Monday, 8/21/00 10:50PM

To: Kelli

From: Ara

...I may be cancelled due to a possible vaginal infection. The blood test showed a borderline indication. This happened once before and the follow-up cervical test came back negative. I am on antibiotics regardless. I won't get the final test results back in time to do a second test to see if it is positive, or rather, to see if the antibiotics cured it. So in one week, I will either still be on -- or bumped to the next round to begin again. Praying God is holding me again this time....

Thursday, 8/24/00 12:15PM

To: Kelli

From: Ara

...Yesterday the nurse called. She was sort of freaked out. In her over 8 years of working there, they have never received cervical culture results in fewer than 6 days, usually a week. In 48 hours they had my NEGATIVE result -- so we are still a go to continue with this cycle -- WHEW!!!!! Between this incident and the crazy occurrence at the pharmacy, where I was the only person whose drugs came in this shipment, I am most certainly feeling protected right now.

We can talk tomorrow about the California visit. All I know right now is that we are leaving Christmas Day and spending most of our time with our friends David and Holly. David is Michael's friend who is more like the brother he never had. Michael and I figured I could fly ahead of him and see you and then he and I would meet in SF.

Ever so much love and blessing for you in this cycle.

Ara

Ara Lucia Ashburne

```
Saturday, 8/26/00 1:04PM
To: Ara
From: Kelli
```
   I predict either the 12th or 13th for egg retrieval. I like the no. 13, so I am hoping for that day....

```
Wednesday, 8/30/00 5:25PM
To:     Kelli
From:   Ara
```
   ...My horse riding lesson went extremely well today! Although we are going to have to see how this goes. I have another lesson next week, but last time once I got to the stim stage with the swollen ovaries and the pounding up and well it was pretty rough. Will have to see how it goes.

```
9/1/00 8:28AM
To:     Kelli
From:   Ara
```
   Kelli, I can't believe how much the leuprolide shots hurt. We are icing the spot and doing everything we are supposed to do. Today we plan to do a short meditation right before to see if we can both calm down. It is really stressful for both of us. Michael doesn't like causing me pain and of course, I don't like being in pain. The whole shot business seriously sucks.

    We had decided when we started IVF that Michael would administer the shots. He had the steadier hand, and his presence calmed me. However, it also meant we would be joined at the hip for the entire process—multiple stages required a series of daily shots.
    The worst phase was the daily leuprolide shots. It was critical that these be given between 4 and 4:45pm. Plus, the injections burned, not only on the way in but for almost a half hour afterward.
    As the days taking the leuprolide wore on, we both found ourselves dreading the four-o'clock hour. Michael hated so to see me hurting; I felt bad because I couldn't suck it up better. I felt as though he was already going the distance making himself available to do the shots, allowing me to live my life as unencumbered by this process as possible. He couldn't take the pain away, but he was infinitely tender and sweet.
    We did the shots in some crazy places. A couple were in parking lots. We

feared we were going to have to explain ourselves to an officer or security guard, "We weren't doing drugs, honest!" Once we had to use a friend's father's bathroom who we had met for the first time minutes before. We did it twice on a moving Amtrak train, on our way to and from one of my graduate school seminars in Louisville, Kentucky. Once we thought we were going to have to do an injection in the cramped bathroom of a commercial airplane. We knew how that was going to look! Luckily, a flight delay allowed us to do it in the "family" bathroom of the airport instead.

During this time, Michael accompanied me to my graduate program's tri-annual conference meetings. It was on the lengthy train trips from Chicago to Louisville that we shared Marcel Proust. I'd gone to see the play *Eleven Rooms of Proust* on my own and was so captured by it that I convinced Michael to go with me to see it again the next night. It captured him, too. Soon after, I bought copies of Proust's books (English translations) to explore first-hand. Michael read passages to me. His glorious, better-than-broadcasting voice reading the delicious prose as we rode the train down to Louisville and back allowed me to transport myself to Victorian Paris and the French countryside. I soaked it up, as I doubted we would have time for this kind of thing once we had a child in our lives. Instead of Proust, Michael would read stories to our forthcoming baby whom we had come to refer to as our "Little Particle."

During my first two cycles, I often read on the IVF board about how often couples fought during the IVF process. Frequently, it was because the unbearable urge to be a mother was one many of the men in the couples could not ever fully understand. Therefore they couldn't appreciate the emotional ramifications of all the highs and lows that come throughout the process of fertility treatments. Often the costs and ongoing disappointment of repeated failures to conceive also put increased strains on marriages relationally and financially. Many didn't make it. Michael and I had our stresses, but they were due to our operating styles being antithetical to one another. They weren't about IVF.

We had only one fight, and it was my fault. Michael was in the middle of band practice, rehearsing with two additional musician friends the group hadn't worked with before. He left the first-floor music studio to come up to our third-floor apartment to give me the shot. He needed to make it a quick one, as everyone was downstairs waiting for him. Their show was in two days. I needed more time to rally to withstand the pain. We had never really done one quickly, and I couldn't pull it together. Then he snapped, "Do you want to do this or not? Because if you don't, we can quit this right now."

He glared and me, and I glared back.

I was stopped cold. He was giving me an out. Did I want it? I thought about why we were doing this. We both knew before all this began I had wanted to adopt. We originally chose this route because Michael had wanted —even felt obligated—to have a biological child, but right there in that moment he was giving me an out. For Michael, going through IVF and having a biological child was all about his parents, Jack and Patty. The truth was, I had been friends with them for the same seven-and-a-half years that I was friends with Michael, before that fated night when we became a couple. For years, I had long talks with Patty over the phone as I moved about the country. In the final months of Jack's life, he and I had forged a genuine father-daughter relationship, so I had become close to him as well. I may not have loved and respected his parents in exactly the same way as he did, but I certainly understood his devotion to them. I knew how truly amazing they were. And I, too, wanted, in some abstract and profound way, for them to live on.

"Give me the shot."

"Are you sure?"

"I'm sure."

I was in. Now it wasn't for him, it was for both of us.

"Let's do this."

*　　*　　*

```
Monday, 9/4/00 2:17PM
To:    Kelli
From:  Ara
```

Well, when I calculated my retrieval it was when I thought I was going to be starting my stims on the 5th, but they actually started me on the 31st. That has me starting the stims two days earlier than the last time and if I have to go the full fourteen days on the stims (and prayerfully don't need more days and get cancelled) then that has me retrieving on the very same day as you, the 13th! We really are cycling together on this one!

How are the stims treating you this time? How many eggs are you hoping for this round?

I'm hanging in there, but I'm definitely starting with the lower back pain part of the process.

Missing you,

Ara

```
Monday, 9/4/00 11:01PM
To:    Ara
From:  Kelli
```

This is too cool that we will likely retrieve on the same day!!!!

Stims are okay. I am hoping for 16-17 eggs. I had 13 the first try and since I'm on a higher level of follitropin, I am greedy and want more, more, more. Andy will go to the final two sonos before retrieval and of course retrieval and embie transfer.

Wednesday, 9/6/00 9:17AM
To: Kelli
From: Ara

My doctor's office just nixed my riding lessons. The last clinic didn't restrict my activity, other than what I felt restricted by during the stim stage because I was uncomfortable, so I'm not happy. Unfortunately my riding is the sanity component of my life and now I'm rendered without it. I'm going to try and work it into an academic blessing with the extra time.

Wednesday, 9/6/00 10:26AM
To: Ara
From: Kelli

Oh, I am so sorry. I know we need all the stress relievers we can get these days!

I am having a hard time even walking at this point, this flare protocol sure has my little ovaries loaded up and I have probably another six days before I get to unload these little guys.

Wednesday, 9/6/00 11:38PM
To: Ara
From: Kelli

I hit the FEAR wall today and my therapist helped a lot with that: it was about living in the past and the future and worrying about both. To cope for the next 3 weeks, I have to stay in the present moment. I do not have enough info this cycle to feel it will not work, so worry is pointless.

9/7/00 2:16PM
To: Kelli
From: Ara

I'm hurting!!! How 'bout you?

How are your sonos looking? Were you able to make your greedy parts happy with some extra eggs?

It looks like I'm running the risk of being cancelled again! It is nerve-wracking. They will not retrieve until the majority are 18-20mm in size and each time it takes me the full 14 days to retrieve to make it just under the wire. It appears as if this time will be no exception. So I will retrieve Wed, if I get to. Are you able to guesstimate your retrieval date yet?

So, how are things coming with the nursery? Our friend Wendy is moving into ours tomorrow. I'm going to be so grateful to have her life force by my physical side.

I met Wendy in the mid-eighties when I was living in East Lansing, Michigan. Over the years she had become one of my closest friends. There is no one in the world like her. She is the most delicious package of intelligence and quick wit, bundled up with an insatiable curiosity about the world and a love for new experiences. Her curiosity gave her a way of listening deeply, and it was really hard to get to bed, because we couldn't stop talking. Wendy was going through a difficult post-relationship, post-career transition in her life, and we had unhesitatingly offered to let her move in with us while she sorted things out.

Thursday, 9/7/00 4:09PM
To: Ara
From: Kelli

Well, things are looking quite good so far. I have a lining of 7.5 which is good, E2 of 752 and approx. 20 little follies in various stages of development. Not bad for being so old, huh?

So now is the juggling game of getting enough little ones up there to make it a good harvest and not overstimming the others. I continue on 2 amps of follitropin today and Friday and return for bloodwork and sono Sat morning. I could retrieve anytime from Monday to Wed next week.

AAAAAHHHH, THE NUMBERS GAME, I am already dreading it. I am off for a nap as I did not sleep well last night. My Alfie dog had a nightmare and woke me up crying and I took forever to fall back to sleep.

Thankful and grateful,
Kelli Bear

Thursday, 9/7/000 7:49 PM

To: Ara

From: Kelli

I feel I will probably retrieve Tuesday. They say anytime between Monday and Wed. Intuitively I feel Tuesday, but I am open to whatever is to be. I am staying on two vials so that should give the little guys enough juice to catch up to the larger batch.

I sure do wish we could be together physically during this time. I would use all my Cancerian Maternal energy to soothe your soul, make you tea. I am holding you close as you walk this difficult part of the hike with me.

Keep the faith.... It is all there is in front of you Ara.

Friday, 9/8/00 11:44PM

To: Kelli

From: Ara

I'm praying for you as your retrieval is so close now. I get Saturday and Sunday off from the sono and the stabbing. I too am incredibly uncomfortable, so much so that I actually rescheduled the workshop I was supposed to teach tomorrow, because there is no way that I can pretend that I'm not in pain.

Muches of love to you and Andy and your baby-making materials.

Ara

Saturday, 9/9/00 2:21PM

To: Ara

From: Kelli

E2 level today was 1495 and there are about 4 follies a little on the small side so we will stim tonight, return to the lab in the a.m. to do one more sono and E2 & progesterone level, and I should get the trigger shot* Sun night. My lining was an 11 which is the best at this stage that I have had.

I am sore and tired, but glad to be getting to the end of this process!

How are you doing? Hanging in I hope, and staying hopeful.

---

* An injection of hCG, which induces the final stage of egg maturation and allows for proper retrieval. Timing this shot during the IVF sequence is crucial. It is administered when eggs have reached a certain size and levels of estradiol (a sex hormone) are greater than 2,000 picograms per milliliter.

Ara Lucia Ashburne

Sunday, 9/10/00 5:02PM
To: Ara
From: Kelli

   Well, we have lift off soon; trigger tonight at 8:30 and Retrieval Tues morning! My estradiol* is 2040 and I have approx 10+ eggs possible. The left ovary is not producing much, no surprise as it has been the victim of surgery 3 times, so there are 3 times the number of adhesions. But Mrs. Right Ovary is a champ and FULL OF EGGIES!
   I am feeling hopeful and good, hope this trend continues.
Love,
Kelli and Eggs

Monday, 9/11/00 3:17PM
To: Kelli
From: Ara

   My experience at the new clinic was too hideous to try and describe written. Michael and I both hate that place. We will definitely go to the first clinic to get the beta, true that it is closer, so we were given that option, but certainly I don't want to deal with the nightmare of the new clinic for results.
   Much love from me to you and all the soon-to-be Embies.

Monday, 9/11/00 7:59PM
To: Ara
From: Kelli

   I am tired and sore in the ovary dept and my breasts are tender too, but also hopeful and full of faith.
   So friend, off I go into the wild blue yonder and then walking up the trail to the Suspension Bridge, I will be waiting for you there with open heart and arms -- and we can wait there together for the final word.

Wednesday, 9/13/00 11:02AM
To: Kelli
From: Ara

---

* Administered to support growth and maintenance of the endometrium (uterine lining), to prepare for the embryo's implantation.

I am going to take the full 5 day bed rest this time. How long are you going to spend in the bed rest phase? Do you go to the beta test by yourself or does Andy go with you?

Our beta will be one day after Michael's father's birthday and 3 days before the anniversary of his death. Michael is always acutely aware of the anniversary of everything, so this certainly won't pass him by. It will be a big one for him.

My investment in this process is escalating which always happens to me at this stage.

Loving you ever so gently from here,

Ara

P.S. I will be huggin' upon you after all this is over regardless of the outcome. Honestly, I can't wait to finally be in the same physical space as you. I cry every time I picture it. I certainly do love you, sister.

Wednesday, 9/13/00 5:39PM
To: Kelli
From: Ara

OH YEAH KELLI! I GOT YOUR VOICE MESSAGE!

THAT IS AWESOME! 7 ROCKS! I am so very happy for you and praying this is the early signs of the one that is going to take you to a delivery date in JUNE!!!!!!!!

If I am able to be conscious on my retrieval day I would like to call you in the evening to tuck you in from your transfer. That is my plan. Let me know if you would rather I didn't, if you would rather hold the sacred space privately.

The clinic called me with my Retrieval time, it will be on Friday at 7:30am. We will have to get up at 3:00am to be there by 6:00am.

I love you and I am sending love to your little incubated embies hanging out in the lab waiting for their clearance to come on home.

Peace be with you.

Ara

*   *   *

I was alone in my office. Michael was in the control room of his music studio. Almost everyone in our lives knew today was the day we would get word from the lab. We had wanted more privacy, but we soon learned it was nearly impossible. Just like people having natural pregnancies, everyone wanted to know when the "due date" was, so to speak. The only way to have more privacy would require immense gyrations—like the manipulations of a high-level addict—because the scheduling demands of the IVF process had made us virtually unavailable for months at a time over the last year. We had to explain to my family and our friends, otherwise they wouldn't understand why we couldn't be present at important events in their lives. We missed weddings, we missed birthdays, we missed memorials. Everybody knew and everybody was waiting for the word.

```
Friday, 9/15/00 4:50PM
To:     Kelli, Diane, Yvonne
From:   Ara
```

　　Hello All My Precious Friends!
　　I had a horribly traumatic experience today at my retrieval. I learned some information about transfer. I am too out of it still from the anesthesia and I'm still processing the implications, so the whole story will have to wait. I don't mean to be a tease, but say a prayer for me, because I'm freaking out right now.
　　Here is my good news. We got more eggs than expected. 10, which is not ideal, but our best yet. So, we are happy with that. I'm scheduled for transfer at 9:30 CST Monday.
　　I'm mostly, but not completely, out of my funk from the anesthesia and my pain is the lowest yet from retrieval, so aside from processing my traumatic experience, I'm my best yet.
　　I want to share about the wonderful concert that we went to last night but can't at this moment....
　　Loving you all, with a special note to Kelli (whose transfer was today). Praying your transfer was smooth and you are well on your way to a new life.
　　Ara

```
Saturday, 9/16/00 12:55AM
To:     Kelli
From:   Ara
```

　　First, I go in for my transfer on Monday. But Kelli, here is the deal about the trauma. I don't know what your clinic says about sex after the bed rest period, but our first clinic said three days. Now, as I'm sure you will understand, we wanted to have sex as close to the transfer as possible, sort of symbolic, "this was the time that we did it and got pregnant." So, as I am sure I told you after both transfers, I felt this buzzing, an energy inside my uterus. Now to be clear, I'm not saying that there is a spirit in there, because quite frankly, I believe that the spirit enters the body at first breath, that is my belief, but that the biologic "life form" has its own energy. I know people might think I was crazy, but I have always had a very high sensitivity/awareness of my body. When I get bodywork or massage and they are working on one part of my body, I can often feel it having an "energetic" shift or impact somewhere else in my body.

So anyway, to get back to what happened at the clinic today. Before the retrieval, Michael had already been removed from the room and the nurse was running over the details about the bed rest and she said that there was to be absolutely no intercourse or masturbation for 10 days, 10 DAYS, KELLI! I questioned her about it, because that is NOT what the first clinic in the city told me. She said that when the body has an orgasm it cuts off the blood supply for a few seconds to the uterus and it could be just long enough to hurt the embryo!

Now here is the mega-freaky part. I never said anything to anyone about this, because I figured everyone would think I was nuts, but BOTH TIMES the day after we had sex I didn't feel the buzzing in my uterus the next day. In hopefulness, I prayed that it had taken hold and somehow I was going to have a different sensation or I was able to perceive the new sensation, but the truth was I was freaked out both times, because I had a nagging fear that we had put an end to the embryo with the sex. But like I said, I kept telling myself I must be making it up, because first of all no one was going to believe me that I could feel the energy of the embryo in my uterus, and secondly, the first clinic had said it was fine to have sex after the third day.

As you can imagine, I am going out of my mind. I'm so upset, I'm dreading telling Michael. There is nothing we can do about the previous two attempts, but, when I tell him what the new clinic says on the subject, he is going to do the math and wonder too, even if I never say anything about the buzzing and then the not-buzzing. So, of course, I can't stop thinking about all of this and I'm horrified. I'm reeling from the sinking feeling that we went through this entire tortuous process twice only to have destroyed the outcome ourselves, but not knowing! But now having this information and maybe this is the missing link, so we can do it differently and "assure" a different result this time!

I love you and I am praying for the twins that you and Andy are holding.

Ara Lucia Ashburne

Saturday, 9/16/00 9:29PM
To: Kelli
From: Ara

   Hey There Embie Holder!
   Wow, I am so pleased to hear about your high-quality embies. I know you would rather be in a situation where you had to figure out what to do if you had more babies than you thought you could handle vs. not being PG so hang in there....
   ...As far as our fertilization results: We had 10 eggs, 9 mature, and thus 9 embies. So we will see where we end up on Monday.
   What are you doing during your bed rest? What movies, books are keeping you afloat?

Sunday, 9/17/00 4:44AM
To: Kelli
From: Ara

   It is 4:30 in the morning. I can't sleep. We went to this workshop earlier today, then I came home and fell asleep and Michael woke me up for my shot. Then I couldn't get back to sleep. I've been thinking about creating a workshop around the concept of Authentic Action, the process of transforming inner impulses into real-world changes in one's life. I've been up making notes.
   It is such an amazing place to be, this place between Retrieval and Transfer. The light at the end of the tunnel.
   Loving you, Andy and your embies too!

Monday, 9/18/00 1:48PM
To: Kelli
From: Ara

   ...The lab tech guy came in and explained all the embie stats to us. We had 8 live embies, but the three top ones were only a 9 cell, a 7 and a 6. He explained that although it certainly is possible at that point to have more cells, he was really impressed with the clarity. Less than 25% fragmentation is considered Grade I and we had 2 embies with less than 5% which he considered exceptional. He rated us at more than a 50% chance of having a singleton, about a 40% of twins and less than a 5% of having triplets if we went ahead and dropped in all three which of course we did. By far our best odds to date on Transfer day,

30

so I guess despite how horrible the process was at this new clinic with the aggressive and rude staff, they do in fact get better results.

So, I'm holding the Three Musketeers presently. Michael read to us from Harry Potter and it was quite delightful. We are finally playing the baby name game again and having a grand time.

I'm loving you and looking forward to belly hugging. My Musketeers are with you Kelli. Let round 3 be our charm!

Love,

Ara

And Threesome

We were having a hard time agreeing on names. We decided if it was a boy Michael would choose the name, and I would only have veto powers if I truly hated the name. The problem was, I truly hated his first choice, Malachi. He was attached to the name since high school. It was a character in the first Kurt Vonnegut book he read. I knew I wasn't going to be able to veto it. I was still working from a short list which included Gabriella, Raphaela, and Quinn. I believed it was dangerous to decide on a name before the child's arrival as one might find out that the name didn't fit. I figured I should still come up with one or two more tomboyish choices and would hang on to my short list and see who showed up.

Tuesday, 9/19/00 11:45AM
To: Kelli
From: Ara

Hello Sis,

How does the view look today? You are ever-present in my thoughts as we wave to one another from parallel bridges.

This morning when I woke up I could feel the light buzzing or humming or energetic activity in my uterus. I really couldn't feel much physically yesterday, I think it was because of the medication.

I was looking on the Internet for an apple cider mill/pumpkin patch that Wendy and Michael and I could go to next month to honor Autumn. I came across the pumpkin festival in Half Moon Bay which I attended back in 1991. Oh, do I love HMB, and I do wish I could go there to get my pumpkin -- Meet you there! ;-)

Again, I am appreciating having you to share my inner workings and "growings" with.

Please tell me how you and your embies and husband are today.

Muches of loveness for you and all,
Ara

Tuesday, 9/19/00 4:57PM
To: Kelli
From: Ara

When we talked today you really sounded like you were in a good spot, spiritually speaking. One week away from beta day. So how does that get handled with you? Will you be alone when you "get the call" from the clinic? How will you tell Andy?

...I'm feeling like I'm in a "God's will" place. I'm having fun and I'm okay at this point with either outcome. This is the first time I have felt that way after transfer. I really am in the state of acceptance. I suspect I will be back into my natural state of attachment soon, maybe even tomorrow, ;) but I'm enjoying this moment where I am just able to trust in All That Is.

Wednesday, 9/20/00 7:39AM
To: Kelli
From: Ara

Good Morning My Precious Cooker-Friend,

Well, I intended to call you last night, but I passed out watching the Olympics. So how early do you get up on the west coast, and how late do you go to bed?

Well, I will be available in my office on your beta test day -- waiting for the word from you.

My uterine signal is louder now, I think that is a good sign. Michael is still way more present with me. I have enjoyed that over the last few months, but especially the last few days.

Back to the books for me. Today I hope to write my first abstract for the week and begin reading the next book; bed rest has of course put me behind schedule.

Wednesday, 9/20/00 12:26PM
To: Kelli
From: Ara

I can never figure out those birth calculators. If we get a positive this time, when are we due?

Wednesday, 9/20/00 12:59PM
To: Kelli
From: Ara

Hey, thanks for the help with the calculations on the phone today. I also read today that 75% of IVF babies come two weeks early, and three weeks early for multiple.

Wednesday, 9/20/00 3:51PM
To: Kelli
From: Ara

I felt my first little twinges in my uterus. I know that, to be accurate, the twinges could be good or bad, but since feeling the buzzing and then nothing later was always bad, I hope that feeling buzzing and then these itsy bitsy twinges are going to mean a positive result. So, here we go, I suspect.

Oddly, Michael, who refuses ever to speculate about anything ever, is talking as if this time it is going to happen. He is kind of freaking me out.

Loving you and all our embies.

Friday, 9/22/00 8:16AM
To: Kelli
From: Ara

I really enjoyed hearing your voice last night. Now I am just waiting for you to call to say, prayerfully, "I'm pregnant!"

I transferred on Monday, so today is only four days post-transfer, but this morning when I woke up my uterus felt tight as a drum.

I was thinking this morning about how, being pregnant now and staying that way would mean that I would be pregnant with both you and my bio-sister Julie, as she still isn't due until January 1st. That certainly would be fun.

Today, your feeling-pregnant friend, Ara

Michael is a bit of a collector. He kept all his toys from childhood. He has action figures that are well-loved from many years of adventuring, games still in their edge-worn boxes, and a very matted and loved Winnie the Pooh. His parents had given it to him for his first Christmas, when he was only a couple of months old. There are pictures of him as a toddler, cuddled up and sleeping with his Pooh bear. He loved the classic Pooh, he was very specific about that, not the Disney Pooh. He had bought hardbound copies of the A.A. Milne books as an adult. We agreed we would have to get a new Pooh for our little one. I was grateful for this decision, as his Pooh had been repaired several times by his mother, and well let's say it certainly was in no condition for passing on. The Particle's Pooh was one of the items we would put in the nursery. I'd started collecting children's books, too.

```
Friday, 9/22/00 3:40PM
To:     Kelli
From:   Ara
```
    Counting down with affection for your day on Tuesday.

    I ordered the classic Pooh that I'm going to give to Michael if we make it (still PG until the end of the next week).

    I'm going to make tea after my meditation in a few moments. And like you did the other day with me, I'm going to "have it with you."

    Prayers and love to your family.

```
Friday, 9/22/00 11:50PM
To:     Kelli
From:   Ara
```
    Kelli!!!!!

    Owwwww! I am really having cramps! Really! I don't get cramps with my period. These are increasing in intensity. I'm not freaking out, because this is different and the word is it is mostly likely a sign that this one has taken. But Geez Louise, they really hurt! I'm not sure I'm going to be able to sleep if this keeps up. Michael talked to them and told them they could do what they needed to do, but if they could do it any quieter, we would really appreciate it. I do adore him.

    Wow, Kelli you are at the point where you can start counting hours instead of days.

    Love, Ara and the "Block Party" in Chicago

```
Saturday, 9/23/00 4:26PM
To:     Kelli
From:   Ara
```

Kelli, I'm losing my mind. I was fine and now quite suddenly I am not. I want to know right now if I am PG or not, and I want to know how many -- NOW, I WANT TO KNOW NOW! I could maybe be more relaxed about it if my body wasn't causing such a ruckus, but it is and I want to know what it is all about. If it is good I want to enjoy it and if it isn't I want to let go of the idea. This is maddening. I have no serenity, none.

Monday, 9/25/00 12:24AM
To: Kelli
From: Ara

I'm glad you called last night. As usual we tend to freak out in sync. It is hard to know if staying positive is sane, staying detached is sane, or being pessimistic is sane. I think the only thing we can do is be honest about where we are at the time. I certainly do hear your fears and they are just. The one thing I do know is that you are on your way to becoming a mother. Hang in there. Andy is with you. I'm with you. You may feel scared and alone in your heart, but we are by your side, holding your hand. You are not alone. You are loved, in your hopefulness, in your dreams, in the true state of the mother that you already are. This process is just what you are going through to bring your baby to you.

Now you only have to get to tomorrow. What time exactly is your blood test?

You are so very close to stepping off the Suspension Bridge into the place of knowing. Prayers that you are stepping off into an incredible, brilliant new land on the other side.

Monday, 9/25/00 7:40AM
To: Kelli
From: Ara

Is there anything I can do to support you and Andy in the final hours? Consider it and let me know.

As for me, my uterus is burning. Last night it was a campfire and this morning it was at least 4 times more burny than when I went to sleep.

I am so with you. Today I held you during my entire morning meditation.

Ara Lucia Ashburne

Wednesday, 9/27/00 6:15PM
To: Kelli
From: Ara

My Dear Kelli,

Since your call, I have of course been thinking of you all day and, to be honest, I can't stop thinking about Jesus -- his prayers to God in the garden, "Please take this cup from me," and asking God, "If there is any way that I could not be in this situation, please, God, take it...."

I'm loving you and feeling the desperation of your situation. I unfortunately don't know when and where your solace from this pain will come or when and how the joy of your baby is coming, but I am praying that you can surrender to God on this one.

I want to continue to be by your side as you travel on this path, but I certainly understand that you may need to seek shelter for awhile.

Know I love you deeply.

Thursday, 9/28/00 1:17PM
To: Ara
From: Kelli

My Dear Ara,

I am overwhelmed right now, I don't know what is next for us. I can't see out of the darkness. I don't know a future where I am not a mother and yet I am so deeply exhausted from the journey that has taken us to this place where still we have no baby. I don't know how long it will take to heal from being struck down again and yet I know that without the healing I can't be open to the path that will bring our baby to us. We knew that this was the last cycle with my eggs, so we know that our next cycle will be with donor eggs, but right now I can't bring myself to even think about it.

But my current pain does not in any way change my connection to you and the journey we are sharing together. I may have to secure myself in a cave during some periods as I move through the coming days and weeks, but I want you to know that you can still reach out to me whatever your outcome is. Nothing can change the soul connection we have, the sisterhood that we have created.

Thursday, 9/28/00 3:29PM
To: Kelli

From: Ara

   Your letter was deeply moving. You have "gone under" each time you have had a negative and I knew with this one being the last one with your eggs, that it was going to be especially difficult. I honestly didn't expect you to surface for another week or two, regardless of my outcome. I would have been worried sick about you, but I would certainly have understood, and still will if you change your mind. I don't want you to be without one of the few people you have felt like you could lean on in this process.

   But, I also know that my desire to be a mother is very different from yours and the women on the IVF or most other infertility "sufferers," and that can or could be crazy-making for you or them. This was, in part, why I didn't participate in the board this third time around. I was being treated like a Buddha freak of sorts or like I'm disinterested, neither of which is accurate. Your spiritual focus allowed us to share in this process in a way that is meaningful for both of us even though our intent about mothering or parenting is different.

   I pray that you will find a way through this horrible mess you have been dealt. I'm so sorry that the things that Andy said when you got the news only made things more difficult, all I can say to that is, this process is a very different journey for the men that are on it and that disconnect hurts us both.

   Each of us are working through our life and the people in it. You are ever so important to me, and I know that this freak twist of fate is likely to put some kinks in both of our styles for awhile, but I know that it will work its way out, because we have a real friendship. Please know that I want to be available to you, as much or as little as works for you.

Friday, 9/29/00 11:45AM
To: Kelli
From: Ara

   As usual, I'm pissed at my doctor's office. As it turns out the suburban clinic works with a different lab. If I had come in before 7:00 then I could have my results[*] by 9:00, but because I didn't get there until 9:00 I won't have them until 3. Instead of apologizing for the misinformation that was given to me when I was there for my transfer, the bitchy nurse actually berated me. And I hadn't given her any attitude, I was trying to understand what was happening. I know they have to deal with a lot of stressed-out, hormonal women, but they need to do something to

---

[*] From the office pregnancy test.

deal with their own stress apparently, because they are constantly going off on me and other people that I see there for honestly no reason whatsoever. So there will be an extended wait time for the hardest wait of them all.

I sat in my office and stared at the clock for twenty minutes, waiting for the second I was allowed to call for results. I knew other women were doing the same. We had the number memorized.

"Your name?"

"Ashburne, Ara Lucia."

"Birth date?"

I answered as mechanically as she asked. I knew I was the only patient with that name, but this was the procedure they used to verify who I was and that they were going to give me my results and not someone else's.

"Please hold."

There was no music. It seemed to take longer than usual. Then it turned out I wasn't actually on hold—I could hear nurses talking in the background, but I couldn't hear what they were saying. It was a casual conversation between them.

I stared at the phone, then looked to my day planner. After all of the abstract debate about whom I would tell first, if it would be my mom or Kelli, now—in the moment—it was clear. Obviously, it would be Michael.

Then, all of a sudden, she said, "You are pregnant."

"What's the number?"*

I knew a minimum number of 5 was needed for pregnancy and anything over 45 could mean twins. It seemed like everyone who went through this process prayed for twins. Most wanted more than one kid, and to be able to land two out of this hellacious process would truly be the pot of gold at the end of the rainbow.

"I can't tell you the number." This was unusual. We were always told our numbers.

"Is it high?"

"No, it's not high. You are going to have to talk to your doctor."

"Is it low?"

"I can't discuss it with you. You need to talk to the scheduler and see your doctor to discuss the number."

"Then it's low. Is there a chance it's a false positive?"

"No, you are pregnant. I'm not saying anything else. You have to discuss this with your doctor."

"Is there a problem with the number?"

---

* The specific number depends on how many days post-transfer the test is performed.

"The doctor said he is comfortable with the number."

"Comfortable?" I thought. *What could that mean? Odd but acceptable, I guess? But still, what else could it mean? That aside, she said I was definitely pregnant.*

So there it is.

I didn't know how I was going to tell Michael, but I knew what I was going to do.

We had created a nursery. My friend Diane and I painted a mural with a big tree and a rabbit. There were a few toys in the room with all the books on a high shelf. I went upstairs to the third floor to the nursery and picked up a child-sized musical instrument, the toddler's keyboard. Then I walked down the three flights of steps to Michael's music studio.

I walked in with a smile. He seemed to be in the middle of something, but it didn't matter to me.

"You're gonna need this," I said, handing him the keyboard.

"Why is that?" he asked.

How could he ask? He knew I had been waiting for the call, so how could this be anything other than my way of telling him the yea or nay? I had figured this would be so much sweeter than blurting out, "I'm pregnant."

He honestly looked confused, so I said, quietly and calmly with a smile, "We're having a baby." He stretched his arms out to me, and I straddled his lap and gave him a hug.

We didn't say anything for a very long time. Neither of us cried or laughed. We silently held each other.

Then he asked the question he so frequently asked when we were done with a meal or an activity: "Now what?"

But this "Now what?" was actually different because I had to tell him something was up with the number. I said that the nurse explained that I was definitely pregnant, but we would need to see Dr. Kesson. He wouldn't be available for two more days, so we would have to wait and see what the issue was.

```
Monday, 10/2/00  9:20AM
To:    Kelli
From:  Ara
```

I want to call you, but it is too early for you. I thought they were going to make us come in for an appointment. It was bad enough having to wait through the whole weekend wondering what the hell was wrong.

So here is the deal. The number is 22. As you know, anything over a 5 is pregnant. So without a doubt I am pregnant, but for 10 days post-transfer, they really expected to have something more like a 40 or 45, or around 100 for twins. So a 22 is suspicious.

It could be what Kesson called a "slow starter." He wanted me to get another beta on the 6th, but I'm going to be in D.C. at my training. So, he actually wants me to go to another hospital down there. He is a little concerned that it will be a different lab, and so he won't be able to compare the data exactly, but we will need to have the number go up considerably by then to be sure that everything is okay.

He told me that with this as a starting number, we have a 50/50 chance that it will make it.

I asked him if he thinks there is something wrong with the baby and he says that if that were the case, the body will usually miscarry, so I don't really have to worry about that. I just have to wait and see. The body will either expel it on its own or the numbers need to go up appropriately.

Now I'm in a real waiting game. And I thought that damn Bridge was bad.

Wednesday, 10/4/00 1:47AM
To: Kelli
From: Ara

I have never for a moment doubted our friendship and I completely understand that you may need to go under for spaces as you go through your grieving process. Please take care of yourself, know that I will be here for you whatever shape that takes, truly.

I don't know much about the donor process, so I can't be much of a technical support, but let me know what I can do to support you as you step on this new road. Songbird on the forum seemed to be very knowledgeable about the process, so she might be a great resource if you are starting to gather the information.

Please give your Alfie-dog a hug for me for being by your side when I can't.

My news may be grim. I haven't yet had a doubled number. I prayed to God that I would never be in my present, iffy situation. I always said that I could deal with a negative result far better than I can deal with a maybe, which is where we are now. Michael and I had a good hard simultaneous cry tonight -- our first ever (we usually take turns). He is in a huge and horrible funk. The current situation is amplifying his anger and self-hate about several aspects of his unfulfilled life.

Reconstruction

As for me, I rescheduled my client for tonight. I want to reschedule the client I have tomorrow, but I don't think they could handle it. I haven't been able to do much in the way of homework for a week and so I cancelled my advisor meeting (I've never done that before) until I can get caught up.

So these are the facts. My first beta on 10 day post was only 22. Day 12 beta at a different hospital (different lab) was 35.8 and my 15 day beta was only 72. I don't have another beta until Friday. I know it is not over. It is either:

- a very slow-starting embie which I'm told is "not uncommon"
- an embie on its way to dying
- an ectopic pregnancy

If this round doesn't bring us a baby, I'm done with IVF, I can't do this again. This is truly torture.

Friday is the next beta. I'm supposed to be on a plane to D.C. for my weekend meditation training. I have no idea if Kesson will recommend that I go or stay, and expect it will depend largely on what the tests say. I'm obviously going to do whatever he says even though my ticket is non-refundable and we have to pay for the training regardless.

Wednesday, 10/4/00 11:11PM
To: Kelli
From: Ara

I wonder how you are at this moment.

I watched my West Wing and it was wonderful.

I'm having medium level cramps. Obviously it either means progress or the end and there is no way to know which. Not ever having had cramps in my life, I don't know what to make of it.

I don't have much focus. I'm okay with clients because that requires intense concentration, but I'm having a hard time studying. I'm sort of hovering without emotion. I'm not optimistic or sad, only waiting.

I may try and read some Harry Potter before bed.

Life is strange.

I don't want you to have to wait any longer for your baby to come to you.

I love you and am grateful for you every day since you entered my life.

Ara Lucia Ashburne

Thursday, 10/5/00 1:24PM
To: Ara
From: Kelli

   This is one of those times where the distance between us DOES feel like a hindrance. I am a person who can support others much better in the flesh. I am a hugger and someone who likes face to face, eye to eye contact.
   I ache for the pain you are going through, as it feels so familiar to me. This limbo crap is the part that makes me CRAZY and I imagine the same for you. Hang in there. If you have no bleeding, signs are good that you are not miscarrying.
   I am starting to be pro-active in my own sorting out of facts and feelings, and of the seeds of planning for the future. I just made an appointment for the 20th for an ob/gyn my shrink has been recommending for months. I'm also going to make a follow-up appt with the Infertility Counselor.
   I am doing a lot of external clearing out today at home, the clutter level has risen again and is affecting my ability to have clarity in my head. I am also sending in the form to request more info be sent on the donors we picked so we can start reading and thinking and praying about this.
   We are going to the travel agency to look at plans for our 2nd honeymoon for the end of December. We are taking off for 2 weeks to an exotic locale to be lovers and friends and reconnect. Please remind me what days you will be here in my neck of the woods to be sure we plan to leave after that time.
   Though I am far away in body, I am there with you in spirit. Email me with any requests you may have that will help today. Glad you are seeing your therapist, this is such a hard time.

Thursday, 10/5/00 5:21PM
To: Kelli
From: Ara

   You are really moving through such a thick transition with the end of this cycle and the beginning of whatever is next for you. My goodness. It is really rough waters. I believe you are doing everything you can do, counseling, relationship building/nourishing, but that doesn't make it easy, it just makes it possible.
   As for the California dates, we arrive on the 15th and depart on the 26th. We have no set plans in there yet, so whatever works for you.

Thursday, 10/5/00 5:21PM
To: Kelli
From: Ara

My body hurts, cramping. I'm fatigued. I'm tired. Yesterday I took two naps. I don't nap! Tomorrow is the test. Now that I know that my odds are fifty/fifty, basically what they were at the beginning, I'm back to my normal self again. I will be invested in either outcome and accepting of either. Again.

Thursday, 10/5/00 9:18PM
To: Kelli
From: Ara

I'm cramping something terrible.

So, I'm in bed. I took acetaminophen and I'm watching the debates which I have loved since I was a teenager. So fun.

I'll be going to DC for my meditation training for psychotherapists with Rudy this weekend. So, I'll see Yvonne (who is also doing the training) and Diane, because we stay at her place. My doctor wants me to get a beta at the local hospital. I'll check in with you when I get back.

Monday, 10/9/00 7:06PM
To: Kelli
From: Ara

I'm sick. Isn't that just dandy. It is almost comical, like cartoon comical, as I'm constantly sneezing and blowing my nose. I'm going to see my regular doctor tomorrow, doubtful he will be able to help me as it might be a cold, but I'm going to see.

You really are pulling it together on all fronts with alone time, journaling, consciousness around food and exercise, and making so many nourishing, but difficult, choices for yourself.

I can only listen or gently encourage you. You call it.

Your California proposal sounds perfect. I would love to get picked up by you at the airport and spend the night. I would also love to go to your church with you. It sounds like a plan to me, but I want you to continue to check in with yourself, and if, at the time, you need it to be shorter or different you just call it. David and Holly are flexible, so they can get me if need be, we can work out whatever.

Michael met me at the airport with the Pooh that I got for him to give to the little Paratrooper. It was very sweet. He also got me a half a dozen of my favorite brand of lip balms, and aloe tissues, and took me to the Thai restaurant we have made a tradition of going to when he picks me up from the airport. So, I ate healthily and heartily.

Tomorrow I go hang out at the doctor's office and pray they can get me in with a doctor before 11, as I have 3 clients tomorrow afternoon.

After that I have to gather myself and focus as I have to write the first draft of my paper for the seminar this weekend. Prayers I can make this happen despite feeling crappy.

I love you ever so hugely, gently, preciously and forever.

Monday, 10/9/00 11:26PM
To: Ara
From: Kelli

I am sooooooo glad that your beta went up so nicely. I have kept you in prayer all weekend. I sent special prayers up while at Unity yesterday. I will continue holding you, Michael and the baby til he/she makes her/his arrival in this world.

I am aware I have not journaled for a week despite all that is going on. So, I am going to make it a routine each morning for 30 minutes to have the journal and pen ready. Getting back to pouring it all out on the page then I can sort it out better.

I started exercising today, a 40-minute walk. The medication I am going to be going on soon will not do all the work, I need to do my part with healthy eating and exercise.

Continuing to be in a place in life to practice setting boundaries. A friend of ours sent an email this weekend full of unsolicited advice, almost to the point of reprimanding me for allowing this IVF process to affect my marriage. Also telling me I should not take this whole baby thing "so seriously" and just move on to adoption! I meditated on the note, knowing it was not meant to be malicious. I wrote back and told her that Andy and I were fine and looking forward to more time together during this break time. That whatever we choose to do next, it was a very personal decision and Andy and I would be making it between the two of us. And that I appreciated her caring for us and her support of our journey.

Give the baby a rub on the tummy for me. Hugs to you and Michael. You did such a good job of being present and yet calm this past weekend. I am proud of you.

Monday, 10/9/00 11:46PM
To: Kelli
From: Ara

    Wow, you handled that friend's issues with your trying to conceive quite gracefully. It is mind-blowing the opinions that people have and their arrogance in sharing. I'm sure we could entertain each other for days with stories. I don't think I've ever mentioned my favorite one.

    A woman called me, who happened to be an M.D. but she practiced more alternative therapies. She was calling me to get a therapy referral for one of her clients. I forgot how it came up. She asked me something personal, I think she asked if I had any children, and I mentioned that I was going through IVF. She didn't ask any questions about why, she launched -- and I mean launched -- into this intense lecture about how women need to relax and do this, that and the other, and they could conceive naturally, but how they jump into these technical processes. There was no way to interrupt her because she was talking so fast and with such intensity, so when she finally stopped, I said

    "Are you finished?"

    She said, "Yes, but --" and she kept going.

    And because my tone was very stern when I said that, she got defensive and started in about resistance and how women were resistant, blah blah blah.

    Then I interrupted her, and said stronger, "Are you finished?"

    Then she said, "Yes."

    "My husband had testicular cancer. His sperm are frozen."

    "Oh my God, I had no idea, I am so sorry, blah blah blah."

    And that is exactly it. They have no idea, but they think they do and they want to tell you all about what they have no idea about. It never ceases to amaze me.

Wednesday, 10/11/00 5:53PM
To: Kelli
From: Ara

    Paratrooper died. Beta dropped from 279 Monday to 240 today. You know what that means. We will be isolating for a couple days and will probably resurface on the weekend.

    I love you and thank God that I have you, a single friend, that has some concept of what all of this process means.

Ara Lucia Ashburne

Wednesday, 10/11/00 7:18PM
To: Ara
From: Kelli

   Bad news.
   I just got in and ran to the computer. I started to cry as soon as I read your subject line.
   I am SO sorry you had to go through this Ara. My heart is breaking for you and Michael. Life is not fair sometimes, you and I are such living proof of that.
   I have no words of solace as there are none. I only have words of support, love and understanding. You let me know what you need as the days go on and I will honor and do all in my power to meet your needs.
   Love you,
   A very sad Kelli Bear

Wednesday, 10/11/00 8:54PM
To: Kelli
From: Ara

   As you know I thought it all ended on Sunday when I had the dropped beta, so we all began grieving. But we were required to take one additional beta, and this one is somewhat higher, so now I'm a little confused. I'm waiting to hear back from the doctor.
   I love you, too! I will be in touch through this process. It is healing to have you, but also to now have Wendy here too. We are able to laugh and cry at the same time. Earlier I was saying IVF is like an expensive raffle ticket, except when they call your number you might not win anything which we found hilarious. Then she said it is more like an expensive scratch off lottery ticket, but you only get to scratch off a little part of each number every few days before you find out if you won anything or not... then we couldn't stop laughing.
   Luckily my client for tonight canceled, but I have four tomorrow.
   The living room is filled with about twenty lit candles. Michael is at therapy. It was already scheduled. Wendy and I are waiting for Indian food to be delivered.
   Living life one moment at a time.

Wednesday, 10/16/00 2:21PM
To: Kelli

From: Ara

My Dear Kelli,

We have been laying low, moping around waiting for my period to start given that, as you know five days ago my beta dropped from 279 to 248. We thought it was over, well apparently it isn't over. Today my beta was 964. Now this isn't as high as it should be at this stage, but I'm told the term is that it isn't "uncommon," believe it or not "not uncommon" is actually a technical term with a definition meaning "not rare" or "it happens sometimes." I'm not kidding, this is what I was told by Dr. Kesson. It can mean that this little guy is taking his sweet time "catching" so to speak.

So all we can do is wait. And I thought waiting on the Bridge was horrible. I couldn't imagine that there could be another waiting that could be oh so much worse. Well, I knew there could be, of course, because I watched your second cycle when it looked like you were miscarrying. The agony you were going through and the way you were handling it was what made me feel so connected to you. It is why I reached out to you. But, I, just like everyone else on the board, never thought it could happen to me. It really is crazy making, because everything, every physical experience could be a positive sign or a negative sign. So there is nothing to look for, nothing to anchor one's self to with regard to reality. There is only prayer and hope and love and our friendship and Michael and Wendy and hanging on to one another rather tightly.

Obviously, I will keep you posted.

Unheard

FOUNDER'S MEDICAL CENTER OF CHICAGO
10/17/00 4:23 p.m.
<u>Emergency Room Visit Synopsis</u>:
Patient Report: "Increased stabbing pain post IVF"
Ultrasound examination, unable to locate pregnancy in uterus (pregnancy 7-8 weeks)
Discharge Orders: Recommend patient contact primary IVF physician in a.m.

Tuesday, 10/17/00 11:04PM
To: Kelli
From: Ara

    Sorry about Michael earlier. He must have been completely out of it to not even tell me you called. As for me, I'm trying to distract myself. I made a huge pot of soup, some of which I shared with our neighbors. I watched dumb tv.

    Again, I'm so proud of you for the steps you are taking to build a whole life. But you have to remember to cut yourself some slack when you can't keep up with even all the good stuff you have on the docket to do.

    Much love to you.

Ara Lucia Ashburne

RIVERBANK HOSPITAL, CHICAGO, IL
10/18/00, 6:25 a.m.
<u>Emergency Room Visit Synopsis</u>:
Patient Report: Sharp left lower quadrant pain starting at 4am. Sharp, constant with intermittent exacerbations. Saw primary IVF doctor last week who told her she had 20% chance of ectopic. Patient claims slow-rising beta-hCG with a lab result of 900 two days ago.
Current beta-hCG: 1406.3 mIU/ml
Ultrasound: Inconclusive

Wednesday, 10/18/00 8:10AM
To: Kelli
From: Ara

This is a quick note. I've been to two different ERs. First to the one associated with our IVF clinic and then to our "home" hospital to get a second opinion. Our home hospital is where Michael and I both have internists and I have my psychiatrist, Segel.

Kelli, it is maddening. We still don't know anything. The stabbing pain is increasing in intensity. I can't imagine this is what a pregnancy is supposed to be like. I've also looked and looked online and I don't see reports about IVF pregnancies being different in this way. I can't help but think something is wrong with the pregnancy, but my doctor says every woman is different and every pregnancy is different, so there is no way to know. I'm praying this is the little guy burrowing in and he finds a good spot and settles in quick, because the pain is wearing me down and I can't see clients or do anything if all of a sudden I get this sharp stabbing pain. It honestly is ridiculous.

So, our IVF doctor made arrangements for us to go back to the ER again and get a direct admission and he is going to come over and talk to me later today. I'm sure they will run another beta and then prayerfully he will have some kind of answer.

Wednesday, 10/18/00 10:54AM
To: Ara
From: Kelli

I had to work some magic to book my trip with Andy and not interrupt our time together, but I did it. We can work out the remainder of the details soon....

Off to walk the dog.
How is your uterus today?

FOUNDER'S MEDICAL CENTER OF CHICAGO
10/18/00, 6:40pm
<u>Emergency Room Synopsis</u>:
Patient Complaint: Sharp pain in lower left quadrant. Increasing throughout day.
Post IVF. Patient approx. 7-8 weeks pregnant.
Ultrasound Examination inconclusive

FOUNDER'S MEDICAL CENTER OF CHICAGO
10/19/00 6:50 am
Admission Report
Patient Complaint: Increased pain in lower left quadrant.
Physician Notes: Consider diagnostic laparoscopy
Meperidine 25-50 mg, plus promethazine, intramuscular 4-6 hours for pain

Thursday, 10/19/00 9:10AM
To: Kelli
From: Ara

 It was the weirdest thing. I was shuttled from the hospital ward over to the private practice building, where the IVF doctors have their clinic. Dr. Kesson had told the ER the night before he wanted to see me in his office in the morning. So they had to transfer me from the hospital to the private offices. The young guy who was pushing my wheelchair seemed like he would rather be sleeping so he could skateboard in the afternoon.
 It was like being at a border crossing. We get to the corridor that connects the hospital from the various clinics and the skater isn't allowed to go any further, apparently. So he looks at Michael and says, "Do you want to take her from here?" I felt like I was being passed off in a bizarre travel drama.
 I had put my street clothes on, because I thought it was going to be freaky enough to be in Kesson's actual office in a wheelchair with an iv. You know, once IVF starts we are only ever at the lab or if one goes back in for a consult to start another round, right? So I figured all those baby-wanting women and

51

couples would be super-horrified to see me there in a wheelchair and with an iv in my arm in the doctor's lobby. I was not the least bit surprised when the nurse escorted me out of the lobby and into an exam room as fast as possible.

It was all routine. Another vaginal ultrasound and they still can't see anything in my uterus. Another blood draw for a beta which we got the call about. My beta had gone up from 1400 yesterday to 1800. This, Kelli, is what is so confusing. It is still going up, but not at the rate it should and still no spotting. All indications are it is one which is slow to take, but it doesn't explain why I am having this ridiculous stabbing pain in this specific spot on my left side.

The plan is to keep me here for today. Give me pain meds, and then take another beta tomorrow. If it goes up then likely more of the same, if it goes down then there is a medication they can give me to expel the pregnancy (rather than a D&C* which, quite frankly, seems pretty icky to have to go through). With the number being so much lower than it is supposed to be, if it drops again, the compound situation would indicate that in fact, something is very wrong with the pregnancy. If this happens, I will have to give up on my solemn vow to endure the pain and I will take the medication to expel the pregnancy despite all we have done to get here.

Thursday, 10/19/00 1:40PM
To: Ara
From: Kelli

I am so so so sorry you are having to go through this. I am praying for you and Michael to know one way or the other soon.

Much love and prayers. Call if you need to. I may be out, but I will keep my cell close at hand.

Thursday, 10/19/00 1:47PM
To: Kelli
From: Ara

I'd never been admitted to a hospital before. It was weird to be in a hospital gown. I've always refused to wear them in the past in a regular doctor's office or in the ER. I wore them for

---

* A surgical abortion, short for *d*ilation and *c*urettage (the latter word stems from the French verb meaning "to scoop").

the actual IVF procedures, but that is it. I deem them dehumanizing.

But, here I am, not at the clinic, but actually in the hospital, in a ward, in a bed, in a hospital gown. Worn down from being up all night and from a week of stress not knowing if this baby of ours was going to stick with us or not. Now, I watch the clock pass its minutes and wait for Dr. Kesson to show up sometime today to talk to me about my situation.

Normally, Dr. Kesson was bold, energetic, and confident, almost to the point of being offensive, but today he entered my hospital room with his head down. He started speaking so quietly my heart sank. I figured he was getting ready to deliver the "all hope is lost" news, but he surprised me. He wanted to have a heart-to-heart.

"Ara," he began, "you and Michael have been through so much to get pregnant. At this point you have completed your third cycle, so you've been through over a year of tests and shots and now you are pregnant. I can't assure you this pregnancy is okay. It might not be, but today's beta is 1800. That's up from 1400. You might have what we call a 'slow starter.' I can't tell you what to do; the decision is up to you. You can have a D&C if you need to put an end to this, with the indeterminate pain. With the number climbing, if it were up to me, I would give yourself one more day, one more day to see what happens. Let's get another beta tomorrow and see what you think then."

"Of course," I replied. "Do you think that the slow number might mean there is a higher probability there is something wrong with the pregnancy?"

"It is possible, but more often at this stage the body would miscarry and that isn't what is happening here."

I nodded, solemnly declaring to myself, I could take the pain. Pain is just pain. If this embryo needed to cause me pain to do whatever it needed, I would take it.

"I know you haven't been able to sleep with this intense pain. Why don't you rest here this afternoon. The floor isn't that busy right now, so you can stay here until the end of the day. I'll have them discharge you around dinner time. Try to rest, okay?"

I nodded, and he squeezed my hand.

Thursday, 10/19/00 6:13PM
To: Ara
From: Kelli

Ara Lucia Ashburne

    I am praying whatever the outcome is for you, that the journey eases up soon. I am here for you. Sending so much love to both you and Michael from afar.

*　　*　　*

FOUNDER'S MEDICAL CENTER OF CHICAGO
Medical Record
10/19/00 10:51pm
ER Attending Physician Note:
- Patient Complaint: Pain Scale 10 out of 10.
- Pain in lower left quadrant.
- Patient's husband indicates had been discharged earlier today.

10/19/00 11:45pm
Patient Admitted

10/20/00 8:30am
Physician Order from Kesson: medications
- Methotrexate 75 mg STAT
- Meperidine 50mg, hydroxyzine 25mg
- Beta-hCG history:
    10/18: 1400
    10/19: 1800
    10/20: 1600
- Patient aware of purpose of medication

Friday, 10/20/00 11:04AM
To: Kelli

From: Ara

We have reached the end of the road. This time the Little Particle has given up. Today the beta dropped significantly, from 1800 yesterday to 1600 today. This, combined with the pain, means my body is trying to miscarry; it hasn't happened yet. Kelli, the stabbing pain is so bad.

I took the medication to end it all. The doctor said it could take 24 to 48 hours. I will have a heavy period and the pain is likely to become even worse. He said it is up to me whether or not I stay here in the hospital or go home, but honestly if the pain is going to be even worse, it seems crazy to go home. And that is saying a lot, because being here is unpleasant in every conceivable way for both Michael and me. But if I'm definitely going to be worse than what I've already experienced, then I'm definitely going to need pain meds.

Michael is being the most dear. Neither of us has had any sleep now in five days and yet he keeps running to get take-out or go home to get anything he can dream up that he thinks might possibly make me more comfortable. We keep coming into the ER hoping for some kind of answer and each time thinking we are going home, but twice now, I've been admitted. We hadn't planned on hanging out in a hospital room for two days, waiting for the most horrible period of my life.

Friday, 10/20/00 3:40PM
To: Ara
From: Kelli

Oh, Ara. I so wish I could be with you. Sometimes this physical distance hurts. Please know I love you and I am here for you in any way that would feel supportive. I understand if you need some time or if you want to talk, either way.

I am glad you and Michael are able to connect while all this is going on. So often when IVF couples hit the stressful patches, the stress tears them apart instead of bringing them together. I've noticed, over time, when you two are faced with challenges you always support each other so faithfully and respectfully.

Again, I love you and I am so so so sorry about the deep loss you are feeling right now.

Love, Your Friend,
Kelli

Ara Lucia Ashburne

> 10/21/00 4:00pm
> Assessment:
> - Pain, 7
> - Monitoring for bleeding

Saturday, 10/21/00 4:46PM
To: Ara
From: Kelli

    My appt. at the new ob/gyn was discouraging. He was great, he took 1/2 hour to just talk before the exam, but the news is not great.
    I told Andy I want to start adoption proceedings.
    Was depressed last night, feeling somewhat better today. Andy is being much better about being with me when the depression hits so I do not have to retreat.
    With you still,
    Love,
    Kelli

> 10/22/00 8:00am
> Assessment:
> - Pain, 5
> - Will check beta, if dropping will discharge home
> - Still no bleeding
>
> 10/22/00 9:00am
> Assessment:
> - Beta rising
>   10/19 1806
>   10/20 1651
>   10/21 1768

> 10/22 2135.7
> • Dr. Larson notified

Sunday, 10/22/00 3:50PM
To: Kelli
From: Ara

   Hi Kelli,

   This is Wendy,

   I'm taking dictation for Ara. She is in pretty severe pain, but she wanted to connect with you and give you an update:

   My pain is now even worse. I was writhing and twisting about in the bed in the early morning hours.

   The beta has risen again, so now the only reasonable conclusion is that the pregnancy is ectopic, but they won't know until they go in to actually do the laparoscopy.

   I continued to take the meperidine through the night but it wasn't enough. I've never experienced pain like this in my life. I can't tell you Kelli, it is nuts.

   I felt so badly for Michael having to see me agonizing.

   Now Wendy is back in town, so now she can help with the management of staff, which is more than it should be. Yesterday a nurse came in and asked if I was bleeding and when I said no she said, "Good, because we wouldn't want that!" Obviously, she looked at my chart and saw I was pregnant, but didn't see anything else. Nice, huh?

   Now Michael and I haven't slept for, I don't know, seven days? Hopefully, we will find out it is ectopic. They say the surgery is in and out. I should be able to go home a few hours after. All I have to do after is pee and they will discharge me and then we get some sleep and try to put our lives back together.

   much love,

   ara

*   *   *

Ara Lucia Ashburne

> 10/23/00
> Physician's Note: Brown, M.D.
> - Patient has Bipolar Disorder
> - Was on Lithium.
> - Discontinued during ivf. None now
> - Will follow-up — may be affecting reaction to pain and condition

I was so frustrated and upset, words failed me. They fail me even now.

I was in so much more pain than before the surgery, and that made no sense. It was a different kind of pain than before. Those were the only things I knew for certain, I couldn't get anything to happen. I couldn't get anyone at the hospital to *listen*.

The nurses did the best they could. When I told them I was in terrible pain, they were as responsive as the rules and regulations and hospital hierarchy allowed them to be. I felt as though the nurses believed me when I told them I was in pain, and they did what they could to help me. Most of the time, all they could say was, "I'll tell the doctor."

When the doctors arrived, they asked questions and felt around in my abdomen, but they seemed to think something else was going on. Obviously, I can't know what is in other people's minds. All I know is what the doctors did and said. Things amounted to, "You shouldn't be in this much pain."

It wouldn't be until many years later we would see the medical records that confirmed my suspicions. I now believe the October 23rd report was a red flag and marked a pivotal moment in my fate: the doctors' responses were colored by their take on this information, the fact that I'm bipolar, or whatever bias they may have had about my mental health status.

I don't think it would be overstating things to say this one small note, made by Dr. Brown on the 23rd of October, was one part of a synergy of events, the cascade of which would derail the life Michael and I had built together. Despite the losses we'd already suffered, we had no idea what was about to hit us.

*

Operative Report: ASHBURNE, ARA LUCIA
Operation Date: 10/23/2000

PREOPERATIVE DIAGNOSIS: Left ectopic pregnancy post methotrexate, abdominal pain.

POSTOPERATIVE DIAGNOSIS: Same.

SURGEON: Dr. Susan Brown, M.D.
Assistant: Nadine Townsend, D.O.

OPERATION: Laparoscopic removal of ectopic pregnancy.

FINDINGS: Left ectopic pregnancy approximately 1-2 cm in diameter in the ampullary portion of the left tubule. Removed.

10/23/00 6:15pm

Physician's Order:

- transfer to 7th floor once stable
- Diagnosis states post-operative laparoscopy with left salpingostomy
- Condition stable

10/23/00 9:20pm

Patient Complaint:

- Patient complains of pain with movement
- Patient asking for more pain meds
- Discussed with patient risk of poly-pharmacy narcotics including addiction, plus risk of respiratory distress.
- Patient understands and agrees to use meperidine every four hours overnight as previously described.

10/23/00 11:15pm

Patient Complaint:

- Patient afforded no relief from pain medication
- On call doctor paged.

10/24/00 1:30am

Patient Complaint:
- Patient wants more pain meds
- "Intense abdominal pain, worse than before surgery."
- "Worse than earlier today."
- Tenderness over entire abdomen
- Patient complains of pain, possibly low pain tolerance.
- No evidence of infection.
- Awaiting call from Dr. Brown..
- Will give meperidine 25mg.

10/24/00 6:45am

3rd Year Gyn. Resident Note:

Patient Complaint:
- Patient complaining of "excruciating pain"
- Patient "severe pain with movement or touch" and Patient describes pain "before pain was piercing in a single spot, now it is diffuse and throughout my entire abdomen"
- Patient needs to void before discharge

10/24/00 6:50am

Nursing Note:

Patient Complaint:
- Pain
- Patient unable to urinate
- Offered bed pan; Patient refused, stated she didn't want to move, "didn't think it's a good idea"
- Has not voided tonight

> 10/24/00 9:30am
> Physician's Order:
> - No iv/im pain meds only hydrocodone+APAP 1-2 tabs every 4-6 hours as needed

> 10/24/00 8:10pm
> Attending physician's order:
> - Please give patient pain meds now

> 10/24/00 9:10pm
> Nursing Note:
> - Patient voided, leaking in chair
> - Blanket wet with urine
> - Plan: Notify M.D.
> - Patient voided 10cc in bathroom
> - Patient incontinent

> 10/24/00 2:30pm
> Physician's Notes: Dr. Larson
> Plan:
> - Ambulate; catheter if needed
> - Discontinue meperidine
> - Discontinue hydroxyzine
> - Discontinue hydrocodone+APAP
> - Oxycodone + APAP 1-2 by mouth every 6 hours for pain.

Ara Lucia Ashburne

- DO NOT CHANGE PAIN MEDS
- Clear liquids

10/24/00 4:10pm
- Case discussed with RN
- Still with abdominal pain and inability to void
- Discharge plan is for patient to return home when medically stable

---

10/25/00 6:20am
Nursing Notes:
- Patient doesn't tolerate oxycodone+APAP
- Nausea and vomiting
- Temperature 100.4°F
- Abdomen distended
- Still complains of pain
- No oxycodone+APAP for 2 hours
- Will give acetaminophen (extra strength)

10/25/00 8:05am
- Complains of abdominal post-op pain
- Acetaminophen extra strength — 2 tabs
- Stable

10/25/00 4:30pm
Psychiatry Junior Medical Resident Notes:
- Patient lying on bed, very restless, appears in pain
- Medical history of bipolar disorder

- Lithium discontinued one year ago when patient went for ivf
- Psych evaluation requested by patient to assess psychological component
- Patient's psychiatrist Dr. Segel was contacted on phone by ob resident who prescribed hydromorphone and anxiety med
- After first dose at 2:40 she was able to sleep for half hour, but woke up in pain
- On questioning on why she wanted to see in-house psychiatrist, she said she wanted to make her physicians know that her pain is real," and that "she is not a drug addict" of which she has been accused
- She also said that her pain medicines are being delayed, that "they don't think I could have this much pain after surgery for an ectopic"
- RN notified, who thinks she looks paler than before

Vitals:

Blood pressure: 92/64

Pulse rate: 128

Respiratory rate: 20

- Advised to contact ob senior for further management
- CBC vital charting suggested.
- Discussed with Sr. Clinical Specialist, Lillian Jacobs
- Contacted Emily Ahon, RN for Assessment of Pain Management
- Mental Status exam could not be done at this time due to patient's condition of pain; will re-evaluate in am

---

10/25/00 5:30pm

Clinical Nurse Specialist Note:

Ara Lucia Ashburne

Ms. Jacobs:
- Patient visit related to dissatisfaction with pain control
- Patient is post-op Day 2
- Also with medical history of bipolar disorder
- Patient alert, oriented and reports abdominal pain
- Expresses concern that staff believe her pain is real
- Aware that this level pain is unusual post op according to physicians
- Psych here earlier
- Vital Sign: 98/64, Pulse 130-140, Respiration 20
- Patient not walking related to elevated pain

Recommended pain med change to ketorolac, oxycodone, oxycodone IR, & naproxen and evaluate response over next 12-24 hours

---

10/25/00 5:45pm
Pain meds administered

10/25/00 11:00pm
ISSUE: Pain
- Encourage Ambulation
- Ambulated with sister

10/26/00 6:00am
Nursing Notes:
- No Nausea
- Complains of lower abdomen pain
- Blood pressure 103/68, Pulse 135
- Abdomen distended and tender

Thursday, 10/26/00 11:50AM
To: Kelli
From: Ara

Hi Kelli, it's Michael here taking dictation for Ara:

Kelli, I'm in way too much pain to say much, but I know you are hanging there wondering what is going on. I've been worse since the ectopic surgery. The doctors keep telling me I'm not supposed to be in pain, but when I tell them my pain is worse they either accuse me of being "drug seeking" or hint around that my being off my lithium is making me unable to interpret this agonizing pain. I would think there could maybe be something to what they were saying, maybe, if the pain itself wasn't different than before the surgery. It feels completely different, but they don't seem to care.

They are trying to tell me it must be gas from the surgery or something, but there is no way in hell this kind of pain is gas. It isn't humanly possible. I even demanded a psych evaluation in an attempt to prove I'm not crazy and so they would know the pain is real, but the psych person COULD NOT DO THE EVAL BECAUSE I WAS IN TOO MUCH PAIN! WHAT THE FUCK! SERIOUSLY!

It is clear they want me out of their hair and to go home, but I want to know what is WRONG and I can't get anyone to listen. Oh and the psych person even sent up a pain specialist to monitor the situation, because the doctors were trying to take me OFF pain meds, because of the whole drug addict accusation. Anyway, she at least got me back on pain meds, but this whole situation is insane. We can't seem to get anyone to listen to me no matter what we do. It is maddening.

Love you,
Ara

*   *   *

Over the next four days I have diminished recall of what occurred. I've heard these stories told many times by both Michael and Wendy, so the narrative which follows is a combination of what I remember and what I've been told.

*

10/26/00, 11:20 a.m., Thursday

Dr. Larson came to my room to assess my condition. Once again, I attempted to explain I was still in pain, but the pain was different than before the surgery. Not sharp, in one specific place, but intense and diffuse throughout my entire abdomen and far worse than when I originally came in.

"You have already been here four days. We can't keep you here any longer."

"But we don't know what is wrong."

He walked over to me and slapped me on the back of my shoulder, "Tincture of time, Air-rah," he said, using my least-favorite mispronunciation of my name, "tincture of time!" The jarring effect of his slap sent a vibration of pain throughout my abdomen.

"I need to look at your chart," he said as he walked out of the room.

I thought he was going to take a look at my pain medication and return.

We waited more than 20 minutes. Finally a nurse entered with a handful of papers. "I have your discharge papers!" she said with a big smile.

"What do you mean, 'discharge?'" I asked in a panic.

"These are the doctor's orders. He is discharging you with a prescription for oxycodone and acetaminophen."

"But that's the one that made me throw-up. You can't be serious."

Despite the physical agony, I pushed myself up out of the chair and struggled to the door, thinking I might be able to catch him in the hall.

"What are you doing?" the nurse asked.

"I need to speak with the doctor."

"Ma'am, he's gone."

"I can't be discharged. I don't understand. I'm still in tremendous pain, and we don't know what is causing it. I don't understand how I could be discharged? I can't go."

"Well, you can't stay here. You've been discharged."

I looked at Michael and, not knowing what else to do, signed the papers.

It took Michael and Wendy forever to get me into the car because every movement hurt. I moaned and gasped during the bumpy ride home over Chicago's pothole lined streets. Michael was able to get a parking spot ten feet from our place. Since our apartment was a third floor walk-up, we agreed I would spend the night on the couch hide-a-bed in my first floor office.

Michael helped me out of the car. Even though it was October, there was ice and snow on the sidewalk. I held his hands for support, and he walked backwards in front of me. As I crept along taking four-inch steps, I felt like we were doing a sad version of pairs skating. He set me up in my office. Despite the prescriptions, the pain left me with no appetite. I slept on and off all night.

*

10/27/00, Friday

The next morning, we managed to reach someone at Dr. Kesson's office to notify them I was still in pain. Michael and Wendy were with me all of the time, though they would occasionally take shifts so one or the other of them could nap.

By the afternoon, I was unable to complete a sentence without nodding off. One of them would tap me on the shoulder, and sometimes I would be able to finish my sentence, sometimes not. They were trying to get me to eat. I was snowed under. They would confer and decide to make something they knew I liked even if it was a bit of trouble, but I would refuse to eat it.

After rounds of calls with no answer and trying to chase down multiple doctors, it was decided to take me off the breakthrough pain meds and stick with the time-release oxycodone and naproxen. There were concerns that I had been over-medicated, which led to my extreme drowsiness. Michael and Wendy were instructed to get me eating, drinking, and moving. They were also told to relocate me to normal surroundings, meaning our apartment, even if it was challenging. It took more than two hours to get me upstairs and into the recliner, but they managed it.

*

10/28/00, Saturday

I slept the entire day in the green rocking recliner. Michael expected as much after a week of sleepless nights at the hospital. Wendy and Michael tried to get me to eat myriad items, all of which I refused for one reason or another. At one point they managed to get me to the dining room table when Wendy had prepared tilapia, a favorite choice of mine under normal circumstances. I complained the fish was too dry, everything was too dry. Michael dunked a piece of the fish in my water glass; now the fish was too cold. Wendy made me a berry smoothie. I complained it was too thick. Wendy dumped a little water from my glass into the smoothie and stirred it. I yelped, "Now there is fish juice in my smoothie." Eventually, I wound up back in the chair and passed out again.

That evening was the much-anticipated Ninth Annual October Birthday Bash. This was a party Michael and several of his friends held every year to honor their collective October birthdays. Several friends came from out of town to attend. Michael had committed to providing the food. He planned to drop off a giant party sub but not to stay. It was also a chance to explain to Frank, his friend and bandmate, he might not be able to perform at their upcoming show in a couple days if things didn't turn around.

While Michael was away, I asked Wendy to help me get to the bathroom. She helped me out of the chair, but I stumbled, fell to the floor, and passed out. Wendy wasn't able to get me back into the chair by herself, so she tucked pillows under my head, knees, and arms to try to make me comfortable until Michael got back. When Michael returned a couple of hours later, I could hear her explaining how I wound up on the floor. He came over to me and gently asked if I still wanted to use the bathroom. I shook my head, "No." Together they lifted me up and put me back in the chair, where I remained through the night.

*

10/29/00, Sunday

At various intervals, I groggily woke up and felt a panic set in as I was very disoriented. Michael, concerned I was still so out of it even after a "full night's sleep," paged Dr. Kesson's clinic around noon. No one responded. More time passed. Michael wondered if I might still be "over-medicated," so he called our pharmacist and asked how long it might take for these pain meds to get out of my system. She said it could take a few days. Eventually a doctor called and suggested discontinuing all of the narcotic meds and to only take naproxen.

Though I was very out of it, things were quiet. Michael and Wendy agreed she should run a couple of overdue errands. In the mid-afternoon, Michael came in to check on me, still passed out in the easy chair. He pulled up a chair and sat by me, resting his hand on my forearm. He recoiled in horror. He later described my skin as being "hot and cold and wet and dry, all at the same time."

Michael sat there, wondering what the hell was going on with me. He noticed, because of the angle I was reclined in the chair, he could see the pulse in my neck. He watched the tiny fluttering movement and was concerned by the speed of it. It seemed to be too fast. Since there was a clock right there by my side, he decided to check my pulse. He counted for 10 seconds: twenty beats. Multiplied by six, that's 120. One hundred twenty beats per minute? That didn't seem right. That's an aerobic exercise rate, but I hadn't moved from the chair in over twelve hours.

He figured he should time it again. This time he counted for fifteen seconds and got 32. Multiplied by four, that's 128. He hadn't miscounted before.

Michael decided to page Dr. Segel, my psychiatrist, who almost always called back within twenty minutes. Michael explained the way my skin felt, his pulse calculations, and my general state. Dr. Segel asked a series of questions. Once he heard I hadn't gotten up from the chair to use the bathroom in at least twenty-four hours, he calmly told Michael it was time to get me back to the hospital. This time, Michael wanted to be certain I would be at Riverbank Hospital with Dr. Segel and our normal team of doctors. Dr. Segel explained that Michael would have to sign a document indemnifying the ambulance company since Riverbank was not the closest hospital. Dr. Segel said he would notify the emergency room we were on our way.

Although Michael wasn't more than ten feet away from me when he was talking to Dr. Segel, I didn't hear a word of their conversation. I do remember the paramedics shouting at me as they tried to rouse me while they moved me onto a special gurney designed for navigating tight stairwells. After the trip down the stairs, I was unconscious again. Wendy, meanwhile, had returned, and Michael explained the situation to her. She packed up food for what would inevitably be more waiting, and drove off to meet him/us at the hospital.

Michael sat in the passenger seat at the front of the ambulance, filling out various forms, including the request to go to Riverbank Hospital. The medic in back with me, took my vitals and struggled to get an IV in my tiny, collapsed veins.

After a time, the medic said to Michael, "I'm sorry, sir, but we can't take her to Riverbank."

"What do you mean?"

"She's in critical condition. By law, we have to take her to the nearest hospital." The nearest hospital was Founder's Medical Center, where we had just left three days before.

Michael screamed out, *"Noooooooooo!"* as if I was being ripped out of his arms.

"If you want her to go to Riverbank you would have to take her."

He considered it, but knew there was no way he could maneuver me by himself, and Wendy had already left. Besides, if what they were saying was true, I might not make it all the way downtown. Founder's was a mere ten blocks away. He had to let them take me.

Once at the hospital I was wheeled directly through the emergency room into the trauma area. Michael spent several minutes on the pay phone in the lobby, trying to reach Wendy to tell her to turn around, that she was on her way to the wrong hospital.

Between

> 10/29
> ER Admission
> - History: Bipolar, ectopic pregnancy (removed)
> - Physical: Blood Pressure 77/41
>   resting Heart Rate: 130
> - Abdomen tender and distended
> - Septic shock
> - Internal bleeding
>
> 10/29 11:30pm
> Post-Op
> - Intubated
> - Restraints
> - NG* tube inserted; check every 4 hours
> - Foley catheter; check volume of urine drained every 4 hours

---

* Nasogastric; a method of intubation. A flexible tube is inserted through the nose, past the throat and into the stomach. Here, used primarily for feeding and administering oral medications.

Ara Lucia Ashburne

- IV — standard — one in right arm, one in left also
- IV catheter — right Femoral Artery*
- Finger-mounted pulse oximeter to track blood oxygen level
- Respiratory — on ventilator
- Blood pressure cuff — check every 20 minutes

- BP 109/62
- Jackson—Pratt tube drains inserted in abdomen during surgery — check collected fluid drainage periodically
- 3 units of red blood cells ordered + started
- Hypothermia blanket
- Intermittent pneumatic compression (IPC) boots to prevent blood clots

Administered:
- Antibiotics: vancomycin, gentamicin, metronidazole, aztreonam
- Morphine for pain
- Midazolam for anxiety & to induce amnesia

Moved to Intensive Care Unit
- Labs to be drawn every 6 hours

    Michael and I are waiting for our flight to Telero, Mexico. It didn't seem like a place he would choose to take me, but we had never gone on a proper honeymoon, so I was up for anywhere. I know there are often great deals to coastal Mexican resort towns—one of my sisters and her husband have taken advantage of them repeatedly. Maybe this is the reason for a surprise vacation. I

---

* The major blood vessel in the thigh supplying the leg. This kind of IV is used to quickly move large volumes of fluid into a patient's system and can also be used for additional blood work or to check levels later.

don't care where we are going. I'm excited to have time off and to be alone with Michael. I grab his arm and snuggle up to him while we wait for our flight to be called.

After an uneventful flight and check-in at the hotel, we decide to go for a walk to a small town inland from our hotel. The road is dusty, and there is no one around. As we stroll down the road, the pavement turns into a dirt path. The view begins to look like the desert with only dusty red rocks until the horizon. Although the scenery change feels somewhat alarming, I treasure time when Michael and I are alone in the world, separated from our everyday concerns in a physical seclusion.

A small wind-worn building appears out of nowhere. The wood is gray from the sun. Cracks in the wood are as big as some of the spaces between the unevenly-nailed boards. The building reminds me of a saloon from a Wild West movie, with a pair of short swinging doors. Two drunken men fall out, each singing a different Spanish song to the other and laughing simultaneously.

Are they cowboys or people from the neighborhood? But where is the neighborhood? This saloon is isolated out here in this huge expanse of dirt.

They are holding each other up and laughing. The heavier one grabs the other, and they slide down the wall of the bar, falling asleep on one another's shoulders. We decide, lacking any other option, to enter the saloon.

The wooden doors smack shut behind us, announcing our arrival. Our eyes attempt to adjust to the darkness as we enter the one-room tavern. Two light bulbs cast a hesitant light across the room. When we sit at the bar, the bartender walks up to us and stares without a word. Michael orders us each a beer. Although I wouldn't usually drink beer, I assume he has chosen the least-noteworthy beverage in an attempt to diminish the awkwardness of our presence.

There are two men at the far end of the bar. I can feel their gaze on my back, but I keep my eyes on Michael. I can see through the dark haze there are also three men at a small table in the back corner, playing cards. I can't tell if they are watching us or not.

After a few sips of our beers, Michael and I nod to one another. It's time to make an exit. He reaches to his back right pocket and his eyes go wide.

"My wallet, it's gone," he says, raising his voice above the whisper which feels safe in this place.

He is ritualistic about his departures—keys, cell phone, wallet, iPod. There is little chance he left it behind. I replay our entrance into the bar: we weren't bumped on the way in, but somehow, someone must have taken it. I try to survey the room casually and see now two men are standing guard over the door with their arms crossed in front of them. It had to be them, I just can't figure out how they did it.

"Tell them you need to go back to the hotel to get your wallet and cash. I'll wait here."

"I'm not leaving you here," he declares as he gestures for the bartender to come over, "I'll see what I can do."

```
10/29  11:40pm
• Stat chest x-ray
• Vecuronium* 10 mg IV push x1, then vecuronium drip at
  3 mg/hour
```

"Sir, it would seem that my wallet is missing."

The bartender nods to the men at the door. At once, they, along with the three men from the back table, surround us. They grab Michael and in a flurry begin to beat him.

The men from the other end of the bar grab me from behind and drag me behind the bar. I'm screaming and thrashing, but I can't get away. Unconcerned about my fight, they do not attempt to silence me, but throw me through a door. I quickly scramble to my feet, but as I reach for the open door it disappears into a marble wall.

I turn around to see a huge room with marble walls and floor. A stepped pyramid lies at the far end, surrounded by lush plants and trees that seem to grow right out of the floor. On each step are servants whose oiled and supple bodies are clothed in red fabric that covers only their shoulders. I can hear the chatter of exotic birds and monkeys.

The pyramid is topped with a tent draped over a huge man on a king's throne. He has a Buddha-like body, but his face bears an expression of slight pain. Many leis hang around his thick neck, each one a single color.

Suddenly, the King laughs. I hear his booming voice in my head—his lips do not move. Against my will, I feel my body moving toward the pyramid. My eyes scan the room, looking for an exit or anything that could be used as a means of escape.

His voice echoes in my head, "We have no tolerance for your kind here. Your punishment will amuse me." I'm moving up the steps toward him.

"But it was an accident," I stammer, "the wallet—we have money back at the hotel. Just release my husband," I plead with more confidence than I actually have, "I'm sure we can resolve this."

---

* A paralytic drug which blocks signals passing from the nerve to the muscle at the point where they interface (as compared to a drug which might act upon the muscle directly). It was explained to Michael that this was administered so Ara's body could direct all of its energy toward fighting off her infection.

I reach the top and stand before the King. "Your husband will not be released until you satisfy my desires. Prepare yourself."

From behind me, a servant grabs my upper right arm and squeezes hard.

He hustles me through a trap door in front of the King's throne. "I'm going," I say through clenched teeth, "you don't have to hurt me." He squeezes harder, ignoring my protests.

Down more stairs and into a small room to a marbled sauna with stone seats. I see what appears to be a reflecting pool at the center of the room, but I soon realize it is an entrance to the dark ocean below. Another servant, waiting in the room, rips my clothes from my body.

I cry out, but the sound is distorted as if something is covering my mouth. I cannot stop the servant. I stand in front of him, alone and naked and angry.

He speaks for the first time. "The King will see you take these flowers into your body." He pulls out a large orange flower from behind his back, like a magic trick. I remember it from the botanical gardens upstairs, it's called the Parrot's Beak.

What is happening?

The first servant wraps a large rope around my waist with his free hand and drags me to the edge of the pool. Being without my clothes has taken some of my strength, and things are happening so quickly I don't even have a chance to look for a way out. He dives into the water and takes the end of the rope with him. I fall in, choking and gasping, until I realize I am somehow able to breathe under the water. He swims downward, dragging me deeper. Soon I feel the pressure of the water inside my ears and wonder how deep we have gone.

There is a huge flash of light from above. The trap door has opened again, and I can see the King above us on his throne. A small fire has been started in a pit at the King's feet. He plucks a flower from one of his leis and hands it to another servant who plunges it into the flames. Instead of burning, the flower holds its shape and glows like molten fire. The servant grabs the fire-flower somehow, without burning his hands, and dives into the water toward me. The molten flower is not cooled by the water, and it continues to glimmer and blaze as he swims closer.

The first servant holds my mouth open while the other servant shoves the burning flower down my throat. My screams are silenced as the flower burns its path from my mouth into my belly.

Now I see a third servant swimming toward me with another burning flower. I am held by the first two servants while the third forces the next one into my nose. The searing flower burns a passage through my nose into my throat and down into the center of my body. I scream again, but I cannot hear my voice.

> 10/30 5:00am
> - Oral care — repeat every 2 hours
>
> 6:00am
> - Bath — repeat every 6 hours
> - Perineal care: wash front of vagina to anus, then dry to prevent yeast infection

    Two more servants bring burning, pulsing flowers. The first three men are holding my arms, legs, and head. These last two swim lower, and at once I feel violated. Again, I scream, and again, there is no sound.

    The King is laughing. He has been satisfied.

    The first servant drags my beaten body to the surface.

    "You will be delivered to your husband," he whispers.

    I crawl out of the ocean onto the marble floor. A door, previously unseen, is now open in front of me, leading back to the bar. I run, wet and naked, through the doorway, out onto the street, screaming for Michael. The dust from the road covers my body. I'm running for what feels like forever, back toward the hotel, but I feel weak and soon fall to my knees.

    The hotel seems farther away.

    I can't crawl that far.

    I collapse, face first into the dust, and my spirit falls away behind me.

> 10/30 6:50am
> Nurse's Notes:
> - BP 100/30
> - Respiratory failure

> 10/30 8:00am
> • Aggressive resuscitation overnight

Michael is carrying me.
Are we crossing a threshold? Is this our honeymoon? Why do I feel so weak?
My spirit is far away, but I can hear him talking to the border guards as he holds my body in his arms.

"No, sir, our passports were taken. We need to make it back to the States. You see, my wife is very ill. She needs medical care urgently."

"There is no way back to the States from here without a passport. You cannot cross the border."

"I would offer you compensation to help us, but my wallet was taken with our passports. Can you direct us to the American Embassy?"

"There is no American Embassy here in Puerto Rico."

"I haven't much time. Please, help us."

A tall thin guard with more metal across his pocket walks up and asks, "What is the trouble?"

He speaks quickly in Spanish and waves the guards away. The superior officer then ushers Michael into a small, windowless room with a table, two chairs, and a telephone. He rests against the wall and shifts my weight in his arms. The guard speaks on a telephone in Spanish and gestures for Michael to sit down. Michael drags a chair out with his foot and sits in the chair, still holding me. He squeezes me and breathes like a prayer.

A young boy enters the room and hands the guard papers. Glancing only briefly at the papers, the guard explains we will have to take a Korean medical ship to China. From China, we will go to the American Embassy and receive papers to get back to the States.

"This is your only option."

Michael leans my limp body against the table for a moment as he takes the papers from the guard. With difficulty, he stands and follows the young boy outside to a taxi. The boy drives the taxi to a dock where a cruise ship waits. The boy speaks to him in Spanish and rushes him to the bridge where he gives brief instructions to the attendant there. Michael carries me aboard.

Immediately a gurney is rushed forward and Michael is relieved of my body. He holds on to the edge of the sheets covering me and races with the medics down a maze of corridors. We enter a gigantic, brightly lit room that is divided into cells by numerous curtains suspended from wires dropped from the ceiling. I am wheeled toward one curtain, and it is quickly pulled aside. This "room" is divided in half by another, smaller curtain, and an empty gurney is on the other side. We are in a giant triage area, the curtained cells lined up row after row—ten, twenty, more than thirty down each aisle—each cell with two beds and only a curtain between them.

"You are going to be okay," Michael says, trying to reassure himself as much as me. "The guards explained the care here is good. They will stabilize you until we can get you home. You have to hang in here with me, Ara. You have to hang on."

I can't respond to his words. I am quiet inside. I can hear him, but my spirit is so very far away his voice is tiny. I am aware of my weakened body, but my spirit is above it, spinning and rotating like a gyroscope, as if drunk.

After a time, while I hover over Michael looking down at my body on the gurney, the spinning stops. A nurse comes into the room and lays her hand on my forehead, then my wrist. She mumbles, counting to herself, then leaves quickly. She comes back with a doctor, an Asian woman with short black hair and a lab coat with a military insignia over the pocket. She places Michael's hand on that same wrist and counts again. Then, the doctor puts the nurse's hand on my heart and moves to the end of the bed, taking hold of my feet, and begins counting again.

She dismisses the nurse and pulls out five very long acupuncture needles. The doctor begins inserting the needles, one at a time, into my chest. I can feel the needles penetrate deep into my lungs, through to my spinal column, and out my back. Another needle pierces my neck, through a vertebra and out the other side. It is strange, feeling pain from the needles in my body while being outside of it. It is immense.

The doctor speaks to my body on the gurney, telling me in Korean to remain still and to keep my breath shallow. Somehow I understand her, despite not knowing her language.

She turns and speaks to Michael too. His expression changes from one of concern to one of determined resolve, and his grip on my wrist tightens. He understands: the responsibility for keeping me alive is now his. Until China, he must keep hold of me to keep my spirit in this world—all by my wrist. This is something he knows he can do. Pushing past the curtain, she leaves abruptly.

There must be another way out of this mess besides this boat, but I can't see anything beyond this little curtained area.

Michael leans in close, speaking quietly. "Ara, listen. Keep listening. As long as you can hear me, you are still with me. It doesn't matter about the numbers. Odds have never meant anything to you before, and I'm sure they don't mean anything to you right now. I will stay right with you. You can't go as long as I have you here, and I will never drop you. It is a long ocean to cross, but we are going together, so you needn't worry—remember, you and I are our own universe. Do what the doctor said, breathe low and steady. Keep listening, and I will keep holding you. I have you, Ara. I have you right here."

* * *

Reconstruction

Operative Report: ASHBURNE, ARA LUCIA
Operation Date: 11/01/2000

PREOPERATIVE DIAGNOSIS: Necrotizing fasciitis and spreading bacterial infection of the subcutaneous tissue and preperitoneal tissue.

POSTOPERATIVE DIAGNOSIS: Same as above.

SURGEON: Dr. David Han

OPERATION: Extensive debridement of dead soft tissue, abdominal wall: consisting of subcutaneous tissue, some strips of skin edges, preperitoneal adipose tissue in the suprapubic region and right lower quadrant of the abdomen wall; on the right side some rectus muscles in the outer part of the abdominal wall.

Translation: A large amount of soft tissue was removed. This included some skin and the layers of tissue under the skin. Additionally, some fat tissue was removed from a couple of places: next to the front of the cavity which contains most of the abdominal organs, and from just above the pubic bone area. On the right side, some fat tissue was removed from the lower part of the abdomen as well as some of the muscles from the front of the abdomen.

* * *

Operative Report: ASHBURNE, ARA LUCIA
Operation Date: 11/02/2000

PREOPERATIVE DIAGNOSIS: Necrotizing fasciitis and necrosis of the subcutaneous tissue and mild necrosis.

POSTOPERATIVE DIAGNOSIS: Necrotizing fasciitis and necrosis of the subcutaneous tissue and mild necrosis.

SURGEON: Dr. Han

OPERATION: Debridement of necrotic muscle, subcutaneous tissue, skin and preperitoneal necrotic tissue from both flanks.

INDICATIONS: This patient required debridement because of the very fast-spreading necrotizing fasciitis on 11/01 and also one day previous to that. Patient was examined again today and with Dr. Farion we inspected the wound and decided that the patient will need more debridement. It was also felt that probably this patient will need debridement every day. After the decision was made, the husband was contacted and he gave consent.

PROCEDURE: It was also felt that on further examination that this infection was also spreading to the retroperitoneal area on both sides of the flank. This area was exposed and lots of necrotic tissue from the preperitoneal fat was removed. Having done this, the wound was packed. I should also mention that previously given sutures were removed and it was found in the upper part of the wound there was a defect measuring about 6 cm in diameter. The defect in the peritoneum could not be closed, therefore Gore-Tex graft was placed to prevent the extravasation* of the small bowel. This Gore-Tex was not fixed to the abdominal wall through these stitches. All the edges of the Gore-Tex were pushed under the peritoneum to protect the small bowel from the dressing changes and/or irrigation when the dressing is changed. Having done this, the wound was then dressed and the patient was taken to the Intensive Care Unit.

I should mention here that the patient seems to have a very poor prognosis, and she may need more debridement in the future.

* * *

My bed is a large boulder, sending severe pain through my spine. I cannot move and am unable to speak.

The Elder Woman will usher me to the Other Side: "You have reached the edge of your life. Your body remains with your people, but your spirit is being held here by us. You must step into the darkness, and there, you will see your own light. You need not fear, my little one. Yvonne and I are here to watch you cross, but you must go alone. The crossing can take many hours. We will not tire as we remain here beside you. It is time to begin."

We're in a cave lit by a small fire beside me. A group of women from a small village in Ecuador are keeping candles lit while singing a dark chant in an ancient language—it's this chant that will pass me through my spirit's tunnel to death.

I'm disoriented. I only feel the pain in my back. Aside from this, I can't feel my physical body. I don't know where it is in space or where the boulder bed has gone. My body isn't moving, but I have a sense that my body is spinning in a corkscrew spiral to the right. I feel as if my arms are in many places at once, like a stop-motion camera image of my arms moving around me as I spin.

I scream with my mind, begging the Elder to move my body into any position to stop the pain, but she doesn't respond. Hours pass, and the women

---

* Emergence of the bowel into the peritoneal cavity.

sing the song of death over and over, until I know the sound of their low ululations from memory.

The youngest woman draws a handful of colorful ribbons out of a fold in her dress and passes them out among the others. Once each of the chanting women has chosen a ribbon, they take turns holding it over my body and offering wishes for my safe passage into the darkness. One by one, they delicately place the ribbons on me.

My chest has become heavy, and I have to draw in each breath with intention. I believe I am slipping away as their voices become quieter, more remote, and yet the pain in my spine intensifies.

Oh God, that's it: I'm dying. Of course—that explains everything. Why didn't I figure this out sooner? Well, dying is something I can certainly do, and then this searing and unbearable pain in my spine will end. I'll fall into the pain, into the darkness, the black, and release. I will become the pain. I will...

...depart.

I sink into the pain. I let it surround me, consume me, become me. I feel my spirit slip out of my body and hover overhead.

Now, I will lift away.

But I'm stuck.

What the hell is holding me? What is happening?

I relax, let my mind float in the spaciousness of time, and release—softly, gently.

Letting go.

Instead, I feel a physical tug, right next to my heart.

Dammit! I don't understand!

I hear steps behind me and Yvonne emerges at my side. Without a sound, she takes hold of my left arm. I can feel that physically, too.

Enraged, I try to scream at her in my mind: *Yvonne, I don't get it! The woman in the cave said I was dying. I tried to cooperate and die, but I'm stuck here! It doesn't make any sense. I'm in terrible pain, my spine hurts—this is unbearable! Please, move the rock in my back, or slide me to the ground, or push me over. Anything.*

I want to cry, but the air I feel in my lungs and the tears behind my eyes never make it to the surface.

The chanting stops. Everyone has laid their ribbon on my body, and the Elder Woman sits at the end of my bed.

A multi-colored dust is thrown into the fire beside me, and many little flames swell up. It is exquisite, like an aurora borealis caught in the campfire. The women are chanting again, a murmur of a song this time, more melodious, and the old woman speaks to me with her eyes. Her words enter my mind in silence, but I understand her in my heart: "You are free."

I am? What do you mean, "I am free?" Did I pass some test? Does this mean I am going to live instead? Is that my task? Is that why I'm stuck, why I can't die?

Okay then, what do I do next? Do I just transform myself into the light? Is that where Life is?

I can try.

I fill my heart with light. I'm aware of every cell in my body and bring each to life. I acknowledge their power for renewal. I breathe into them the power of rebirth. I throw myself fully into living. I rest in a light cast by thousands of fireflies into the sky.

Nothing. *Really?*

I'm caught. Somehow, I'm caught between these worlds. I can't get back to Life, I can't get to Death. I've somehow fallen into a crack—Between. And this time, I can't find the way out. If there is a portal that leads back to Life, I don't know where it is.

The flames reflected on the wall and the fire on the ground blow out in an instant.

From: Wendy [mailto: wendy@email.com]
Sent: Thursday, November 2, 2000 12:41 PM
To: Allgroup
cc: michael
Subject: Ara's Situation

My name is Wendy. I am a friend and current roommate of Ara and Michael. I am acting in my role as executive assistant to Michael at this time, and sending you the first update on Ara's health. Many people are calling the house at this point, interrupting a much needed 20-minute nap or leaving a message. Michael really appreciates all the care and concern and love expressed for him and for Ara. However, as the number of phone calls is becoming increasingly hard to manage, and as Michael needs to be able to focus on Ara, we are trying to get info out via e-mail. Those of you receiving this e-mail know Ara, and so you can perhaps imagine what your life might be like if you suddenly had to handle your own life, plus all the activities and responsibilities of HER life, all while managing her 24-hour health care, and worrying about your wife being ill besides.

Here is what is happening: Ara had an ectopic pregnancy that was surgically removed last Monday (Oct. 23). She was discharged from the hospital on Thursday. She had a lot of pain and was on medication for it through Saturday. From Friday through Sunday, her abdominal swelling did not go down as expected and she became more disoriented even once off the strong pain medication. On Sunday we checked in with her doctor via phone and it was decided she needed to be taken back to the hospital.

It was determined she had an infection in her belly. An incision was made to clean it out. For those of you who like detail, the infection was above the peritoneum (the membrane that holds in your organs), which means that it was not affecting her organs directly. From outside in, the order is skin, fat, muscle, fascia, peritoneum. That was Sunday night. She was stitched closed and transferred to the ICU under heavy sedation.

On Monday, signs of necrosis appeared (hard, red areas on the skin, in this case, the skin of her belly). She was opened up again because it was suspected she had necrotizing fasciitis (literally, dying cells of the fascia—and you don't want to have that). She does indeed have a variant of necrotizing fasciitis. Imagine that you have a deep wound that needs to be cleared of nonviable tissue periodically until it is healing properly. So, as I said, they opened her belly a second time and cleared all the necrotic tissue. Then they packed her and returned her to ICU, where she is closely observed and monitored by both humans and machines. The process is to be repeated until it is determined that there is no more necrosis, at which time they will close the incision.

Let me answer some common questions at this point. No, you cannot visit her, for two reasons. One, she is totally unconscious, so you would not be comforting her, only freaking yourself out. Yes, there are some machines involved and it looks a little like a TV set. She is medically sedated and paralyzed (so that her body will relax and do what it is supposed to do), so when I tell you that she is unconscious, I don't mean she's groggy and might not recognize you; I mean unconscious.

Feel free to send a card or note of support to Ara or Michael. Do not send flowers or perishables unless you intend them for Michael and me at this point. Prayers and loving thoughts are incredibly appreciated.

Know this is now a long-term situation. It is likely Ara will be unconscious and be in the ICU for several more weeks, and then be in a hospital room, and then be recuperating at home. So, hang in there with us. Your next update will come not later than Saturday; sooner if there is something to report. Feel free to ask questions via e-mail.

That's all for now,
Wendy

Someone is next to me, someone is speaking.

I can immediately tell this is different. I'm not in the nightmare place, the Between place—I'm in the real world, an echoey room, where I can hear everything that's happening but am unable to move, to respond, to speak... I can only think, and that is a struggle.

"Hey there, Ara."

Great, it's Michael! My God, I'm freaking out. I can't figure out how to get out of this place. The only thing I can figure out is somehow I must have fallen into a crack between Life and Death.

"Last night was our New Order cover show."

Oh that's right! Wow, how did it go?

"I didn't want to play with you in here."

Oh my God, I will kick your ass when I get out of here!

"Since, over the weekend, we didn't know what was up with you, Frank came in on Sunday and recorded all my parts, so they could play the show without me."

Oh, Michael, no—unless you could have gotten me out of here, you should have played the show. Oh Michael, I can't believe you missed it. You were so looking forward to playing.

"Last night, I helped them load the gear into the van and then went upstairs. Wendy knew I had gone to help them load but acted surprised to see me. She asked what I was doing there, and I told her I didn't feel like I could play the show. Then she said, 'If Ara heard you say that, she would kick your ass.'"

You're damn right!

"I thought about it, and I figured she was right. People had come in from out of town for the party the Saturday before, a bunch of them had stayed an extra couple of days to see the show. Everybody was going to be there. I hadn't talked to anybody at the party, because I just brought food over and left, but everyone already knew about you, and this ... what was going on."

I feel a rush of heat to my head and ears. Immediately after, I feel the warmth speed into my arms and legs. I don't like it.

This happens periodically, and I suddenly realize that it precedes the moment when I slip away: I feel the heat, and no matter how hard I fight against it, I start to disappear, to slip back to the Between World.

The sounds of the room, of Michael, are getting farther away, getting harder to hear. I already can't see anything, can't move. Sound is my only tie to Life-World, and now the heat is taking it away. Again.

No, I don't want to leave Michael!

I try to fight the heat, fight the slipping, the fading. His words sound like they are coming from across the room even though I can still feel him close, feel his hand on mine.

"It was weird, though," he says, "I felt like a zombie on the way over to the club."

The sound of his voice slips farther away.

"There were people all around, but it was like I wasn't really there. It was all a blur. I dedicated the show to you and played the best I've ever played."

And I am gone.

> 11/03 (no time given)
> Physician's Order: Apply Lacri-Lube to eyes every four hours
> Physician's Notes: Dr. Allenson
> • General status remains unchanged
>
> Nursing Notes: Pulse/ox 90%

Sometime later, I have no idea how long, I'm back in the Real World . . . though it doesn't actually feel any more real than the Nightmare Place. In many ways, it feels less so. But I can tell the difference, somehow.

I hear clogs shuffle into the room.

"Since we couldn't convince you to take a break, I brought you a muffin."

"Thank you," Yvonne says. I can hear the crunch of the bag as she takes the muffin out. The clogs walk away.

I wonder what kind of muffin you buy for someone when you don't know what they like? Banana nut? Blueberry?

I can't smell the muffin, but I can hear Yvonne eating it.

Yvonne read me books when I was old enough to sit up in her lap. She took me to see the *Puff the Magic Dragon* movie and *Escape to Witch Mountain*, but mostly she listened to me with greater attentiveness than any other person in my life.

One summer when she was in high school, we made a paper kite together with a tail made of pantyhose. She kept adjusting the pantyhose tail until it caught the breeze and flew into the sky. I begged her to adjust the tail so the kite could take me with it. She also let me help her with her butterfly collection, even though it was very delicate and I was only five. She was eternally patient with me.

There's a woman in the next room crying. A different woman, younger than the first, says, "I'm sorry ma'am, we can't know for certain, but we don't expect your son to make it through the night." There are other voices, and I can hear Yvonne trying to console this woman.

I heard someone mention a gunshot wound. I wonder about the circumstances —altercation, a drive-by, an accident? His mother probably doesn't care how he was shot, only that he lives.

Yvonne tells her, "It's in God's hands now. The doctors have done all they can. I'll pray for him, too."

Yvonne walks back into my room and sits in a chair at my left side.

I want to talk to her, to ask her what is going on here, but I can't move. I hear a loud, fuzzy buzzing in my ears and my body is heavy. I feel as if there is a blanket of lead like the dentist uses when taking x-rays, but it is much heavier, and it covers my entire body. I'm lying down, and my head and shoulders are lifted up, so it's almost as if I'm looking out at the world, but I can't open my eyes. I see a thin gray haze of dots like dense pixels. They vibrate as if the air itself is a living being.

I feel the quick rush of heat from my heart out to my limbs, and now I am burning up, searing, radiating red. The slipping is coming, I know the signs now. I'm going to disappear again.

My thoughts are fading away. I can't see through the fog.

Yvonne holds my left hand and traps the heat between my hand and hers.

I want to scream out, but I cannot scream or even move my lips.

This can't be.

I decide to try harder. I try to take a deep breath, but I can't. I decide to purse my lips. There is no movement—none. It's as if I'm encased in metal. I decide to move just a single finger—maybe then she will feel me and remove her hand—but I can't. How is that possible? I start to panic and hear a machine beep. I gather my energy from all over my body, drag up my force of will from my feet, into my heart—nothing. My fear spins. I hear another beep. I try to push all of my life's energy into my one finger—nothing.

I surrender to the heat, the slipping, swimming, spinning, fading. The gray dots melt into darkness.

I'm gone.

*

I'm sitting up now. Although I can't see, I hear waves crashing quietly across the shore. I imagine the sand beneath the fog is clean, white sand. It seems at the very distance of my vision there's a coast.

Over my left shoulder, between Yvonne and me, is a man with a low, calm voice. He places my hands in a praying position.

"You will have to keep your hands in this position until the god appears and releases you. If you tire and drop your hands, you will die. Also, focus your attention on the point right there," he points to an 11 o'clock position on the horizon, "and wait for Him to appear. Again, if you tire and let your eyes or attention wander, you will die.

"Lastly, you will have to hold a name for the god in your mind without using any words. If you lapse, you will die. This is what is expected of you and this is what you will do. Do you understand?"

I nod while looking to the horizon. I begin holding the sense of God in my mind while holding the prayer position. The dense gray fog surrounds me. I let my mind hold an expansiveness, a sense of God that is the Oneness of All There Is. I am able to think slowly, and I wonder where I might be. The coast of Mexico? The Caribbean? Another island?

I hold the sense of God in my mind and heart, and maintain my hands in prayer until they burn from fatigue. The murky air buzzes, its tiny gray flecks padding the miles between the horizon and me. I simultaneously feel agitation and a suspended peace. As the focus of my attention begins to slip, I feel a gentle nudge, an outside pressure guiding me back to task.

Minutes pass into days. My eyes make out the suggestion of colors, maybe two figures. They look like wooden puppets—silhouettes acting out a scene. I can see only the faint suggestion of their forms and a flash of red through the gray haze. I maintain my focus on the spot where I was directed, but expand my attention to include the glimmers of the performance in the distance. The burning in my praying arms changes to a numbness that makes it difficult for me to know if I am still holding my hands in prayer or if my arms have floated away from my body.

*

"Hi Ara, this is your Mother. It is Tuesday, and your Dad and I just drove in."

Where is Dad? I don't hear him. Is he right beside you? Dad, please say something.

"Gramma and Grandpa are asking about you, but the weather is too rough for them to travel. You are doing really good, and we are very proud of you. You can do this."

Do what?

What does that mean, Mom? And "do" what? I can't "do" anything. I can't breathe right. I can't talk, and I can't move—not even a finger. I've tried with all my might. What is it that you think I can do?

"You are young, and they are doing everything they can to help you. You are hanging in there and fighting."

Who am I fighting?

"We are all praying. We love you, Ara."

I hear my Mom step out of the room and start talking with someone in the hall, a voice I don't recognize.

Wait Mom, come back. Please explain to me what is going on. I can hear everything. I can hear you. I can hear plastic wrap and a metal chain in the morning. I just can't move. I can't see.

I'm scared, Mom.

I feel the rush of heat again, to my heart, then my arms and legs. It pulses in my ears and slows my thinking. I start to swim. I fade for a moment, it stretches longer...

... I snap back to the room, somehow. It's a relief, but jarring, too.

My mom is talking.

"Julie is doing well. They were watching a situation with the baby, but it looks like it has worked itself out."

Wait? What did I miss? What situation with the baby? How long was I out this time?

"We'll be back in a bit," she says.

Don't go! Please, can't you help me understand?

I'm already falling again. I can't resist the heat, the gray, the slip. I try to tell her, but she's already so far away.

The Tree Trunk God still has me trapped, and if you leave I might be swallowed up. This last thought makes sense to me, as if I'm remembering something that happened but didn't happen. I only know I don't want it to happen again, and if I slip away...

Then I'm lost again.

I can't see the figures or the distant island any more. I'm lying on my back now, and the water is lapping at my feet. Occasionally a wave will come higher, over my stomach. Then, without warning, I feel the tourniquet of pressure on my right upper arm again and pressure around my lower legs. The Tree Trunk God is still holding me. When a big wave comes up to swallow me, he tightens his grasp on my arm and legs, reminding me of his power.

It's been a while since the heat rush that makes me feel so weak, so I decide to fight him again. I'm feeling stronger, so maybe this time I can gather myself and pull away. I wait for his grip to relax, as it always does eventually, and I reach into myself to slowly, carefully pull my legs up and my arm out. I think I've moved just enough to be out of his grasp. I wait quietly to make my next move, holding very still. I have to see if there is a way off this beach. The waves roll over my body again and again, but the sensation is far off, detached. The crashing of the waves in my ears is more intense than the feeling of them on my body.

Suddenly, the Tree Trunk God's grasp on my right arm tightens, pinching. Moments later, his hold on my lower legs tightens as well. He still has me. I haven't gone anywhere. His grip feels tighter than before. He must be angry with me for trying to escape.

Eventually, though, his grip loosens, and I decide to try a different strategy. Since I couldn't escape, I decide next time I will surrender. When he squeezes my upper arm or grips my lower legs again, I will not cringe or cry. I'll allow the pain of his grip to ride over me. Maybe then he will relax his attention on me, and I can escape without his noticing. I relax into the sound and distant feeling of the waves as they wash over my lower body, and I float in the rolling sensation, waiting.

Tighten… *Here we go. Ara, relax, let it hurt your arm. It's okay, you've felt it hundreds of times now. Let the pain go. Be still. Be easy.*

"Tree Trunk God, You and I are one. I feel you on my arm and my legs and we are together, You and me. I am a part of You, just as You desire."

Suddenly the heat rushes into my heart, and I know I only have thirty or forty seconds before I pass out again. Even though I'm in the Nightmare Place, I'm more afraid of being nowhere, of not being at all.

"No, no," I plead with him, "Tree Trunk God, don't take my awareness away. I was surrendering to you. I'm not trying to leave you, I promise. You don't have to make me slip away. Don't put me out."

I feel the heat move throughout my body, the blood pulsing in my ears, the fuzzy burn and thickening fog, and fade, and I know it's too late. I'm already fading, and gray becomes black.

*

"Yvonne," my mother says, "we're going to get a bite to eat at the Italian place on the corner. Why don't you come with us?"

Oh my God, Mom, do you not remember you forbade me to have anything to do with her? How is it you're now asking her to dinner? I would need to be there to run interference! Is Michael here? Michael, could you go?

I'm vaguely aware I'm back in the room with everyone. The line between this world and the Nightmare Place feels more blurry every time I transition from one to the next.

"Yvonne," Wendy interjects, "all you've had to eat today was the muffin the nurse brought you for breakfast."

Oh great, Wendy, at least you're here, but you are not helping! Stop! Honestly, just stop! This is the worst case scenario of worlds colliding! Can't somebody go with them? Maybe both you and Michael could go?

"No, I'm fine," Yvonne says, finally. "I want to be with Ara right now."

Michael pleads, "Yvonne, we need you with us for the long haul on this one. You aren't going to be any good to her or anyone if you don't take care of yourself, and eating is fundamental to that."

Michael, so you are here. Why aren't you with me on this one? I mean, Yvonne and my parents, seriously? You think it's a good idea for them to go to dinner together? Do you want to be at that dinner?

Wait, if you all go then I'll be all alone here with the Tree Trunk God.

I feel tears well up in my heart, but I can't feel them on my face. I feel the pressure of breath in my lungs, but I don't feel my lungs moving.

They're already gone. It's quiet again, and the line between worlds stops mattering. I can't control anything, I'm at the mercy of… I don't even know what. Everything.

Ara Lucia Ashburne

I feel the tourniquet-like pressure on my right arm, followed by gradually increasing pressure all around my calves. The Tree Trunk God is letting me know he still has me in his power.

Rush burning through veins to heart to face and arms then legs ...

Once again, I am losing the strength to pull away.

There is a thickening of the ever-present gray light. The Tree Trunk God has sucked away my power again, and now I am moving so   much   slow er   in my   head.

Blackness.

*

I hear my Mom's shoes enter the room. "Okay Ara, we're going to get the tree in a couple weeks. As always, I'm trying to get your father to not get such a ridiculously tall tree. They're always so hard to decorate when they're that big, but you know how he is."

Are you going to weigh in on this, Dad?

"Okay, well, we're going to drive back now, but we'll see you again real soon, okay? You keep fighting, and we will keep praying. Okay now, bye."

Mom, I am fighting, but I can't get out of here. I wish you were staying. Can't you and Dad stay in a hotel and not drive back? I can't get away from the Tree Trunk God, please don't leave me with him.

"I love you. Goodnight."

Maybe if you stay he won't come back.

"Good night, Ara," my father says.

So, he was here.


```
Operative Report: ASHBURNE, ARA LUCIA
Operation Date: 11/03/2000

PREOPERATIVE DIAGNOSIS: Necrotizing fasciitis.
POSTOPERATIVE DIAGNOSIS: Necrotizing fasciitis.

SURGEON: Dr. David Han

Assistants: John Krueger, M.D., Samuel Thompson, M.D.

OPERATION: Additional   debridement   of   the   necrotic   soft
    tissue from the abdominal wall, subcutaneous, skin and
    retroperitoneal area on both flanks.

INDICATIONS: This patient has been having debridement of
    the necrotic tissue because of necrotizing fasciitis for
    the last three days. The patient was brought to surgery
    today for further debridement of the necrotic tissue.
```

Translation: Additional removal of dead soft tissue (the skin, soft tissues under the skin, and likely musculature) from the front of the abdomen.

Additional removal was performed near the back of the cavity that contains most of the organs. Specifically, in the area on both sides of the back, roughly between the bottom of the ribcage and the top of the hip bone.

* * *

Attending Physician's Notes:
Pulse/ox saturation 90% — probable Acute Respiratory Distress Syndrome

11/4 4:00pm
Acute Metabolic Acidosis — could be contributing to respiratory issues

---

"Ara?"
Michael, what a relief to hear your voice.
"I'm on my way over to the polling place. I've decided to vote on your behalf."
After all the political disagreements we've had, it is hard to believe you would forgo backing your third-party candidate.
"With you in here, well, I want to vote on your behalf. I thought I would tell you."
I don't know why, but that seems so sweet. I guess it's because we both feel so passionately about our politics. It just seems so generous. Thank you.
I wish I could give you a kiss.

*

The television is on in my room. I can hear Tom Brokaw announcing. "Good evening, I'm Tom Brokaw in New York. It's been a long campaign. It appears it will be a long and exciting evening."
Cool, Yvonne, I didn't know you liked Brokaw too. So, here we go. After a year of reading salon.com and slate.com and holding my breath while reading every poll, we get to find out what is really gonna happen.
I hear a "thup," then Dan Rather says, "We could be in for a long night."
Wait Yvonne, don't change the channel yet. We don't even have any news yet.
"Thup."
Brokaw: "Stay with us. We are about to take you on an exciting and bumpy ride."

Ara Lucia Ashburne

Thank you, Yvonne. I can see already this is going to be a frustrating evening for me.

"Thup."

Peter Jennings: "There's every chance, as you know, that in many ways this is going to be an unusually interesting election night."

"Thup."

Rather: "So, tonight, if the race is as close as advertised, the three most important things are turnout, turnout, turnout."

Okay, I get it. This is going to be a kind of Zen exercise for me, accept whatever information comes my way.

I can't. Please Yvonne, stick with Brokaw until he says something significant or noteworthy, then you can shop around to see if the others are saying the same thing or something different.

I hate how other people channel surf. I understand random switching when you are looking for something to light on, like when you are too exhausted to watch something interesting, but *this* surfing is important surfing. Until you have something you can compare to, don't change the channel.

"Thup."

Well, I guess since I'm not going to get to follow this election the way I want, I may have to see if there is some actual pattern to your changing, but I have a feeling it is futile. Oh, wait, I have one other idea. You could change to the BBC and just stay there. How about that?

The rush of heat quickly pushes toward my heart and then throughout my body. *Oh no, I don't want to fall into the gray. I can't, not yet. This is really important to me.*

Fade.

*

I can hear the news in the distance. I feel slow and heavy. I want to sleep, but I feel tired, like my mind is on a treadmill I can't control. I listen to the distant sounds and think I hear the chair to my left move just a bit. Yvonne must be here. I know I am in the same place, but the sounds are echoing several walls away.

Oh, that's right, the election.

Yvonne, what did I miss? What states are in? God, I wish I could see from where I am. I'm sure the television where you are is something you can see and not just hear.

...Peter Jennings says, "We are now able to make a projection in the state of Florida. ABC News projects that Al Gore wins the state of Florida and its 25 electoral votes, giving him the first big state momentum of the evening. This is the biggest state where the race has been close, the fourth-biggest electoral prize."

So that is it, right? Yvonne, why aren't they saying? Does that mean Ohio and Pennsylvania are already in? That would be two out of the three needed. So Gore won, right?

I can't believe it. I thought it was impossible. I mean, I did hope, but in the end, I didn't think he was going to win. Wow, to think: a President who is going to repair the damage done to the EPA, who will do what can be done to repair the education system, and who lives in current times.

By the way, you know he doesn't think he invented the Internet. That was a comment taken out of context. And yes, I know, he does suck on camera. I think it's unfortunate this has become a litmus test for a politician.

I don't even know who I'm "talking" to, exactly. It doesn't really matter, I'm trying to reach someone beyond the blackness inside my own eyelids. It lets me pretend I'm not so alone.

Oh, good ol' America, democracy at its finest. The truth is, I would be saying that even if "we" had lost. I would just be bummed out.

Heat rush.

No! No, no, no!

I try to resist, even though I know it's impossible.

Yvonne, God, I wish you could stop this.

The heat burns out into my limbs, the world turns gray.

You know how I hate being left out...

The gray becomes black.

*

Peter Jennings says, "Governor Bush has just called Vice President Gore to retract his concession."

I can feel that time has passed, but have no idea how long I was gone. My brain lurches forward, trying to make sense of what I'm hearing.

What? What do you mean, "retract his concession?" How is that possible? Is this a network mistake?

"Thup."

Dan Rather says, "Florida pulled back into the undecided column due to computer and data problems. This knock-down, drag-out battle drags on into the night. Turn the lights down, the party just got wilder."

This isn't a party, this is freakish!

I feel the tears of frustration in my chest.

Why do I have to be Between when something like this is happening? I can't talk to you, I can't ask anything, you can't hear me, and I want to scream.

Wait, oh, I think I finally figured this thing out.

I'm not Between life and death; this is Armageddon. Presidents in America aren't chosen and then unchosen. That's it, I finally figured it out!

Heat rush.

But wait, if this is Armageddon, then I guess this would be happening to us all.

Ara Lucia Ashburne

> The heat burns out into my limbs, the world turns gray.
> *In this hell, it's only me.*

*

Tom Brokaw says, "George Bush is the President-Elect of the United States. He has won the state of Florida, according to our projections."

"Thup."

Peter Jennings says, "ABC News is now going to project that Florida now goes to Mr. Bush."

*

```
Operative Report: ASHBURNE, ARA LUCIA
Operation Date: 11/05/2000

PREOPERATIVE DIAGNOSIS: Necrotizing fasciitis.
POSTOPERATIVE DIAGNOSIS: Necrotizing fasciitis.

SURGEON: Dr. David Han

OPERATION: Debridement of the soft tissue of the abdominal
    wall because of the necrotizing fasciitis.

PROCEDURE: ...There were some areas of necrotic tissue and
    subcutaneous tissue and they were excised... We had been
    trying to preserve the umbilicus,* but at this time the
    umbilicus also looked necrotic, therefore it was also
    removed.... There were some loose necrotic tissues taken
    on both sides about the inguinal ligament** and some
    loose necrotic tissue was taken.


From:       Wendy [mailto: wendy@email.com]
Sent:       Sunday, November 05, 2000 12:41 PM
To:         Allgroup
cc:         michael
Subject:    Ara Update 2

    Hi, it is me again with an update on Ara's health. I am afraid
it is not much of an update, as things are much the same. She
continues to be kept unconscious in the ICU and her wound is
looked at frequently. She periodically goes back into the OR for
daily debridement (duh-BREED-ment), that is, removal of nonviable
tissue. So far there have been four of these procedures. The plan
continues to be alternating debridement until there is no non-
viable tissue forming.
```

---

* The navel, or belly button.

** A narrow band of dense supporting connective tissue in the groin.

Meanwhile, there are multiple cultures taken and tested as the doctors continue to refine their understanding of the specific bacteria involved. They have isolated one, but continue to test. Tests of this nature are lengthy, some taking five days or more to "set up;" there are still additional tests being performed on cultures taken on Sunday. This does not delay treatment, as she is receiving broad range antibiotics. But if they can in fact isolate more bacteria, they may have even more focused antibiotic treatment options.

So, we are still in a wait-and-see mode. Thanks for being with us in your thoughts and prayers. I will give you another update on Wednesday, sooner if there are any developments to report.

Wendy

11/5 7:50–8:30
Nursing Note:
• BP dropping again 80/50
• HR 110

"*Om namah shivaya…*"

There is an entire choir of women singing like angels.

I remember the words from when Yvonne and I were flying to DC every other month, studying meditation with Rudy at the Washington Center of Consciousness Studies. I think about what Rudy might have told me to do if he were here to guide me. So I listen to the chant and focus on my breath.

11/5 1:45 pm
Physician's Order: Ipratropium+albuterol via nebulizer every 4 h.

My breath feels quiet. I think about when I called Rudy and asked him about being in the pilot Ph.D. program they were creating with the Union Institute.

He laughed and said, "No, Ara. This program is for the social workers and psychologists that have been coming here for years and need to be encouraged to write articles. You don't need encouragement. You're in a speedboat! You keep doing what you're doing."

I don't know what I'm doing Rudy. Or what I'm speeding toward.

11/06/12 05:00 am
Physician's Note:
- Administered total of 4 units packed red blood cells
- Pulse very faint — had to get a Doppler to find pulse
- Nail beds pale, bluish

I remember how in meditation we would enter into what Rudy described as The Field of Awareness, and he would tell us to extend our awareness to connect with loved ones, teachers, the sacred archetypes.

I'm extending to you Rudy. I'm dropping my attention into my energetic awareness.

I feel my energy, but it is much slower than usual. My thoughts are slower. My awareness has difficulty attaching itself. I drop my attention lower; I move to a cellular awareness. The space between my thoughts, between the words, is minutes. I can feel my cells. I try to offer them my intention. I try to charge them with will. I can't feel any motion. They remain unchanged.

Rudy, if I cannot live, then I cannot stay in Between any longer. The demons keep finding me and tormenting me and my body is in agony. Rudy, I'm going to let my awareness fall into the pain and let go.

The pain spikes. I see black.

11/6 6:00 am
- Administer dopamine to increase BP to 90/60
- HR 116

I hear beeping on the outside. I fall and fall and fall and fall. My spirit lifts above my body. Though I can't see my face, I see my body in a medical room with Yvonne beside me. I pull on my spirit, but it's locked into place. The machines are holding me. I slam back into my body with fury and frustration.

*

Operative Report: ASHBURNE, ARA LUCIA
Operation Date: 11/06/2000

PREOPERATIVE DIAGNOSIS: Necrotizing fasciitis.
POSTOPERATIVE DIAGNOSIS: Same as above.

SURGEON: Dr. David Han

OPERATION: Re-debridement of soft tissue of the abdominal wall consisting of adipose tissue, portion of muscles and fascia covering the muscles of the abdomen.

PROCEDURE: This patient is having debridement of the soft tissue of the abdomen every day.

The specimen was sent down for aerobic and anaerobic culture, for fungus and gram stain, as well as quantitative culture. During the procedure, Dr. Metz from trauma service was there and he felt that the progress of the debridement is better and would have to do this every day until the wound looks very clean.

Estimated blood loss was about 75 to 100cc. The wound was packed. The two large Gore-Tex grafts were applied to cover the exposed viscera of the abdomen.

* * *

"We are waiting for the cultures to come back in hope of pinpointing the kind of bacteria. This would allow us to use a more specific antibiotic. In the meantime, we are using six wide-spectrum antibiotics. It is the best we can do. These things take time."

"I understand," Michael says calmly. "Without identifying the source there is nothing you can do to speed up this process."

"We are still concerned about her kidneys. They are working very hard to process out all this medication. They could just give up, and if they do, sometimes they can come back on-line and sometimes they don't."

Michael responded, "If they shut down, we will do what we have to. I've seen two different dialysis places not far from where we live."

What the hell, Michael! Dialysis? I don't want dialysis! What are you saying to him? That's crazy. First of all, I don't know how you could even be worrying about a thing like dialysis with me in this Between place. You guys should be working on a plan to get me out of here. Assuming you already have some kind of a plan, are you gonna lose my kidneys on the way back? Is that it? I'm willing to go with it for a minute here.

Screeeech!

I hear that familiar noise, the metal against metal sound, and make a new connection. It is the first in a sequence of events. I'm constantly trying to make sense of what's going on around me, what it all means. *Michael, listen! Did you hear that? The metal against metal sound?*

I desperately want Michael to understand. Maybe If I can explain it to him, he can figure out how to get me back.

Every time, after that sound, someone rustles plastic, and then they put the gum in my mouth. It lasts for a whole day and is the reason I can't talk to you. Worse, it's always followed by Fernando.

I think the name before I even remember what it means, who Fernando is. I feel a rush of terror, remembering what I didn't want to remember. In the Nightmare Place, Fernando is the most nightmarish of all.

He comes, and he tortures me.

"Feel free to have them page me if you have any other questions," the man says. "I will be back the day after tomorrow and see how things are going. Do you still have my card?"

"Yes, I do. I appreciate your availability."

No, Michael, listen—over here! ME, *not that guy. This isn't the time for your professional politeness! I've been waiting for days for you to be in the room when this happens so you could free me from my frozen mouth and the torturer.*

Then I hear the crinkling of plastic, followed by the shoving of the gum.

No, please—

I can feel the tears well up inside my chest, but once again, my throat doesn't tighten because I can't cry.

I can't even cry.

Okay, okay, Michael, so you missed the metal thing and the person freezing my mouth, but just stay here a few minutes. He's gonna be here any second.

I hear Michael move away, and as soon as he's not beside me the rush of heat comes, relentless, unstoppable.

No, Michael, wait—don't go, please... no....

Before I know it, I'm back in the cold metal room, the one in the Nightmare Place, and everyone is gone, and I'm alone, waiting.

*

He pops up by the side of my bed, like a jack-in-the-box.

Fernando is back.

"How is my little pretty today?"

He smiles. His cracked, dry lips peel back to reveal yellow, crooked teeth. They're the same color as the rheumy eyes he peers at me with. His head and hands are too big for his hunched, decrepit body. His skin is dark, creased, and leathery. Though it looks like he must be very old, his hair is black as jet and his gnarled hands have a grip like a vice.

I want to shake my head or pull away from him, but I still can't move. What will his torture be today? It's always a prolonged, abstract choice.

Everything happens the way he wants. Wherever he goes, he has complete control. I don't know how or why this is, only there is nothing I can do. I have the impulse to cringe, to draw my head to my shoulders, but nothing happens. I feel vulnerable. I hate this feeling of being assaulted, forced to participate in his perverse games, but I'm open to him, exposed, powerless. I can only pull my spirit away from him. My body is his.

"I heard you talking to Michael." The humorless smile has left his face. "He didn't hear you now, did he? How many times do I need to tell you that you are mine, and I won't have you reaching out to the other side?"

He lifts my hand up and presses it against his bony chest. It is such a relief to feel my arm move, but I'm angry he is the one moving it.

"Now, I told you what would happen the next time you did this. I told you, I can see everything and hear everything and there is no point in your continuing to fight with me."

I hear a snapping sound and see he has flipped open his jackknife. For a few seconds, then minutes, he presses the edge of the knife blade against my pinkie finger, between the last two knuckles.

He waits. I can feel the knife, but he hasn't broken the skin yet. He's letting me anticipate the loss of my fingertip.

A tiny smile plays across his lips.

"Whisper my name. Say, 'I am here for you.'"

I ignore him. I know refusing to respond will result in more pain, but I hate the idea of anyone or anything lording over me, controlling me. Call it stubbornness, but I can't shake it.

"Say it," he hisses insistently. "I want to hear my glorious name. Say 'Fernando.'"

Suddenly, I feel a clean cut. The pain shoots into my spine, but the cut is so sharp and quick that I wonder if maybe there isn't any blood.

He releases my hand, and my arm drops clumsily, bouncing off the bed and hanging awkwardly off the side. He shows me the end of my finger.

"I will be keeping this."

He tosses the finger into his pocket and pats the pocket twice. He grins and vanishes.

*

```
Operative Report: ASHBURNE, ARA LUCIA
Operation Date: 11/08/2000

PREOPERATIVE DIAGNOSIS: Necrotizing fasciitis.
POSTOPERATIVE DIAGNOSIS: Necrotizing fasciitis.

SURGEON: Dr. David Han
ASSISTANT: Samuel Thompson, M.D.
```

OPERATION: Debridement of the soft tissue of the abdomen including the edges of the skin, necrotic subcutaneous tissue and dead muscle.

PROCEDURE: ...Starting from the right side the retroperitoneal area was examined and there were a few areas consisting of necrotic tissue which were removed with sharp dissection. There were some left over muscles and edges of the muscle so the external and internal oblique and transversus abdominis were also removed. In the retropubic area on the neck of the bladder there were some necrotic tissues which were removed...

I see a thick haze made up of pixels. The pixels are like broken glass, organized in a kaleidoscopic pattern. It is as if each piece is pointing to the center of my vision. I cannot see through this haze; the light bounces around the completely sterile environment. Voices echo around me as if I am in a cavernous metal room.

This place is really scary. It is like no human has ever been here. I know somehow I am even farther from home than ever before. I hear voices, but the sounds don't resemble language.

Several sets of eyes appear around my body, all looking down on me. They are talking among themselves and I don't understand. Their eyes are somewhat luminous, and their form, somewhat fluid.

Oh my God, they're aliens! I never knew what to believe before this, but that would explain everything—the physical pain, the reason I feel trapped, how I can't get back to Life. What are they going to do to me?

Suddenly I feel an electric shock to my abdomen, like a sharp jab. Pain shoots up my spine and burns my eyes. I scream, but, as always, there is no sound.

There is another shock, then another. They are coming faster now, each stronger than the last. The pain in my spine is immense.

What are they doing to me? Why can't they do whatever it is without hurting me?

PROCEDURE: ...On the lateral side there was a pocket of pus at the neck of the bladder which was opened and some necrotic tissue was found and removed. The rectus muscle on the right side appeared dead, it did not contract when current from the electrocautery device was applied, therefore it was removed.

...The aliens are neutral to the pain they are causing me. The shock-jabs are coming so quickly now. The sensation is more like a belt sander being held to my abdomen. My spine is on fire.

Will I know what has happened to me when this is over?

The electric sander shock-vibrations soon rise to the level of a jackhammer. My body convulses. The blows come faster, faster.

I realize I will never know. My thoughts are shattered by the pain.

PROCEDURE: ...A portion of the skin flap on the left side appeared dusky and maybe by tomorrow it may need debridement. The lateral flank was okay, however a new finding today was that the iliac crest muscle on the left side was found to be necrotic and it was removed. On both sides the iliac vessels could be seen and no attempt was made to debride especially on the left side, the area was covered with a slight amount of necrotic tissue covering the vessels, some of the necrotic tissues were removed without exposing the vessels completely....

11/9 6:30pm
Nursing Note:
- Issue: BP 80/40
- Dr. Baker at bedside
- HR 130
- IV bolus morphine (lower heart rate)
- Minutes later 80/40 a second time
- Doctor still at bedside
- Gave albumin and fresh frozen plasma
- BP went up to 122/65
- HR 125

Michael leaned in close and said, "Ara, I love you so much, and you just have to pull through this. I can't have you in my life and then lose you."

So, I actually might die.

"You are the only one any of us knows who could live through something like this. I know this will be the hardest thing you will ever do, but you need to pull through. You have to. We all need you. I need you."

I have tried! I used all my might, and I can't move or talk or come out of this place, this place where I can hear you, but not see you. I don't know what else to do or how to get back. Can't you come over and get me? Can't you help me break away from here? Can't you tell me how to escape?

"I would do anything for you, I swear, anything. I will take you anywhere in the world you want to go, I will do anything. Please, Ara, you have to live. I need you to live. I need you."

*   *   *

My naked body is suspended between two interlocking metal rings like a circus performer. Tubes extend from the metal rings into our bodies. The tubes maintain all of our bodies' organs and lungs, allowing us just enough breath to remain alive. The only tubes I can feel run into my nostrils and up my nose. They are uncomfortable, and I continuously feel pressure in my lungs I cannot control.

Our bodies are still, but not lifeless. We are still alive, barely, and breathing. The tubes facilitate our connection to one another, and to him. Breath is the key; our breath is his breath. In this way, he knows us, but we know him, too. We are aware of his presence, or at least I am aware of it. The Breath Lord is always with me, though he is not in the room.

We wait to perform for him, to become his plaything for a single night, and then we are disposed of. He keeps 41 women, bodies in row after row like a morgue of lifeless forms. Always 41. There is always another girl coming, one each night, replacing the one who has disappeared. We never know whose turn it will be.

The room is dim with only one metal door to enter or to leave. It makes a sucking sound when it opens and closes. The Breath Lord is somewhere beyond the door. There are often technicians shuffling about the room in short green robes, always in pairs. They are young men, not quite adults, but not children, either. They clean and maintain the tubes. They move with hardly a word, but when they do speak, it is only to each other and in another language that sounds partially Korean.

When we arrive, we learn the Breath Lord was once a deity trapped in stone, a statue of a man-lion in a temple on the highest mountain in the Zhoulang Pass. One day when the moon crossed in front of the sun, the deity somehow came to life. Now he takes what is owed to him.

The technicians slowly clean the metal rings and our bodies with cold water. We are kept clean and quiet until we are chosen by the Breath Lord. Each time we hear the big metal door, we know someone new will be brought in and someone will be taken away. I can't hear anything on the other side of the door. From fragments of the technicians' conversations, I understand that the Breath Lord uses us as concubines. But as none of the women are allowed to talk, and the technicians speak only to each other, I do not actually know what will happen on the day when I am eventually chosen.

My back and body ache from the torture of being held in the same position. Once, during a time when no technicians were around, I was able to rock the metal circles back and forth a little, but nothing came of it. I am unable to move my body. I am frozen, hovering.

One day, one of the technicians speaks to me directly. He is a young and attractive boy. Without missing a beat, while cleaning one of the metal rings, he leans in and says, "Michael is coming to see the room. Pretend you do not know him or you risk both of you being killed."

A few hours later, a technician walks into the room. He is taller than the rest and I instantly know it is Michael.

He approaches my metal ring and cleans it with a substance that emits fumes, reminding me of rubbing alcohol. He doesn't even give me a glance, just goes about his work as if he doesn't know me. I don't know what he's planning, but I fear for how much danger we must be in. Next, he moves to the metal rings and equipment of two other girls before leaving the room as unremarkably as he entered.

Days pass before I see Michael again. When he appears, he approaches my rings and cleans them along with the respiratory apparatus. This time he whispers to me: "Later I will disconnect you. You will have to continue breathing as shallowly as you did on the equipment, no matter how your body is moving or what is happening. If you do not, he will kill you instantly."

Another tech enters the room to bathe one of the other girls. Michael moves to her breathing apparatus, cleans it, and leaves.

I try to control my nervousness, to remain calm, so I do not betray his plans to the Breath Lord. Waiting for Michael to return again is its own kind of torture. Finally, late the next day, Michael arrives. He crosses directly to me and says, "It's going to be quick. I'm going to disconnect you, and you must continue to breathe quietly. I'll carry you out of here. If we don't make it, know I truly love you. Here we go."

He disconnects the tubes from my nostrils, and air rushes into my lungs. I was prepared to breathe quietly, but the moment he disconnected the apparatus, a gust of air filled my lungs with a tremendous force. "Put it back," I plead with him, my voice hoarse from the dry tube air. "He's coming. I can feel his presence rushing toward us. He'll kill you for taking me."

"It's too late. I'm taking you out of here."

Michael pulls my body from the center of the rings somehow, and instantly I hang limp in his arms, with no power to lift my head. Then, he runs with me in his arms, stumbling. We wind our way through a thick nighttime forest. He stumbles over logs and branches, moving as quickly as he can. The roots of the trees trip him along the way—several times he drops my body, but I feel nothing. Each time he picks me back up and continues our arduous flight.

I can feel the Breath Lord closing in on us. Each breath I take is a marker, like a sonar echo. I can feel his presence, closer and closer. I can hear Michael gasping for air.

The Breath Lord is slowly drawing the air out of both our bodies.

Soon Michael collapses to the ground, still holding me. He gasps, "I love you, Ara."

"Michael, it's not too late. Give me back to him before he kills you."

Suddenly the Breath Lord is upon us. He has taken the form of a demon, looming over us, embodied in the twisted trunk and branches of an ancient tree, glowing like molten lava.

Blood squeezes out of my mouth and eyes as my head falls back on the soil. I feel Michael's arms around me, but I no longer hear him or see him. I see only the face of the luminous, angry Breath Lord. I feel his hold on my lungs. He's crushing me from the inside as a punishment for trying to escape him. I sense Michael's spirit slipping away, and his grip on my body loosens. The Breath Lord has taken him. My face is covered in blood, and my last breath has been taken from me.

Operative Report: ASHBURNE, ARA LUCIA
Operation Date: 11/10/2000

SURGEON: Dr. David Han

OPERATION: Examination of the wound and irrigation of the wound. No debridement performed today, but there was a small perforation in the bladder and urologist Dr. Michael Yates took care of that part and he will dictate the operative procedure separately.

After the procedure, Dr. Yates and myself talked to family including her father and mother and husband and aunt. The whole procedure was explained.

Operative Report: ASHBURNE, ARA LUCIA
Operation Date: 11/10/2000

SURGEON: Dr. Mark Yates

OPERATION: Cystoscopy and repair of bladder fistula

...At this time, urological consultation has been requested for continued evaluation of the patient's pelvis. General Surgical Service has previously explored the retroperitoneal space. The bladder has been identified to be intact and previous studies were all unremarkable. A urological consultation at this debridement is now being obtained.

PROCEDURE: ...It was only after approximately 300 cc of methylene blue stain was placed in the bladder that indeed leakage could be seen from a region on the dome of the bladder consistent with the previous cystoscopic findings.... The defect in the bladder which was felt to be perhaps 1.5 cm in length was then closed in two layers, the first layer being a mucosal muscular layer utilizing 2-0 polyglactin 910 in a running fashion to obtain a watertight seal, followed by 2-0 polyglactin 910 in an interrupted figure-of-eight fashion for the outer serosal muscular layer. Having accomplished what appeared to be an excellent repair, once again the bladder was instilled with methylene blue and at this time the bladder was filled to 400 cc. Indeed, no extravasation of methylene blue was identified consistent with a watertight closure.... Having accomplished this, the bladder was then drained and the General Surgical Service then continued with their evaluation of the pelvis.

Estimated blood loss was minimal.

Operative Report: ASHBURNE, ARA LUCIA
Operation Date: 11/12/2000

PREOPERATIVE DIAGNOSIS: Necrotizing fasciitis.
POSTOPERATIVE DIAGNOSIS: Necrotizing fasciitis.

SURGEON: Dr. David Han

OPERATION: Examination of the wound and dressing change.

INDICATIONS: The patient has been having debridements almost every day for the past several days. On Friday she had examination of the wound, and repair of the small perforation in the bladder was performed by Dr. Yates. That day, there were no further developments as mentioned in the previous surgical report.

PROCEDURE: Today, no debridement was performed. During the procedure Dr. Krueger came and he agreed that the wound looked pretty good and tomorrow the patient will be brought again to the Operating Room and we will request the plastic surgeon to assess the situation for further closure of the wound.

*   *   *

Ara Lucia Ashburne

```
11/13  7:30am
Physician's Notes:
• ToF 1/4*
• Vecuronium dose 5 mg
```

"To all the fine listeners here in the Pacific Ocean, we bring you Kiriba Radio, twenty-four hours a day, from our secret location! Our fine business travelers will appreciate our alluring women chosen from around the world who are eager to provide you with personal island adventures."

I listen carefully to the overhead radio announcer in hopes of discerning a clue to our location. I know I will never escape if I don't even know where I am.

"Mr. Winston, we hope you had a comfortable flight. During your stay with us, we will provide you with delightful feminine entertainment.

"Papa-India-Two-Niner, vector for traffic. Steer right zero-one-zero, descend, and maintain five thousand five hundred."

I'm trying to place the announcer's voice. It sounds familiar. He starts reading news headlines.

"Manila: American Ambassador David G. Houghton is attending a summit in Manila to stabilize relations between China and Japan."

He talks like a 1930's radio announcer, but he sounds like he has an Egyptian accent. What is he doing here on a radio station in the Pacific? Amelia Earhart's plane was lost in the Pacific and not even the United States Government could find her, so if that is where I am, I'm on my own.

"Stockholm: American Consulate reports Sweden's Prime Minister Osterberg has left the country and is hiding in Istanbul.

"Paris hospital: Actor Simon Moore and his wife Bessie had their first baby, a boy named William.

"Tower, Skyhawk-Eight-Eight-Two-Niner, ready for takeoff. Departure is VFR North.

"Egypt: A newspaper man who returned from overseas reports Egypt has advanced into Saudi Arabian territory and has taken control of the Red Sea."

I'm surrounded by red velvet—the walls, the floor, the cushions on the chairs, even the one-piece swimsuits on all the women. There are about a

---

* Train of Four. A method of assessing a patient's level of paralysis, whether drug-induced or otherwise, using an electrical device that stimulates a nerve. Four consecutive electrical pulses are delivered to the nerve, and the number of twitches that result roughly indicates the percentage of nerve receptors successfully blocked by the drug (a "blockade"). Here, when the physician noted "1/4," this indicated there was only one response out of the four stimuli applied (typically the desired goal).

dozen of us, standing in a line behind a row of stools. With our breasts accentuated, the swimsuits make us look like antiquated Playboy bunnies. Only from here, the Choosing Room, can I clearly hear the constant sound of the radio announcer. We can't speak, as our mouths have been sealed with a clear putty, but we have our eyes, and that's how we communicate with one another.

The most recent flight brings five new women in their early twenties. They are brought into the room naked by the host of the gentleman's club. He gestures to the pile of velvet bathing suits on the floor, indicating for the women to pick them up and put them on. From his place at the podium he checks in each new girl. This new batch is another international collection: one Asian, one Latin, one Caucasian, and two I can't identify. When a group of new women arrives, an equal number are removed from the club and taken to the other side of the island where they strip trees to make perfume.

No one escapes.

11/13 2:00pm
Nursing Note:
- TOF 2/4
- Increased vecuronium dosage to 6 mg per hour

"Pittsburgh: Mob kingpin 'Kid' Mariani was shot to death by federal agents during a sting operation confiscating liquor stills and guns.

"New Orleans: Jazz pianist and singer, Minnie Calloway, died of an unknown cause."

A very large, older gentleman in a tuxedo enters with both hands in his pants pockets. He looks at us with a reserved curiosity as if reading stock quotes in the morning paper. He hopes to determine not only who pleases his eye, but who will give him what he desires once he has her to himself. Over time, we'll be trained to perform in all styles of sexual pleasure, but we are still individuals and some may satisfy his urges more than others. As a long-time client, he knows which girls are new. They are positioned on stools in the front row. He knows the new ones will move with a bigger fire in their eyes, even if it's a frightened fire, but the older girls are more willing.

I quickly gesture to the new girls to keep their eyes down. Only one understands what I mean. Every time I help a new batch of girls like this, I feel conflicted about it because it means someone else will pay the price. Still, it seems too harsh for them to be required to perform so soon after arriving. This time, however, my gesture draws the old man's attention to me.

"Washington, D.C.: Confidential files implicating FBI Agent Monahan of treason were uncovered by newsman James Dewald of *The Washington Post*.

"Tower, Two-Niner-Zulu is departing your Delta airspace and changing frequencies."

He walks up to me, waving a satin handkerchief in his hand, as if he hopes I will agree to a waltz, but there is no music, just the ceaseless rattle of the overhead radio. For a moment, my focus on the announcer is interrupted. I worry that in these single moments of disrupted concentration I will miss a necessary clue as to our location.

"Skyhawk-Eight-Eight-Two-Niner, you are cleared for takeoff, runway thirty-five."

"New York City: Jazz singer Della Ray hits the stage with her hit performance of 'I'm Your Gal' to a rousing crowd at the Washington Playhouse.

"New York City: Mayor Sullivan will be marrying motion picture starlet Margaret Moore. The happy couple will reside in Atlanta at the end of his term."

The man takes my left hand and guides me between the new girls. He gestures for me to turn a circle before him, but I know this gesture is perfunctory because he has already decided I'll be his catch today. He nods to the host at the podium and holds his hand out for the key to his room. With sleight of hand reminiscent of a card trick, he passes me the key. He wants me to lead the way, as if *I* have invited *him* to my private room.

"San Francisco: Aviation magnate Bobby Stevenson has successfully completed the first cross-country flight from New York City to San Francisco in his gyro-plane.

"Boston: Rear Admiral T. A. Frost and twenty-seven others perished when the dirigible *Fontane* was downed by a storm off the coast."

We climb the creaky steps and stop at the fourth door. The radio announcer is piped in everywhere. I continue to listen, to concentrate, trying to catch some clue as to our location in order to eventually figure out a means of escape. I take a deep breath as I open the door to the room. The fat man pushes me into the room and hurriedly closes the door.

Then I notice that the radio announcer, over a speaker in the room, sounds panicked.

11/13 2:00pm
Physician's Note:
- Anesthesia has requested for surgery to be done in ICU

> - Concerned about transporting critically ill patient to operating room

"Eight-November-Lima, I've got opposite direction traffic located about four miles south of you coming opposite direction, same altitude."

Amongst the constant crackle of radio static, I hear a distant voice reply, "I'm Eight-November-Lima... looking for traffic."

The man pauses for a time, while both of us stand in silence. I don't yet know what he wants from me. Is he trying to make up his mind, or is this waiting part of the game for him?

The announcer's voice returns, louder now.

"Eight-November-Lima, his altitude is holding the same. Why don't you give me a descend to about two-point-three, please—you can at least get below, 'cause he's opposite direction. Uh... uh, looks like we've got converging targets going on here, sir. Why don't you descend down for me, please."

I know that there's no reward for making him happy, only punishment if I do not honor his wishes.

The distant voice responds to the announcer.

"Ah, roger, we're descending to two thousand three hundred—headin' down real quick."

I hear a loud bang over the speaker, and then the crackle of static fills the room. I listen for the announcer's voice, for the voice of the pilot, for anything.

```
Operative Report: ASHBURNE, ARA LUCIA
Operation Date: 11/13/2000

PREOPERATIVE DIAGNOSIS: Necrotizing fasciitis.
POSTOPERATIVE DIAGNOSIS: Necrotizing fasciitis.

OPERATION:  Examination of the wound and dressing change
    with debridement of a small area of the subcutaneous
    tissue.

PROCEDURE:  For three days in a row now, examination of the
    wound was done in the operation room and the muscles and
    all of the area appeared very healthy and pinkish. The
    muscles were found to be contracting. There was only a
    small area of one inch in diameter over the subcutaneous
    tissue on the right side of the abdomen that was
    excised. So there was practically no debridement done
    today...
```

Ara Lucia Ashburne

The man draws a knife.

Before I can react, he is on me, gripping my shoulder tightly with his free hand, and I feel a sharp stab in my belly. The strength immediately leaves my legs, and I collapse to the ground. I see nothing but darkness.

Seconds, then minutes pass.

Nothing but static.

My mouth is still glued shut.

From: Wendy [mailto: wendy@email.com]
Sent: Monday, November 13, 2000 10:37 PM
To: Allgroup
cc: michael
Subject: Ara Update 4

Well, today I not only have news, I have cautiously optimistic news! During Friday's debridement, the doctors found no necrotized tissue (yay!). They decided to let Ara rest on Saturday, and then to change the dressings on Sunday and check things out that way.

On Sunday, the doctor used the word "pristine" to describe the wound. Monday's plan is to change the dressing in the OR, where a plastic surgeon can be consulted. If things are still "pristine," the plastic surgeon will be involved in the plan for the next phase of recovery.

Keep praying; it is obviously working. Next update Wednesday or sooner.

Gratefully,
Wendy

11/13 11pm

Nursing Note:

- toF 4/4
- Bolus of vecuronium given, drip increased to 7 mg per hour

I can hear a man's voice in the distance. He sounds calm, sure. His tone is confident. It seems as if he is talking to a group of people about something important.

I hear footsteps on tile. His voice is closer now. "I have a hunch."

Who are you? A hunch about what? Hey, do you know where the portals are?

I've taken to always looking for "portals" between the worlds. I am constantly hoping to find an escape route, in case the opportunity presents itself. Maybe this confident voice can help me.

His voice is farther away again, but more demanding now.

Then nothingness again.

In the Between, there is no time, only gray. And heaviness.

Then there is a distant rattling sound. It is gradually getting closer.

I feel my hair being parted and tabs being placed on my head, one after another. I cringe inside.

Is this an experiment? What will he do to me?

Another poke at another point on my head, then another.

There is a brief pause.

Then, clearly alarmed, the man exclaims, "Oh my God!"

Another brief pause, and then he continues, speaking quickly: "No, she's not sedated—her mind is racing like a thousand horses!"

No kidding! So, you can see in here with your machine? Can you use your machine to come over here to my side?

He starts shouting orders, demanding medications, assistance, equipment —I can't follow all of his jargon. Then he shouts angrily, "I am pulling her out of this right now."

I feel a sudden, tiny thrill. A flicker of hope.

Is this real? Are you coming over to Between? How are you doing this?

Louder still, but more slowly than before, almost sweetly, he says, "Hey Ara, we're going to bring you back. This is going to take about ten to fifteen minutes, and you'll start to wake up."

But, I'm awake right now! Don't you understand? I'm already awake. Oh no, maybe you aren't going to be able to help me after all.

Then, after a moment, something seems different.

Slowly, oh-so-slowly, the gray pixels begin receding.

My heart is racing. I'm thrilled, and terrified. *What if this isn't real? What if it's another trick?*

And then I notice I can feel where my legs are, then my arms. I begin to feel where my body is exactly, for the first time in what seems like forever.

I open my eyes, blinking, and everything is blurry. I can hear the man speaking to me, but I'm not listening to him. I am overwhelmed by the realization—I HAVE OPENED MY EYES.

I see a woman, in scrubs. She is beside me. Another women in different scrubs stands at the end of my bed. Are they nurses?

Ara Lucia Ashburne

Why are there nurses? What is happening?

A man in a long white coat is nearby. If the people in scrubs are nurses then the person in the white coat must be a doctor. He speaks to the nurses, giving orders to them, then turns to me.

"This is Allison. She is your nurse, and she will be here with you as you wake up." He is facing me squarely.

I continue to blink to try to clear the blur from my eyes. I can feel the closer woman hold my hand and shoulder. She must be Allison. She says to me gently, "Ara, you are in the ICU at the hospital. You have been very sick, but you are doing better now. The doctors figured out what is wrong, and you have been getting better every day. Just rest. Rest is the best way to heal now."

I fight to keep my eyes open, but the lids are heavier than my will. I have so many questions, but the words float around in my head and do not make it to my lips.

Now that I have made it to "awake," I can't risk falling back through the portal. Clearly, my eyes being open is the key, and now that I can open them, I can't risk letting them close again.

I push to keep my eyes open, but my eyelids only flicker and close. I am drowsy. The sensation of sleep is overbearing, but not like I'm falling away, not like before. I can still hear everything in the room with a keen sharpness. This sleep is different. Yet, I don't know how close that portal might be and whether or not I could accidentally fall back into it.

What if the doctor leaves, and I can't open my eyes again?

As I fight to stay awake, I hear a machine beeping. The doctor instructs the nurse to give me a medication "to bring her heart rate down."

No, no, no—no medication, that might make me fall back. I can't go back, please, no!

I push my eyes open a crack, but they close and I fall asleep.

11/14 11:45am

Physician's Note:

Neuro Status:

- Medical coma — discontinue vecuronium
- Increase morphine and midazolam

> 11/14 noon
> - Discontinued vecuronium, showed movement within one hour
> - Following commands
> - Moving all extremities, weakly opening eyes to verbal command
> - Patient is still sedated

Time has passed.

Now awake, I realize my thoughts seem louder to me, a bit clearer. The sounds around me are louder, too—much louder.

The numbness I felt around my ears, the buzzing, is gone. I can hear so many sounds: voices in conversations, footsteps near and far. I hadn't realized how much sound I'd been missing. It's as if the air has been cleared of the pixels, the muddiness, and now sounds bounce around me with astounding clarity.

The weight that was resting on my body, on my entire being, has lifted.

My eyes open, and I see a person.

It is a person I know. She has short, dark hair. She is wearing a fleece vest. She has a familiar face with a sparkle in her eye and an enchanting smile. A warm feeling of comfort flows through me. The feeling is clear, uncomplicated.

Wendy.

She looks at me, and I look at her.

Ah, Wendy.

She's there, and, for now, I am with her, not Between.

And then I fall back asleep.

Awake

From: Wendy [mailto: wendy@email.com]
Date: Wednesday, November 15, 2000 11:11 AM
To: Allgroup
cc: michael
Subject: Ara Update 5

    Hi, again. Since your last update, the wound has been clean each time they've checked, so that is very good. Now the plastic surgeon and the trauma doctors are working together from this point out, planning Ara's continued recovery.

    Right now, there are some secondary infection issues causing an intermittent temperature, and the doctors would like that all resolved before any further action. So, she continues to get medication for these, and to be closely monitored. We expect at least 10 days of that before they start measures to facilitate her wound closing. Obviously, we need to make sure everything is crystal clear (infection wise) before we want the wound to close.

    Also, she is no longer getting the drug that paralyzes her, so now her lungs will be active and will start building strength so that she can ultimately breathe on her own. (Technically, she could breathe on her own now; the ventilator is making sure that her lungs inflate fully so that her lungs stay clear and so that she gets enough oxygen into her system.) This new lack of paralysis also means that she wiggles a little from time to time.

    There are some side issues going on as well. Some time soon she will have her breathing tube switched from the tube that goes in her mouth and down her throat, to a tube in the trachea. This is to protect the vocal cords, which don't enjoy the mouth-and-throat tube for too long at a stretch. It is also easier to monitor, keep clean, etc. Another side issue is blood clotting. They will do an ultrasound tomorrow to check for clots, and as soon as her temperature spikes are resolved, they will put a "filter" in to prevent clotting problems.

All in all, despite the day to day fluctuations and procedures, the trend is still upward and slow progress is being made. We can all expect this to last several more weeks. Ara is still kept heavily sedated and unaware. So she still has a restricted visitation list, and we are still stockpiling your cards for her later enjoyment. And everyone is really grateful for your thoughts and prayers for Ara's health, and for wisdom and courage for all those involved in caring for her and loving her.

More again on Sunday; sooner if there is news to report.

Gratefully,

Wendy

*   *   *

Operative Report: ASHBURNE, ARA LUCIA
Operation Date: 11/15/2000

PREOPERATIVE DIAGNOSIS: Necrotizing fasciitis.
POSTOPERATIVE DIAGNOSIS: Necrotizing fasciitis.

SURGEON: Dr. David Han

OPERATION:
   1) Examination of the wound
   2) Irrigation of the wound
   3) Closure of the muscles and skin on the right flank.

PROCEDURE: ...Dr. Krueger from Trauma Service and Dr. Smith, plastic surgeon, were also in the operation room. Dr. Stummons suggested that on the right flank the muscle looked okay so a few sutures were given and the right side was closed with 2-0 nylon sutures.... The wound was examined again and no fresh necrotic tissue was found in any part of the abdomen. All organs appear healthy.

1/16 9:00am

Pain Specialist Note:
- Patient is alert
- When asked about her pain she nodded yes

> - Given this, will increase morphine to 8 mg/hour and decrease midazolam to 3 mg/hour
> - Given long-term use of morphine patient may go through withdrawals if this is stopped acutely
>
> 11/16 9:25am
> Resident Note:
> - Still spiking fever
> - Still tachycardic* — HR 153
> - Edema everywhere
>
> 11/16 1:50pm
> Vent setting: 10 cm H_2O PEEP**

Operative Report: ASHBURNE, ARA LUCIA
Operation Date: 11/17/2000

SURGEON: Dr. David Han

PREOPERATIVE DIAGNOSIS: Necrotizing fasciitis. Respiratory failure, prolonged endotracheal intubation.

POSTOPERATIVE DIAGNOSIS: Necrotizing fasciitis. Respiratory failure, prolonged endotracheal intubation.

OPERATION: Tracheostomy, examination of wound and dressing.

> 11/17 1:00am
> - 7.5 cm H_2O PEEP
> - No spontaneous respiration

---

* Fast heart rate.

** Peak or Positive End Expiratory Pressure. Increasing air pressure in the lungs near the end of exhalation so additional air remains in the lungs. Used to deter their collapse.

Ara Lucia Ashburne

> 11/18 7:30am
> Nursing Note:
> - Issue: patient complained of nausea, x3
> - tube feedings
> - Gave ondansetron for nausea
> - turned tube feeding off
>
> 11/18 (no time indicated)
> Physician's Note:
> - 4 positive blood cultures — may be infection in the heart
> - Ordered echocardiogram

    I could hear Michael talking to a doctor just outside my room, exchanging the usual pleasantries, with the doctor saying he was available and Michael thanking him. Then he walked in. It was amazing to overhear the conversation so clearly and then to see him. To see him with my eyes open. He is wearing his light brown t-shirt under a forest green sweatshirt. He never wears a layer, but I remembered hearing something about how I kept asking for the room to be colder. I'd been burning up for over a month now and finally, through pantomime and head nods, I was able to communicate basic needs.

"Hey Friend," he said carefully.

I'm immediately calmed by the sight of his strong features—seeing him, not just hearing him—it was like a wave of warmth, but I'm shocked, as I had never seen him look so exhausted. His face looked like the prisoners of war I had seen in documentaries. He might not have been as skinny, but he clearly had been to hell and back.

"So, um, do you know where you are? Has anyone told you, or anything?"

I nodded.

I got it. Maybe I should have figured it out before with you talking to doctors and everything, but it seemed like something happening around me, not actually to me.

"Do you remember anything? Why you're in here?"

I shook my head no because the truth was yes and no, and I didn't know a gesture for, "It's complicated."

Michael sighed, "Well, I don't know what you remember or the last thing or how much. You were pretty out of it when we got home. It turns out when you were in all that pain, you were right. Something *was* wrong. Something happened during the laparoscopic procedure… do you remember that? For the ectopic pregnancy?"

I nodded again.

"Anyway, something happened. All the pain you were in before… it was real. They nicked your bladder, and it leaked, and there was an infection."

Of course the pain was real. I'd been trying to convince them of that all along, but nobody was listening.

I couldn't know that in another ten years I'd get to look at my medical records from Founder's Hospital and see what had been written about my pain. More specifically, what they'd written about my bipolar disorder, how my lithium had been discontinued, and how that may be affecting my "reaction to pain and condition." Or the other notes about a CBC test—a complete blood count—that was never done. If it had been, no doubt my white blood cell numbers would've made it impossible to write, "No evidence of infection." But whether anyone knew if my pain had been real or not *now?* That made no difference.

"It's 'necrotizing fasciitis,' the so-called 'flesh-eating bacteria.' They never should've sent you home."

Oh, gross. I don't want to have that. Pick something else. Can you undo? Control-Z? Make it something else! 'Cause that's disgusting. I don't want to have that.

"Well, so, um, so they had to do a bunch of surgeries. They had to cut out the infected tissue in your abdomen. So that's…" he made a vague circle in the air over the blankets covering my torso. "They had to remove all of the tissue from there—from just under the bottom of your sternum to the top of your pubic bone."

I gave him a wide-eyed look. *"How the hell am I alive then if all of my guts are gone?"*

"No no no, all of your organs are fine. They're all still there. It was only the tissue that was infected, the skin, muscle, fat, and fascia." He said the last part flatly, like it was no big deal. Like he'd said it over and over so many times it had lost any special meaning.

Nice, how you did that, Michael. I always loved how you could read my mind. You would know what I was thinking, even when I was looking out a car window.

"So, yeah. Just the stuff that held all your organs in. Heh." He smiled mirthlessly, "You're gonna have to have another surgery, a reconstruction at some point, later on down the line. But that's later, like, a year or something. Your body needs to recover from this round of surgeries first."

*   *   *

Ara Lucia Ashburne

"Oh hello! You must be Ara's father. Do come in."

My Dad seems rushed, almost agitated, as he hands an Englishman a large roll of papers. The man is wearing a sage and brown tweed coat with suede elbow patches.

"What have you found out?" the man asks as my father follows him, wordlessly, into the study.

The door into the study is set in one corner of the room. His den was claustrophobic: book shelves full of aged publications and tomes line two of the walls, while waist-high towers of papers and journals crowd the floor. The Englishman and my father wind their way through the piles, crossing the room toward the opposing corner, where one set of bookshelves meets a long wall made entirely of glass, or something like glass. Instead of being dim, like in the usual cigar-smoke-filled den, the view is exquisite, looking out over a rocky cliff dotted with the occasional tree. Below lies the roaring ocean, stretching off into the distance. The view reminds me of the California coast north of San Francisco.

11/18 noon
Physician's Note:
Restart tube feedings

They reach the only piece of furniture in the room, a sort of standing desk. The desk is a metal slab jutting out from the window several feet off the floor, with no legs supporting it. Although about the size of a drafting table, it appears smaller, dwarfed by its contents. The surface is covered with papers, but also instruments. Some are brass, appearing to be from the late 1800's, and a few are made of other materials I can't recognize. I wonder if they are from the future. In the corner of the desk are a few medium-sized stones in a tidy pile.

Clearly eager to review the roll of papers my father has given him, the Englishman sweeps most of the documents off his desk, sending them tumbling to the floor. He unrolls the papers and places a stone at each corner to hold them open. Now visible, the roll is a series of large maps of the ocean floor.

After considering the maps a moment, the Englishman points at a spot and says, "As I expected, this rendering indicates the creature has her trapped along this ridge, at a depth of about 1200 feet."

My father attempts to contain his concern at this news.

The Englishman adds, "As I understand it, you've been able to keep her head above water, but the creature has swallowed her up to her rib cage and has held its position for several hours. I don't mean to frighten you, but you must know if she is not separated from the creature before it reaches her lungs, well, there will be no recovery."

My father nods.

"Hopefully, we aren't already too late to avert the progression. It's a matter of determining the precise location of the creature's base, and then I can send my gyro device down with a diver to sever the creature, freeing her. This must be done quickly, between the creature's breaths, or else the process will kill the creature and her. If we're to keep her alive, the creature must be kept alive as well. It's a delicate procedure."

My father looks up at him and shakes his head.

"I understand your concern, Mr. Sandmann, as the gyro is an experimental device, but I assure you I can train your diver. It's a risk, but at this point, it's your only option."

Finally, my father speaks: "You've come highly recommended, so I will put her fate in your hands."

"Let's make the necessary arrangements, shall we?"

11/19 6:15am
Physician's Note:
- NG output OK
- Will restart elemental enteral feeds today
- Continue parenteral

11/19 8:50am
Physician's Note:
- Tube feed on hold
- NG output high— patient not digesting feeding

Ara Lucia Ashburne

> 11/22 9:30
> Psych Note:
> - Patient seen with aunt
> - Patient seems anxious
> - Difficult to read lips
> - Difficult to write
> - Patient finds the restraints of compression boots and vent seem to bring up recall of experience when she was young raped/tortured
> - Racing thoughts, anxiety, agitation
> - Patient explains that lithium has helped her in the past

> 11/23 5:30am
> Nurse's Note:
> Psych recommends adding lithium

> 11/23 midnight
> - HR: 190-200
> - Ordered 6 mg adenosine
> - STAT ECG
> - Diltiazem drip

> 11/24 10:35am
> Nurse's Note:
> Begin lithium 300mg.

Reconstruction

Everyone wanted me to sleep, but sleep meant falling back into the hell I had just climbed out of. The scenario with my dad in the old Englishman's office was one of these new delusions which still haunted me whenever I slept. I had no idea why or what this development meant. I fought sleep with all my might. This was another one of the things I was doing which made everyone furious with me.

I also wasn't supposed to talk over the trach.

Three days after the doctors stopped giving me the paralyzing drug, they surgically installed a tracheostomy tube. They removed the endotracheal tube that ran from the respirator to my mouth and down past my trachea, in order to avoid complications like vocal cord damage and to reduce the likelihood of infection. I was still on the medical ventilator, as they did not want me to breathe on my own just yet. Maybe it was better for my long-term health, but it also meant I didn't have any kind of reminder that I couldn't talk. So I kept trying.

The nurses, the doctors, Wendy, Michael, and Yvonne would plead with me not to speak over the trach. Supposedly it was impossible to talk over the positive pressure from the respirator, but somehow I did. I wanted to communicate so badly. I pushed the air out of my lungs up over the trach and out my mouth. It was hard, but I could talk. It sounded very raspy and weird, but it was *sound*—and it was close enough to real words. I was told that doing this would "destroy my vocal cords permanently," so everyone was angry when I would do it, even intermittently.

I did it anyway.

After weeks of being trapped with demons in another world, being able to tell someone when my back hurt and I needed to be pushed onto my side or that I was hot and wanted the blanket to be taken off of me was all that mattered. I didn't care about any "long-term" anything.

Plus, I wanted to share my thoughts. That was harder to do. It required more words and, thus, more effort. The exertion would push my heart rate up over 200 beats per minute, the machines would beep, and then nurses would come rushing in, telling me there would be "plenty of time for talking later," and "now was the time to rest."

But there was no rest.

11/27 11:30am
Attending Psych Note:
- Case discussed with Dr. Segel
- Reports patient does have increased urine output with

> lithium, but no full blown manic episodes
> - We discussed containing anxiety/agitation with lorazepam as it can cause fewer sedation/memory problems than midazolam and can have anti-anxiety properties
>
> 11/27 2:30pm
> Attending Physician's Note:
> - Patient anxious about wound vac
>
> 11/27 3:00pm
> Nursing Note:
> - Many times the patient becomes anxious, complains of pain
> - Added lorazepam

    I wasn't having any luck with writing. My arm was weak, and I couldn't see what I was doing, so I switched tactics and started asking for my laptop, my precious Apple Blueberry iBook. It was my first laptop, and I had used it continuously in my "old" life. I figured, maybe if I can't write, I can at least tap the keys to convey my thoughts.

    Michael brought me my laptop exactly once. It was a large, rounded shape, and weighed about seven pounds, which made it impossible for me to hold or orient in any way, so someone else had to hold the laptop up in front of me. I wasn't able to hold my head up to see the screen, and I couldn't hold my fingers in position over the keys to type. Even just having it closed on my lap gave me a feeling of comfort, a memory of being able to work instead of being immobilized. At the end of the day, Michael took it back home.

    When I asked them to bring it back, I was told it was impossible for the hospital staff to keep track of it, or to change sheets around it, and I "couldn't use it anyway." Michael or Wendy would say they forgot it, or that it was in the car, and they would get it later. They hoped I would forget about it, but each time I was thwarted was devastating to me. Going another day without a means of communicating—now that I was finally in the same world as everyone else—was unbearable. It was painful to not have near me the one thing which made so much of my work and connection to the world possible.

*

Yvonne offered to help me write on a pad of paper with a marker. Initially, I couldn't even hold the marker. After a couple days of trying, I was able to make a few shaky marks. Tears poured down my face because I had no idea how long it would take me to be able to actually write letters.

At first it was impossible to discern a single letter, but eventually Yvonne was able to guess at what I had written. She would say what she thought the letter or word was supposed to be, and I would nod or shake my head. If she guessed right, I'd proceed to the next letter. Wendy and Michael were easily frustrated by the task, but Yvonne was capable of tremendous patience and had an uncanny ability to guess what was coming next. When she guessed right, she saved me an immense amount of energy. When she guessed wrong, she would guess again, then again, often faster and faster before I could even respond, and then *that* would be an additional stress—I didn't have a way of telling her she had been right three guesses ago.

Even once I could write a single letter, I wasn't strong enough to lift my hand off the paper for the next letter, let alone move my whole arm. Each subsequent letter wound up on top of the previous letter. When I made a mistake —as my shaky hand would quiver along—I had no way to erase the error or to explain I wanted to start over *so please move to a new spot on the paper...* It was all scribbling, making it harder to read what would come next or for Yvonne to know when I was starting again. While I struggled, my heart rate would shoot up over 200 beats per minute, and they would insist I stop. The machines would beep, and the nurse would come in and inject adenosine in my IV to bring my heart rate down.

As it was, it took all the energy I had to stay awake, to focus my mind, to remember what I was trying to say, hold the pen, make the next mark, trying to say by increments a small part of a larger idea I wanted to convey. After a few days of struggling, my hand became strong enough that I was able to lift the marker just a little. This allowed me, in some cases, to start a new letter. Eventually, somehow, Yvonne was able to string together my scribbles into simple phrases. While being able to communicate at all was a tremendous relief, it was also incredibly exhausting. About half of the time I fell asleep before we were finished. When I awoke, I rarely recalled what I so diligently tried to communicate before.

11/28 8:30am

Pain Consult:
- Still showing episodes of restlessness
- Deeply sedated, not rousable

Ara Lucia Ashburne

From: Wendy [mailto: wendy@email.com]
Sent: Monday, November 28, 2000 1:15 PM
To: Allgroup
cc: michael
Subject: Ara update 6

First, my apologies for the delay; I was not only having technical difficulties, but the story kept changing and I wanted to make sure I was communicating the latest and most accurate news.

So, the bottom line is Ara is still in critical condition in the Surgical Intensive Care Unit. At this particular point in the process, each step depends on the previous step's results, so there is a lot of waiting.

As for the abdominal wound, things are progressing well. Repeated cultures verify she is infection-free in that area. Monday they put in a "wound vac," which consists of carbon sponges with tubes attached. The tubes are then attached to the vacuum device and the wound gets constant suction. This does two things: it sucks up any residual fluid in the wound, and it literally sucks the wound toward closing. At the same time, the wound vac is stimulating growth of the red, meaty tissue that you need to heal a wound (blood vessels and fibroblasts) and all that is sucked toward proper closing.

On Wednesday, the wound vac is scheduled to be removed, and the doctors will suture a piece of synthetic mesh over the wound so that her belly is "closed." We don't know what happens after that until we see how her healing is progressing, but we do know that the mesh is a temporary solution that will still be followed at some point by reconstruction.

In the good news department, her temperature seems to be settling in, her swelling is down a bit more each day, and the rash that she developed seems to be fading. Her lungs are coming along nicely and she should be off the ventilator in 2 or 3 weeks.

The pressing concern now is the fungal infection in her blood. The spread has been arrested, but it has not yet receded, and the anti-fungal medications are rough on her electrolytes (potassium and sodium). The supplemental potassium that she receives constricts the veins, making it both close to impossible and extremely painful to draw blood (which of course they need to do frequently).

Her midazolam (the anxiety lowering and forgetting drug) has been replaced with lorazepam (an anxiety lowering and sleeping drug). Although I wouldn't want to remember any of this, it is probably a good switch for Ara Lucia, as she likes to be in on things. Having a memory hole later would likely be disconcerting for her.

As I said, all of this is subject to change, and things are quite "one step at a time" right now. Thanks to everyone who is hanging in there, sending cards and prayers. It is nice to know that people haven't forgotten.

Be good to yourselves,
Wendy

* * *

I see a thick haze made up of pixels. The pixels are dense and vary in size; gray, white, and black dots buzz through the air like the snow on an old television. Each particle creates its own sound just within the range of hearing, like a white noise but not. Together, their dense symphony creates a numb hush in my ears.

We are in a small airport a few miles outside of Dallas. I'm lying on a collapsible gurney behind the pilot's seat in a small twin engine plane. On my right, behind the copilot's seat, is the door, followed by three seats beside my gurney. Only the pilot and I are in the plane when I hear him holler "Clear!" out his side window. The engine sputters and then roars.

11/29 8:30am
Pain Consult:
- Lorazepam had to be boosted due to increased restlessness
- Patient wants to manage anxiety in another way due to lorazepam making the patient too sedated
- Decreasing lorazepam, adding midazolam 2–4 mg as needed for episodes of agitation

---

The pilot's safety call brings a wave of nostalgia from my time as a student pilot. I want to talk to him while we wait for the others to board the plane, but I'm too exhausted.

Just outside the plane, my mother talks to a nurse. I can barely hear their conversation over the sound of the engine, but I glean that I'm to be flown from Houston to a special hospital in Chicago. The pilot said the plane can't leave until they get enough blood to travel with me. I'm relieved because it would seem that I've escaped the control of Fernando and so am able to relax for the first time in many days.

Hours pass. I no longer hear my mother talking as I lie in the plane with the pilot up front.

If it's going to be so long before the blood arrives, why is he running the engine and wasting fuel?

The pilot has gauges to monitor my vitals, and he's concerned that if we don't leave for Chicago soon I may not make it. Yet, it's illegal for him to take me into the air without enough blood to ensure that I can survive the trip. Then, another nurse, a different voice, tells the pilot that the blood is on its way and should be here within fifteen minutes.

My brothers John and Dan arrive and tell my mom that they want to go and get a bite to eat. She begs them not to go because as soon as the blood arrives the plane will have to leave. I want them to stay, too. Often, Fernando shows up as the scene is getting ready to change and my hope is that they would be able to see him and protect me. If they are in the other Life-world, then I still don't know if they'll be able to see him, but I'm pretty sure that my mom's voice is in this Between world. It seems that now I can come and go from both worlds. I don't know who is where and whether or not they will be able to see Fernando.

"John, it's too close now. Please, wait here," my mom pleads.

"Mom, the flight is too long. We haven't eaten all day. Dan and I are going to run down to the cafeteria and get a quick bite to eat. We'll be right back. We won't be gone more than fifteen minutes, tops. Honest, mom, it will be okay. You can wait fifteen minutes." I can tell John must be wearing down her resolve. "We'll be right back. Come on, Dan."

I want to call out to them to wait. I don't want to make the flight without someone to protect me from Fernando. I try to quiet my mind, and fall into the center of nothingness.

I cast up a single wish: *Please bring them back, fast.*

The pilot sits in silence. I feel my spirit getting quieter. Hours pass. The particles still buzz along their gray spectrum whether my eyes are open or closed.

What could be holding up the blood?

My breath continues. I can hear my pulse throbbing in my ears. My thoughts no longer hold shapes.

As my thoughts drift, I hear voices. I am unable to discern whether they are male or female, familiar or unknown.

Then I can make out my mother's voice speaking to the pilot. Then his voice, as he replies. She is on the plane with me now. Apparently, the blood arrived.

"Where are your boys?" the pilot asks. "We can't wait for them. We must go."

Oh, no!

I scream. No one can hear me. Still, I can't keep my mind from screaming.

No, I can't go without my brothers! You can't fly this plane and keep me safe from Fernando! I need protection!

I'm afraid that when the plane takes off he will appear, and he will torture me again. I know that with each torture he inflicts more pain, and this time, I might die once and for all here in this crazy hell place. *Please, Please, Please,* DON'T GO. NO!

No...

I can hear my brothers in the distance. My mother calls out to them to hurry. She gets in the co-pilot seat. My brothers climb on board next to me, with John by my side and Dan in the seat ahead of him. Dan is finishing an apple. John reaches over and pats me on the arm.

"You're okay. We gotcha babe," he says with his warm smile.

Then I notice that the seat ahead of Dan is empty.

Dan, shut the door.

He can't hear me. No one can ever hear me.

I was hoping the boys would be able to see him. *If they can't hear me, are they here in this world or not? Will they be able to see him, stop him?*

A figure darkens the doorway. Fernando climbs aboard and casually closes the door. I can see his angry, manipulative smirk.

"You're okay. We *gotcha*, babe," he snarls, mimicking my brother. I look to John and Dan. They do not see him. Fernando climbs, agile as a monkey, onto my gurney, with his feet and hands on the side rails. I've never seen his feet before. They are as brown, cracked, and as over-sized as his hands. His toes are long like fingers and they grip the rails.

"You didn't think you could get away from me now, did you? I had to hold up that blood, because I was tied up with other things. Now we can go."

The pilot repeats his takeoff instructions back to the tower, and we are airborne.

My heart races as those wet, yellow eyes glare down at me.

11/29 10:00am

Nurse's Notes:

- Patient still feeling trapped
- Patient bothered by hospital gown and would be more comfortable in her own clothes
- Suggested distraction with magazines or favorite tv programs

> - Suggested getting things from home in the room
>
> 11/29 8:00pm
> Nurse's Note:
> - Wound vac not working well
> - More transparent wound dressings applied to have a better seal
> - Wound vac working well now

> 11/30 (no time designated)
> Attending Note:
> - Patient awake crying — upset about loss of dignity in ICU setting

    I could only stay awake for a few minutes at a time. I desperately wanted to communicate my concerns, but there were some things I was afraid to ask and some things I was afraid to tell.

    For example, it appeared that I had been given a tattoo on my left thigh, and I did not recall getting it. It was strange, too. A red line crossed my leg horizontally about four inches above my knee, and then a green line ran the length of my inner thigh. The green line intersected the red line, making a kind of sloppy cross. Even after staring at it for several days, I couldn't understand what it represented.

    At one point, after working up the nerve to ask someone about it, I tried to inquire, very casually, about the tattoo. Wendy responded, "What tattoo?"

    How could she not know about the tattoo?

    I pointed to the marks on my leg.

    "Do you mean these lines?" she asked.

    I nodded timidly.

    "Ara, that is not a tattoo. There is a clear plastic wrap on your leg and those marks are where the doctor took a skin graft from your leg to cover your abdomen. Those marks will come off in the shower. They aren't permanent."

    I felt stupid but relieved.

Reconstruction

During my short periods of wakefulness, I could now see. Yet, for reasons I didn't understand, my vision was always a little blurry. It was as if I were constantly waking up and my eyes hadn't focused on my environment yet. I couldn't see the plastic on my leg through the blur.

Well, I had resigned myself to never wearing a miniskirt again because of the sloppy, meaningless tattoo. Now I wouldn't have to worry about that.

* * *

I wanted to explain where I had been, trapped in the Between world, and what horrors happened to me while I was there. I needed someone, anyone, to know, but I was terrified that if I told, once I was free of the ICU, I would be committed to a psych ward.

Many years ago I was diagnosed as having Bipolar Disorder, Type II. The symptoms of Bipolar II generally are not considered to be as severe as Bipolar I. There aren't delusional or hallucinogenic symptoms (referred to as a "psychotic episode"). I've never had a psychotic episode in my entire life. I admit, I've done some pretty wild things—made choices in my youth that didn't come from the most level-headed place—but I've been stable on medication since age 29. When I was first diagnosed, my psychiatrist assured me that if I hadn't had a psychotic episode already, it wasn't going to happen.

Six years later, in my ICU room, I wondered if there could be an exception to this.[*] Could being deathly ill or enduring immense quantities of medication change a person from being a stable, responsible, medicated person to a never-again-to-be-stable-or-trusted crazy person? I thought that might explain what I had experienced.

On the other hand, if I *hadn't* crossed over to being Type I, then somehow those experiences were something else, were somewhere else. I had to find out. It was possible that the mere act of asking the necessary questions could bring about that which I was trying to avoid: being locked in a psych ward forever.

I decided Yvonne was the safest person to tell, primarily because of my experiences talking about out-of-the-box subjects with her when I was a child. From the time I was very young, I'd always gone to Yvonne with my philosophical questions, about Being, God, and spirituality. She always answered me thoughtfully and respectfully. I considered her a safe haven.

I figured Yvonne was my best shot.

---

[*] Weeks passed before I had the courage to ask my psychiatrist about the experiences I had while in the medically induced coma. He explained that the medications I was on, like morphine, could amplify delusions. He also told me about problems that can occur in patients hospitalized for extended periods of time. One of these, called sundown syndrome (more often associated with dementia or Alzheimer's), occurs after the sun sets. Those who face "sundowning" experience increased confusion and agitation, and often don't sleep well. These symptoms are also known to occur in environments that lack stimulation, such as a hospital room or solitary prison cell.

Ara Lucia Ashburne

*

When she came back from lunch, I screwed up the courage to try to explain where I had been.

"Yvonne, I need to tell you something." I hesitated, and she could tell I was pulling myself together to say something important. Even with her, articulating this wasn't easy. There was so much to explain, and I didn't know how long I would be awake to tell her. "I need you to understand. Before... in the coma... I wasn't here."

She blinked.

I took a deep breath, trying to gather enough air to push over the trach for the next part. "I was with God there... I mean, really *with* God... but there were demons too. They tortured me. It was horrifying. It all really happened there." I stopped then, tried to gauge her expression.

"The demons weren't real, Ara. They were like nightmares. You've had a lot of morphine and other drugs which contributed to the intensity of your experience."

I was surprised; she didn't seem to understand. Maybe I hadn't been clear, but it took so much effort to pull together the words to communicate, I feared I wouldn't be able to have a real philosophical conversation, which the situation warranted. I tried again.

"No, Yvonne, it was real. I'm telling you, I was *really there. It wasn't just nightmares.* Those things really happened to me. I had those experiences." I knew that the Between reality was more intense than the ICU room we were talking in—it was hyperreal—more so than the world in which I spent my entire life before the hospital.[*]

Every time I was on the verge of falling asleep, I risked falling back in, and finding myself in Between—in the Nightmare Place. This wasn't speculation, it continued to happen. The only difference was, now I could be awakened and suddenly be in the same world as others. Waiting for someone to wake me didn't make being in the Nightmare Place less painful. But my experiences were ever so much more than "bad dreams." This I knew.

I was stunned Yvonne dismissed me so quickly. I could tell she was trying to reassure me, to comfort me, but it was also clear she didn't believe me. And if she didn't believe me, certainly no one else would.

I could definitely end up in the psych ward.

---

[*] While in the ICU, I did not know about sundowning (see previous note). Regardless, my delusional experiences in the Nightmare Place were nothing like dreams. They felt more real than reality, which is why I described them as "hyperreal." While it is intellectually satisfying to know there's a medical explanation for what happened to me, that does not change or erase what happened. Those events are as much a part of my overall life experience as anything else. I know they weren't in the real world, the one in which this book exists, but what occurred feels *more* genuine—doubly so at that time—than any reality I've experienced before or since.

I resisted everyone's repeated requests for me to rest. Sleep was anything but restful. I was even more scared.

12/2 1:00pm
Nursing Note:
- HR 174, BP 112/56
- Called Dr. Oren — ordered diltiazem STAT EKG
- Family members at bedside asked to leave room
- HR down to 118, BP 110/44

I enter a kind of salon through thick red drapes. Several women in elaborate Victorian dresses are chatting quietly but animatedly with one another.

I've got to find the portal out of here.

I'm a solo voyager through a video game, a kind of test, a puzzle, an interactive world. My goal is to uncover the clues that will lead me to the "exit." They could be anything. I scrutinize the words in the women's gossip, look for a crack in the wall. Any ordinary object could have magical properties. The answer is within reach. I have to find it before he arrives.

I scan the room. Numerous tall lamps with tasseled lampshades are scattered among the women.

Is one of the lamps perhaps different from the others? It doesn't seem so.

Part of the far end of the room is divided by a sandalwood folding screen. I make my way carefully toward it, avoiding eye contact with the women. I need to seem as if I belong here among them. If they work for him, they could tip him off that I'm here.

As I get closer to the screen, I am overwhelmed by its beauty: ornate carvings, East Asian or Indian in style, adorn each panel. Small mirrors are set into the panels, each surrounded by strings of glass beads. The beads call to me. They have a magical quality, but it feels like a trap. I can't tell if they are there for the taking, but I dare not ask one of the women.

Behind the screen is a makeup table with a pleated cloth skirt. An oval glass tray with an ornate metal edge holds antique perfume bottles in purple and red. The sight reminds me of my great grandmother Foster who, I was told, was once in a silent film.

One of the bottles has a little feather boa around the top. My Dad called me "Feather" as a kid, and I wonder if this might be the clue I'm looking for. I reach for the bottle—

Fernando appears over my shoulder and pinches my right ear. "You sneaked away, my little Pumpkin, but I never lost you."

I know he'd like it if I cried out, but I'm angry. I won't give him the satisfaction. He tugs on my ear.

"See? Here I am. I have you right here."

In one fluid motion he turns me around. I now see the room is actually a stage; I entered through the curtains on stage right and am now facing toward the empty seats. There is no audience, the seats are devoid of people. The floor of the theater is filled with colorful glass balls about the size of my palm. It looks like a carnival ball pit of Christmas ornaments. I can only see the tops of the seats poking up from the sea of colors.

Fernando drags me off the stage by my ear and into the balls. They surround me like water. I can't feel the bottom. I fear that I will sink into the balls and suffocate, but they are dense and hold me so only my chest and arms are exposed. Fernando laughs and continues to pinch my ear.

"When will you learn to stay with me? I have no intention of letting you go free. Maybe this time you will learn."

I hear a snapping sound and see that he has flipped open his jackknife again. He holds my ear like a small wedge of cheese, cuts into it and pulls off a segment to show me. I can feel blood trickle down my neck, but I am afraid to move.

"*That* was for leaving my side." He slips the piece of my ear into his shirt pocket. "*This* is to persuade you to stay."

He opens my right palm and says, "Now, leave your hand right there." In a single swift move, he severs my right ear completely. I feel a quick stab of pain and then a numbness as more hot blood rushes down my neck. He places my ear in my hand. The sound of his voice fades into the distance. Then the pain overwhelms me and I pass out. I feel all of the blood rush out of my body, and my spirit, separated from my body, floats up toward the ceiling of the room.

12/4 (no time indicated)
Physician's Note:
- Afebrile x 24 hours — YEAH!*

---

* The physician on duty actually wrote this in the medical record!

I wanted to die. I was exhausted from the fight and from the doctors and machines dragging me across the remains of my life. The torments from the Between world were never going to end. The physical pain in the Real world reached unimaginable heights every time they rolled me to one side and then the other to change the sheets on my bed or to adjust my position. The medication didn't help. I was in hell. When I was in the drug-induced coma, I'd tried to die but couldn't. Now that I was out, I wanted to end it.

I wanted to be disconnected from the machines.

When Yvonne told Michael and Wendy this, they were furious. All this effort had been spent to save me, and now I wanted to die on purpose? Yvonne asserted that it was my wish. At my request, she agreed to investigate how it could be done. She spoke to the nurse supervisor to advocate on my behalf.

Meanwhile, Michael had the staff reference the copies of our Advanced Health Care Directive documents which he had given them the second day of my stay. It turned out that the Directive stated I should be disconnected from life support after being in a coma *for a year*, and now I wasn't in any kind of coma.

I was angry. I signed that document when I had no idea that being in a coma, medically induced or not, could mean devastating physical pain and tortuous delusions, and certainly didn't know that once out of the coma, I could continue to have hallucinations when asleep. I had signed that declaration out of ignorance.

The supervisor explained to Yvonne that the hospital is legally bound to work toward the efforts of life-saving. The hospital would not condone taking a patient—one who was expected to live, as I was—off life support. In addition, any patient making such a request would have to be considered of "right mind," and a person who had gone through such a prolonged brush with death would not be considered of "right mind."

Yvonne entered the room in tears, "Ara, you should be allowed to decide, but there is *nothing* that can be done now. It isn't fair that everyone is deciding for you. I am so sorry. It may not make a difference to you right now, but you will feel better eventually, I promise. I know it will be a long, arduous journey, but if anybody can do it, it's you."

I was crying too hard to speak, deeply moved that she believed in me. There we were, both sobbing, and left with no options. What I wanted mattered enough for her to have advocated for me even though it so strongly opposed Michael, Wendy, and the hospital. I didn't know where else we could turn.

*

I was still so weak that I could only speak a few words at a time. I couldn't move my body other than my hands. Nevertheless, I decided that if they weren't going to let me die, then at least they would not keep me in that hospital prison any longer. I had an idea: the next time Yvonne left the room, I would depart on my own. It was that simple. I knew I could discharge myself Against Medical Advice. I knew that was a hospital "thing." That was what I would do.

I figured if I could scoot myself to the edge of the bed, I would flop to the ground, and then I could crawl out the door. If a nurse tried to stop me, I would say, "AMA," and keep crawling. They would have to let me leave!

When I first tried to drag my legs to the edge of the bed, they didn't move. I decided to start with one leg at a time. I pushed really hard, and I think I got a quarter-inch, maybe half an inch, before I passed out from the effort. I rested, and began again with the other leg. I fell asleep, woke up again, and continued with my mission, a quarter- or half-inch at a time.

So little was accomplished with each increment that a couple of nurses entered and left without noticing that my legs were no longer directly aligned with my body. More moving and resting and sleeping. Eventually, I got my left leg over to the edge of the bed, and the next push sent my heel over the precipice. The weight of my foot pulled down so that my leg, up to my knee, was now hanging over the side. With a few more pushes, I could almost do the same with my right leg.

I rested and fell asleep again. I awakened to Yvonne scolding me, "Ara, you can't get out of bed. You're too weak to stand. You're going to fall and break something and be in even more pain than you are now!"

She pushed my leg back up onto the bed, and straightened my body. Then she pulled up the metal railing on the left side of the bed and left the room. I could hear her telling the nurses what I tried to do and how she wanted them to make sure that the railing stays up on the bed.

Now even my bed had bars.

12/4 3:30pm
Patient's leg placed back on the bed
Patient emotional, crying
Will hold off on physical therapy for today

12/5 (no time indicated)
Physician's Note:
• Recurrence of fever

12/9 5:00pm
Anesthesia/Pain Note:
- States that pain is 5-10 when immobile, 10+ when coughing or being turned to side
- Continuing pain med
- Adding morphine prior to moving patient

12/9 9:00pm
Physician's Note:
- Patient agitated overnight
- Returned from mesh surgery suite agitated

12/10 6:30am
Physician's Note:
- Start methadone — wean off morphine

12/10 10:00am
Pain/Anesthesia Note:
- Pain rated 7-10

12/11 4:30pm
Nursing Note:
- Midazolam is weaned to 1 mg/hr
- Morphine down to 6 mg/hr from 10 mg/hr
- Methadone wean program continued

*   *   *

Ara Lucia Ashburne

I look down from the platform where I stand with the other girls. I keep my knees together, as I'm embarrassed that the Suits make us wear these above-the-knee bloomers with a dress that stops mid-thigh. We envy the women brought into the shop from the outside, with their hair drawn up and the long skirts and coats we all used to wear. Today, though, we are the Display Girls, with dresses gathered over our breasts like a present. The ribbon just below advertises our merchandise, along with the medicine and sweets sold from the counter below the platform.

Our pumps have beautiful ribbons too, lacing up our legs like a ballet shoe. I would love to wear them under a proper floor length skirt. I imagine meeting the Patterly boy in the salon, back home from school over Christmas, with my aunt making trite conversation about how "the Blue Wonder bloomed all through September this year." Without her knowledge, I could let my ankle slip out for a moment so he could see an inch of the ribbon... But here, these disgusting ribbons climb up my legs as if reaching for my knees. There is no way for me to crawl behind myself or the other girls as we stand here: today's chosen.

I keep my eye on the entrance in front of me, on the Door Suits that stand there. These Suits never speak, unlike the other Suits, the Boss's henchmen. They're always talking, telling us what to do and where to go. The Door Suits rest their hands on the guns stuck in the front of their pants—an unnecessary reminder of the presence of their weapons. The tall one has a jacket that fits, but his pants are two inches too short. He shifts his weight back and forth, and I wonder if he is trying to cover his ankles or if he has the nervous sickness. The other is short and has ruddy hands. I've spent many hours, even days imagining all the jobs he held before he worked for the Boss. *Was he a fisherman, an otter hunter, a miner? What would make those hands red forever?*

Two men enter. They're told to open their jackets and lift their pant legs to prove they haven't arrived to cause trouble for the Boss. They are cleared, and the Door Suits simultaneously sweep their hands, indicating to which of the booths the newcomers have been assigned. Two young Worthington Women are waiting in the booth, one on each side of the table.

"Step right in, gentlemen, step right in," the Hawker continues his peddling, stepping out from behind his apothecary counter. "Take your place by these two charming ladies. Worry you not, if these ladies are not to your liking, you will have an opportunity to win the lady of your choice! A game of skill will be comin' your way."

These new customers seem familiar. They are younger than our usual clients and are dressed like barbershop quartet singers, in boater hats (complete with a ribbon around the base), striped pants, and white shoes. Oddly, they are looking around the room and not at us. Then they nod to one another, and I'm afraid to move.

My brothers. These men are my brothers!

Do they know I'm here? They must! What if they don't? Will they think I came here willingly?

I want to pass one of my brothers a note: "You can only have the girl they choose for you. You will have to find another way to get me out." I want to catch their eye, but I fear attracting too much attention to myself. We know that the Suits are always watching. Somehow, somewhere, the Boss always sees and knows everything. If it is suspected that I'm trying to escape, then I will be sent to The Pit for the night.

Spinning around on his heel, the Hawker raises his cane as if revealing a magic trick. "First, I must tell you all, that right here and right now in Worthington's Apothecary and Sweet Shop, we have imported the medicinal answer to the Common Cold. This powerful remedy will break a fever, thicken the blood and expel the cold from the lungs with only three doses. This newly created remedy was formulated in China, but is brought to you directly from England. I believe Mr. Worthington has only two bottles left. You never know when a boat will make it from China to England and right here to you, so you better buy before it is too late! Mr. Worthington's assistant is ready to help you now, step right up there, step right up."

Other customers move about the room, but I remain focused on my brothers. They make polite introductions to the two ladies beside them, then glance at each other and begin to study the room. John leans back in the booth and extends his arm around the woman beside him. My heart sinks: *He hasn't come for me.* I don't think I can bear watching him now. Maybe I should scream and let one of the Door Suits shoot me.

The woman puts her hand on his tie and runs her fingers down his shirt buttons. I call out to him with my heart, *John! Look up here, Johnny!* Gently, he removes the woman's hand with a quick smile. She retracts, slumping in the corner of the booth.

Did he hear me?

She looks angry. It will be another hour before she can attempt to win another tip that might allow her a sleeping berth and a hot breakfast.

I see John looking all around the room, but he stares keenly at the dark glass wall behind the Apothecary to my right. I thrust my hip forward, making sure that my number tag is clearly in sight, as required. John looks at the Hawker, then to the Door Suits and then to me. He offers a quick wink before turning back to Dan.

I suck in my breath and slowly let it out. I no longer know how many days or months I've been waiting for this, an opportunity to escape. I hold in the urge to scream and be sick all at once.

The Hawker holds his cane like a dance partner and takes two small steps, lunging forward, as his tenor voice fills the room:

Ara Lucia Ashburne

I'se got a little baby, but she's out of sight/
I talk to her across the telephone.

I'se never seen my honey but she's mine, all night/
So take my tip, an' leave this gal alone.

Every single morning, you will hear me yell/
"Hey Central! Fix me up along the line."

He connects me with ma honey, then I rings the bell/
And this what I say to baby mine.

Hello, ma baby/
   Hello, ma honey/
     Hello, ma ragtime gal.

Send me a kiss by wire/
   Baby, ma heart's on fire!

If you refuse me/
   Honey, you'll lose me/
     Then you'll be left alone.

   Oh, baby, Telephone/
   and tell me I'se your own!

   Hello, Hello!

   Without missing a beat, the Hawker begins his next hustle. "Next we have a game of skill for all of our town's baseball players. Who do I have here?" He tips his cane in John's direction: "Can you knock one outta here?"

   John nods for Dan to go first. I want to explain to my brothers that the games are rigged. This particular scheme has some poor sap stand at the end of the booths near the entrance and try to hit a ball into a hole in the wall at the far end of the room.

   Dan stands up with a slow pride. He seems to think this will be easy, but I've never seen any man get the ball into the hole. Has Dan figured out a way to beat the trick?

   "Now, you look like a strong gentleman. Pick your lady." The Hawker gestures with his finger for us to turn around.

   If he picks me, will the Suits know something is up?

   "I'll take number eleven, sir."

   Dan has chosen my number.

   "That is a fine choice, our Curly Top, Number Eleven."

He turns back to Dan. "Two chances, that is what you have. You hand me a nickel and I will give you the bat and a baseball." Dan reaches into his pants pocket and hands over the money. The Hawker slides the coin into his vest pocket. "It is simple really. You toss the ball into the air and then swing the bat to knock the ball into that hole in the wall, right over there. You will have two chances, and if you win, then your lucky lady, Number Eleven, will be yours for the evening."

The Hawker doesn't seem to know, or is Dan playing into a trap that will get us all killed? *How can I act as if this game of "skill" is the same as every other?*

He tosses the ball up gently and then cracks the bat against it with a fury.

He's shocked. It didn't go in.

If he were to win me, I still don't know how he would get me out of here. He has another chance, and he seems sure this time he will win. Will he be the first?

Again, he gently tosses the ball up, and the bat slams the ball against the wall—just beside the hole. Dan, clearly keeping his emotions in check, offers up the bat to John, but John tips his chin to the side, shaking off the chance to follow Dan.

"That's okay, mister," the Hawker bellows in mock consolation, "we have many chances for you to win the girl of your dreams. Stay with us here and the answer to all that ails you will be in your hands!"

Suddenly, the lights go out and at once the room is filled with the sounds of girls screaming and scrambling, gunfire, and breaking glass. I'm afraid in the chaos I'll get knocked off the platform. The back door opens and casts a small ray of light into the room. I can see people behind where the black glass used to be. Michael's up there. He has a machine gun, and he's broken up a poker party.

He must've been the one that cut the lights!

That room must be where the Boss has been watching us all along.

I hear John's voice directly below me. "Ara! Jump, I'll catch you."

Without hesitating, I fling myself toward his voice and find myself in John's grasp.

"Michael has taken care of the Boss," he says, setting me on my feet. I look up, but there isn't enough light to see more than silhouettes.

But where is Michael now? Did one of the Suits get him, or is he waiting for me outside?

John grabs me by the wrist, "Come on, I gotta get you out of here."

"John wait, I have to get the rest of the girls from the Waiting Room behind the stage."

"No, Ara, we don't have time. There's a trolley waiting in the street. We have to go *now*."

"I'll be right back, honest." I break free of his grip and race around behind the stage, into our room, just before the open back door. I can hear all the girls crying in the dark room.

"Girls, this is our chance. Run, out the back!"

"You're gonna get us all killed," yells Geraldine, the oldest among us. "This is one of the Boss's traps!"

"It's safe, Geraldine. My husband killed the Boss, and my brothers are watching the door. Now go, this is our only chance."

I find Geraldine in the dark and push her toward the door, then usher the other girls to follow her. The trolley car is a few feet from the door. The girls climb on board, trying to avoid being seen on the streets dressed like the wrong kind of women.

Moving quickly, I run through the shop to see if anyone else is left. The bodies of three girls are in a booth, but there isn't enough light to see who they are. The Suits must have gotten to them first. I hesitate, not knowing what to do.

Should I get John to bring their bodies? I don't want to leave them like this.

John is behind me, at the back door, shouting, "Ara, the trolley is leaving, come now!"

I give up, run outside, and climb on the trolley. John puts his arm around me. I hear the conductor's bell ring, and I look toward the front. A large, leathery hand releases the brake, and I hear the snap of a jackknife being opened.

12/11 9:00am
Psych Note:
- More alert and able to sustain longer and more focused conversation today
- Still reports periods of anxiety, restlessness, nightmares, and fears that she will get manic.
- We reinforced that we have discussed this with Dr. Segel and that she has not shown behavioral signs of mania
- Told her that many people in prolonged ICU with multiple meds can experience mental status fluctuations. She appeared relieved with this.

I could barely open my eyes. There was a man in a white lab coat by my bedside. He held a clipboard and made notes. My vision was blurry. The noises around me sounded like they were vibrating. I was so heavy with a drugged sleep that my eyes close again.

I felt an intense itch by my nose. I slowly raised my left hand to rub it, but something was in the way. I tried to move it, to get at my nose, and I felt a pull inside my nostril—

Owww, that hurt.
What's hurting me?

I tugged at the thing by my nose again. The man with the clipboard grabbed my wrist and pushed my hand down to the bed, at my side. His grip hurt my wrist.

He yelled at me, "If you touch that tube again, I'm going to have to strap your hands to the bed, and you won't like that."

What tube?

He sounded so angry. I didn't understand what he was talking about. My eyelids were so heavy.

My nose itched. I reached up, bumped something by my nose. I grabbed it.

What's this?

"Stop it! You can't do that!" I opened my eyes and saw him looking down, the anger evident on his face. "I'm not going to tell you again! Do you understand me?"

I was so sleepy. I closed my eyes again.

My nose itched. I reached up to scratch the itch and felt something hard by my nose.

Is there something in my nose?

It kept itching. I tried to move the hard object away.

The man grabbed my wrist and squeezed it hard. I reached up with my other hand to try to get him off my wrist, and he grabbed my other hand. Now he held both of my wrists with one hand and pinched them together. He pushed my wrists down into my chest. He held my hands there, and called out to a nurse to get a sedative. I tried to pull my hands away, but he gripped tighter, pressing down on my chest. He was hurting me, and I cried out, but he didn't let go of my wrists.

I didn't understand why he was so angry and forceful.

12/12 7:00am
Physician's Note:
- Attempted to pull NG tube

Ara Lucia Ashburne

> - Now restrained
> - Seems anxious, upped morphine to 8 mg

Some time later, Michael arrived. He was wearing his light brown sweater vest which I love, but he rarely wears it because he is usually too hot for such apparel. I figured now is one of the few times he can wear it, knowing that my room is being kept so cold to try to keep me comfortable. Most of the nurses have layers of sweaters and sweatshirts on when they work in my room. The doctors declared that no matter how much I beg they can't make the room any colder than 65 degrees, that is the lowest they'll go. So, this was a special circumstance that I got to see him in this sweater vest.

I wanted to explain to him what happened with the resident. I'm sure that if Michael had seen how aggressive that doctor had been with me... Well, I don't think he would have treated me like that if Michael had been in the room. Certainly, Michael wouldn't have let him treat me like that had he seen it.

I tried to speak. "That doc-tor... hit... me."

"He HIT you?"

"No, not 'hit'..." That wasn't the right word.

"You said, 'hit'!"

I shake my head, and gesture pushing my hand into my body. I am so exhausted I can only say one word. I say, "Punch."

"He PUNCHED you?!"

I know the doctor didn't punch me like a punch in the face, but the way he shoved my wrist into my body—felt closer to punching than any other word I could come up with.

I should clarify all of this and say, "Crammed. Really hard. With force. Squeezing the bones of my wrists together. Into this place, my chest. Pushed, shoved my lungs. Sternum. Hurt me. Angry yelling," but I can't say any of it. I'm fading.

I wanted to tell him that the doctor frightened me, that he was being too aggressive, but I can't find the words.

Michael left the room to get to the bottom of this.

> 12/12 8:43am
> Attending Physician's Note:

> - Pain
> - She is expressing frustration at the restraints, writes about her interpretation of early morning events when she inadvertently dislodged the breathing circuit

> 12/14 10:58am
> Speech and Occupational Therapist's Notes:
> - Tolerated leaked speech over 30 minutes
> - Swallow ice chips with timely swallow response
> - Good mastication of apple sauce with blue dye — suctioning immediately after did not reveal any blue dye
> - Daily speech therapy

> 12/15 2:30pm
> Speech Therapist's Notes
> - Patient has excellent voice
> - Excellent speech with cuff deflation
> - However she desaturated quickly but recovered with cuff re-inflated also quickly

> 12/16 (no time indicated)
> - Patient off ventilator

I'm attached to a monster from the abdomen down. Five young women in scuba suits are supporting my upper body to keep me from becoming submerged and swallowed by the creature. My head is barely above the surface. All of us are protected from the wind and rain by an eight-foot nylon tarp arcing above us like a tent. They alternate between being underwater, being nearby to support me, and resting momentarily while hanging onto one of the struts of the metal apparatus that supports the tent.

One of the divers breaks the surface next to me and spits out the mouth piece from her oxygen tank. "Your brother Dan is going to do the dive," she says, shouting so I can hear her above the howling wind. "They trained him last night. He is going to have to work quickly to numb the creature and then cut you out of it. The separation is technical, so they are sending a pod for him to use for additional oxygen and to hold all the necessary tools needed to make the cut.

"He did well in training, Ara," she says with a warm smile. "The Pod Team thinks he might be able to do it."

"And if he can't?" I ask, wondering how my brother got mixed up in this.

"Honestly, we can only speculate. This is the only time this particular creature has been identified. We are timing its contractions to determine when a cut can be made. A Navy ship is bringing him in. He should be here any moment."

With that, she was back under the water.

So, Dan is going to dive and see if it is possible to cut through the creature's tentacles to release me, or maybe he plans to unearth the creature.

Pain shoots through my body as another contraction strikes. The women brace themselves against the struts so they can keep themselves and me from being pulled under by the creature.

12/18 6:16pm
Nursing Note:
- Patient Controlled Anesthesia (PCA) started with morphine; took off of drip
- Still on methadone — wean
- Instructed patient on use of PCA

12/19 5:40pm
Physician's Note:
- Patient doing well out of surgery
- Split thickness skin graft

I heard my Dad's voice talking to someone. I'm way too exhausted to talk right now, but it would be great to have him by my side and know he's here with me in the Real world. Maybe I could open my eyes. I think I could open my eyes, but to say any words would be too hard. Maybe I will keep my eyes closed, and he will stay for a while and then go.

"Hey there, Ara. Your Uncle Dennis and I are here to visit."

Oh, it is so great to hear you. I can hear the smile in your voice. It feels like your smile reaches over me and wraps comfort around me.

"We drove up. It's pretty snowy, so it took us an extra hour or so. What time is it, Dennis?"

"Eight-thirty, Eastern."

"Yep, so it took us about 3 hours and 20 minutes."

Wow, Dad, at the speed you drive, it should have taken you no more than an hour and a half, so it must be seriously snowy.

Dennis added, "And you know how your Dad drives, even in the snow, so we couldn't have got here any faster."

I know, I just said that.

Dad decided to change the subject. "Mom wanted me to tell you not to worry about Julie, that the baby is coming along fine. She still can't travel because she is too far along, or she would be here. She is praying for you, too. And because she can't travel, we decided we would have Christmas at Julie's this year." He pauses, then adds, "Even though you won't be with us. We'll be thinking about you."

After a moment or so, Dennis asks Dad, "How long are you planning on staying if she doesn't wake up?"

"Until she does wake up. As long as it takes. I don't have somewhere to be. She'll wake up eventually."

Damn. Of course, my Dad would wait until I wake up. In a test of wills, I guess my Dad still wins.

I didn't want him to think that I was responding to that comment, so I kept my eyes closed for another minute.

Dad sounded a little closer when he said, "I know you know how much I love the winter, but I'm really looking forward to this summer, because I am going to learn how to use the GPS on my sailboat. Your Uncle Dennis and I are finally going to do some racing."

How exciting! I want to go racing, too!

"So, Ara," Dad continued, "I came here to let you know that I'm going to be thinking about you on Christmas. I brought you this wooden sailboat. It's a tree ornament. I'm going to hang it up here on your IV. That way when you're hurting really bad or feeling like you need something to look forward to, you can think about next summer. You'll be out of here and doing better by then, and you can come sailing with me."

Finally, I opened my eyes and said, "Thank you."

"As I was saying, I know it isn't going to be too cheery around here on Christmas, but you can look up at that ornament and remember all the great Christmases we've had, and all the great ones we're going to have again. You'll be in all of our hearts on Christmas."

*

On the beach, I hear a woman shouting into a handheld transceiver radio, communicating with the Navy ship. It's approaching along the Southern Californian coast. One of the divers near me wears some kind of headset, and somehow, over the din, I hear the rattling voice of the reply: "Pod delivery fee of three hundred thousand dollars has been confirmed, delivered by Mr. John Sandmann. Prepping pod for mission release. Will reach destination at thirteen hundred hours. Engineering team will change over with scuba team at thirteen twenty. Compression valve synchronizing with Sandmann diver at thirteen thirty-five. Over and out."

12/19 5:40pm
Nursing Note:
- Agitation
- Patient wanting to turn on side
- Patient picking at dressing
- Midazolam 2 mg iv
- Morphine PCA encouraged for pain
- Bilateral wrist restraints initiated for patient safety
- Instructed not to turn to left side

"No," I shout, tasting the salty water, "someone needs to tell that woman to stop the ship. I know this is an experimental measure. My father can't incur that kind of cost when they don't even know if it is going to work. He'll never get out from under it."

"The ship has already been commissioned. It is done. You need to relax or the contractions are going to be stronger."

"It's okay. Let me go." I feel overwhelmed by the enormity of the situation, hopeless. My voice is barely a whisper now. "Let it take me, please. I can't be the one who curses my father like this. It isn't worth it."

12/22 [no time indicated]

Physician's Note:

- Patient complaint of increased anxiety at around the time she is supposed to get her dose of lorazepam
- Patient feels "panicky" if her dose is a bit late
- She wants to receive her does strictly every six hours
- Patient reports concern about having staff and coworkers see her having anxiety attack
- Intermediate panic-like attacks possibly related to trying to make the best impression possible
- Discussed with patient that it is unnecessary to push herself to be upbeat in front of the staff even when she is not feeling well
- Also recommended some relaxation techniques.
- Will also ask nursing staff to monitor time of symptoms of panic in relation to dosing of lorazepam

---

12/22 3:15pm

Nursing Note:

- Patient reports increased sense of anxiety and sometimes panic since discontinuation of midazolam
- Appears tearful and articulates desire to wean off meds and frustration and feeling out of control at times
- Will start midazolam every 2-4 hours as needed.
- Continuing lorazepam every six hours as regulated by Psych doctor
- Patient agrees to plan

Ara Lucia Ashburne

12/23 6:45pm
Nursing Note:
- Patient with episodes of sobbing, but able to verbalize and able to utilize personal stress reducing techniques effectively
- Lorazepam given at set dose

12/25 7:00am
Nursing Note:
- trach only for suctioning

12/26 9:30am
Psych Note:
- Patient awake and alert and well oriented
- Generally feeling better and not significant mood swings
- Denies significant periods of anxiety or panic
- Describes that she is realizing that much of her anxiety/stress was related to her assumption that she is being a difficult patient as she couldn't clearly communicate her needs and requests we communicate directly to her
- I attempted to normalize this and share this responsibility of communication problems
- Patient appears to be more aware of this and making appropriate cognitive interpretations
- Recommendations for now: I would continue routine lorazepam
- I will convey this information to her outpatient psychiatrist Dr. Segel

> 12/28 2:30am
> Nursing Note:
> • Transfer Note: Patient is instructed to keep left leg straight, avoid shearing of donor site. Do not roll patient on left side or stomach

* * *

I was ready to move from the ICU to the rehabilitation hospital. More correctly, I was "well enough" to be discharged from the ICU, but not yet ready for the rigors of the rehabilitation hospital. In the meantime, I was being transferred to a general recovery floor of the hospital. I had my own room on the 12th floor of the general hospital. Once there, I could receive more visitors than in the ICU. My friends were amazed and delighted that I made it past their daily death watch, but disturbed by the reality of seeing my altered spirit and body for the first time. After the expression of horror on the face of my third visitor, I knew I must look absolutely hideous, so I asked for a mirror.

My coloring was a peculiar yellowish-green. I had deeply sunken eyes with dark black circles. My previous 140-pound frame was skeletal, as my weight had dropped below 100 pounds. My nail beds had turned black and were each, in turn, falling off. About half of my hair, previously a dark brown mop of curls, had fallen out, leaving a patchwork of wispy pieces. My arms were spindly and my body looked like skin over bones. No matter what size clothes I put on, they seemed to billow around me. But for everyone, the worst part was what Michael called the Thousand-Mile Stare: glassy eyes framed by my expressionless face.

My appearance aside, it was a delight to carry on a real conversation. I had always been an energetic person, with a tendency to lean forward when conversing. I wanted to sit up to talk, so desperately wanted to behave in a way that bore some semblance of my old self. Sitting upright required using my hands to pull myself along the bed railing as if I were climbing up a wall on a rope. Once I made it into an upright position I'd cling to the railing with a tenacious grip that lasted for one, maybe two minutes before I collapsed onto the pillows on the bed.

Even this tiny accomplishment brought me great satisfaction. My friends, however, had the opposite experience. With simultaneous looks of awe and horror, they would invariably shout, "No! Don't! Stop!" It was as if they thought I would die from the effort. I hated having to talk to them from a lying down position though. It didn't feel like a real conversation.

At this stage of my recovery, the images from the hallucinations I'd experienced during the drug-induced coma were still more intense and more powerful than any of my other experiences had been at that time. I so desperately needed someone to hear about that world, but Yvonne, Wendy, and Michael had each in their own way made it clear that they did not want to hear the stories. "That's over now, you don't have to talk about that anymore," they would say.

Only one visitor, my friend Doug Chamberlin, would listen to the stories in any detail. He listened in earnest and even asked interesting questions that actually helped to maybe sort out some of their meaning. Unfortunately, Doug was only able to visit a couple of times. I tried telling other friends I suspected had experienced interesting drug trips, thinking they might be able to relate, but it was clear that the tales were too disturbing, and their obvious discomfort convinced me to stop.

The intensity of the trauma from the persistent delusions while in the ICU was so pervasive and overbearing it was all I could think about. I desperately needed something to engage my mind, but there was no other stimulation in my barren hospital room. The nurses kept insisting that I relax and repeatedly encouraged Michael and Wendy to bring me calming music. With nothing to engage my mind, the supposed "calming music" only accelerated my panic. I needed something that I could pay attention to. The only music that could capture my attention was the recent hit "Slim Shady" by Eminem. Michael brought in a portable CD player and headphones, and I would play that song singing along to the chorus and bopping my head to the beat three, four, and sometimes even five times. Then I would be over it.

I desperately wanted conversation, connection. The nursing staff had work to do, and I knew it wasn't appropriate to try to have conversations with them other than managing my immediate needs. The nursing station was outside my room, so during the day there was enough going on that eavesdropping would capture my attention, but at night the place was empty. I could do nothing but watch the minute hand on the clock and wait for morning. I would have an overwhelming urge to call my friends even though it was the middle of the night. I would try to restrain myself, but eventually my resolve would collapse, and I would call Wendy or Yvonne. They would answer in a panic, thinking there was some emergency. When they would ask, "What is happening?" I would realize I had nothing to say. "I don't want to be alone," or, "I just need someone to talk to," doesn't fly at 3:00 a.m. with even the best of friends.

A few days in and I began shaking and rocking. I would repeat over and over, "I gotta get out of here," while flapping my hands wildly. If I were asked a question that required my concentration, I could snap out of it, but otherwise, I resembled a candidate for the psychiatric wing of the hospital.

It was during this period that I noticed a single small tree bereft of leaves outside my window. I felt a whisper of a connection to this sad tree. She and I were both stripped down to nothing and standing in a barren land. At the end of the week, I decided to ask one of the nurses for a piece of paper and a pencil. The pencil they found quite easily, but the piece of paper took a couple of hours.

Despite having spent time in art school as an undergraduate, I hadn't acquired much in the way of drawing skills, but I began drawing the tree. Fine motor control of my hand proved elusive, but I could enjoy the focused observation and make simple marks on paper. As I continued to draw, I was delighted to find that I seemed to be capturing something of the character of that tree. As I moved along, however, I lost control and dropped the pencil. It rolled off my tray and onto the floor. I stared at the pencil, which at a mere three feet away from the bed might as well have been an ocean away. I knew I couldn't buzz the limited night-time nursing staff who were hustling to get patients' medications out to come and pick up my pencil for me. I looked at the clock. It was going to be over three hours before my nurse was going to be back in for her next round. I was back to staring at the clock and looking at the tree with longing.

*

A perky, pony-tailed, twenty-something year-old girl in a blue hospital coat strode purposefully into my room. She smiled brightly and said, "Hi, I'm Jenny, and I'm here to see you sit up."

"I'm sorry," I replied, "I would love to sit up, but you must have the wrong patient. I was in the ICU for sixty days, and all I can do is move my hands up to my elbows, like this." I flopped my hands around to demonstrate.

"No, I'm quite sure I'm in the right room. You're Ara Lucia Ashburne, right?"

"Yes I am, but I'm sure there's some mistake, because there is no way that I could sit up."

"Well, I'm sure you can do it," she grinned.

Turns out, she didn't really mean that I could do it. She had brought a lengthy strap with her which was about four inches wide with a buckle at one end. She wrapped it around my ribs and cinched it tightly, standing right over me in the bed.

"Now, I want you to use all your might and sit up!"

I could see what she was up to. I was going to use all my might and SHE was going to sit me up with this strap. Her enthusiasm seemed ridiculous. She was talking to me as if I was either four or eighty-four and hard of hearing.

"Okay, Ara, on the count of three, ready? One, two, THREE!"

On the count of three I exerted all of the effort I had, which might have been about 2% of what used to be normal for me. She met my effort, bringing the additional 98%, and, sure enough, she yanked my spindly body into an upright position. In one fell swoop, I was looking out at the world from a different perspective, albeit one that was spinning around and made me feel like I was in a drunken stupor. Now upright, sitting in bed, I hung from her strap, barely able to hold up the weight of my own head. I had no balance. I wobbled more like a faltering top than a human sitting upright.

As if this weren't enough, she declared, "Now, you stand up!"

"That is a bit crazy, don't you think?" I was still woozy, hadn't even had a chance to get used to sitting upright yet.

"I'll show you," she said, and gently placed me back on the bed, still wearing the strap. She opened a walker near the bed and scooted my legs off the side of the bed.

"We'll begin the same way. You'll sit up, on three. One, two, three." As before, I used all my might, such as it was, and we repeated the coordinated action to get me into a sitting position. This time, when she pulled me upright, she also swung me sideways so I was sitting on the edge of the bed. I could see out the window: the gray January sky, the chair by my hospital bed, the nightstand, the fan, and out the window—my tree.

I was woozy, spinning more than the last time. She held me as still as she could for several minutes until I no longer felt like I was going to throw up.

"Jenny, I'm exhausted. I think that is all I can manage for today. I gave you all I've got. How about if you come another day for the standing up?"

She wasn't having it. "No, today is the big day. You are going to sit up AND stand up. On three—one, two, THREE!"

Again she met my fierce yet minuscule effort with the remainder of the energy needed to bring me to standing. I felt like a rag doll as I hung in space. My hands clutched the sides of the walker and my feet met the floor as Jenny held on to me from the strap, like a living marionette.

I hadn't realized until that moment how truly weak I'd become. I was discouraged. It was going to take a long time to regain physical capability. And even though the doctors told me that despite having no abdominal muscles I would be able to walk normally at some point, I wasn't so sure I believed them.

As a result, I was amazed at what happened after that. In two days, I was able to get out of bed, pull myself along the wall railing over to the walker, and stand with the walker all on my own. Two days after that, I was able to stumble and bang my walker across the floor, taking the four steps from my bed to the bathroom. In four more days, I showed up at the nurses' station for the sheer joy of shocking them and proving to myself that I could do it. They screeched, and I laughed. A day after that, I met my mom at the elevator—about forty paces from my room.

I felt like I was now in charge of my recovery, and I was ready to kick it into high gear.

*

After I'd been on the general inpatient floor for about two weeks, a doctor and team of physical therapists came to my room to assess whether or not I could transfer to a rehabilitation facility. Was I the kind of case they take on? A couple of my personal doctors (not associated with the hospital) advised that, while I shouldn't lie to the assessors, the goal was not to "try with all my might" when the assessors gave me physical tests, so as not to skew the results and cause them to determine that I was in such good shape I could go to a lesser facility. I didn't think I had much to worry about because I couldn't really do anything.

I was taken by ambulance from the hospital to the Cooper Rehabilitation Facility. Michael had researched the options, and hospital staff confirmed that CRF was one of the best rehab places in the country. They had a reputation for having the most qualified staff and every conceivable kind of equipment to prepare patients for returning to their lives. They had a kitchen where one would learn to stand up and prepare a simple meal and an engineless car sat in one room for patients to learn how to get in and out.

I arrived at CRF on a Thursday, and I was put in a shared room with my bed facing the bed of my roommate. There had been a lot of talk about how much effort is made to put a patient in a room with someone who is about the same age or has a similar difficulty to overcome. My roommate was a 62-year-old woman who had lost her capacity to speak or to understand speech. Her husband was devastated. I was glad we weren't the same age with a similar problem because I didn't want the group therapy treatment. But I was uncomfortable with her inability to make sounds into speech, to ask for what she needed, or to respond to her husband's words. He would have loved her to understand what he meant when he said that he would be making the drive back from Indiana on the weekend. I was told she wasn't likely to make more than a few percentage points of improvement.

An excessively chipper nurse dressed all in white and named James oversaw my orientation. He ran back and forth from my room to the nurses' station, explaining the schedule and the rules and letting me know when I would be meeting with my team. It was late in the day, and he was trying to see if it was still possible to order dinner for me at the same time that he was managing all the calls into the nurses' station. I asked a lot of questions and explained the notes in my chart—how often my abdominal wound bandages needed to be changed and in what manner. In turn, he told me that the burn specialist would do all my bandage changes. He posted the staff schedules, along with the various exercise groups that I would be expected to attend, on a fabric board next to my bed. He also mentioned that my physical and occupational therapists wouldn't be meeting with me until Monday and Tuesday, respectively, of next week.

This was not good news, in my opinion. I had already waited 13 days to get here, and that would be four more days of waiting. I wanted my life back. I wanted to go home. I was sick of waiting, sick of hospitals, sick of everything.

My room looked far more like a hospital—and one in need of some paint, at that—than I had expected. I was encouraged to make the space feel more "like home," with pictures and personal items. Although I knew it wasn't going to happen, I suggested that, since I was facing my roommate's bed, it would make more sense for me to be able to adorn her area, and she mine. My friend Diane had sent two enormous posters, one of Matisse's *Window at Tangier* and one with a view of Morocco, which I hung above my bed. Wendy brought in framed pictures of Michael and me from our mantel at home, and three of my guy friends sent an awesome doctor teddy bear with one of their names embroidered over his lab coat pocket.

Michael bought me a new wardrobe of fitted tops and some sweat pants that came much closer to fitting than anything in my closet at home. He picked out a red and black spandex cap that I could use in a sad attempt to cover what used to be a head of hair. He also found a pair of sneakers that were "in" this season, more like loafers than anything else, as they had no laces or straps. They slipped right on. They were light gray suede, and I almost felt cool in them.

On Saturday morning, I received an unexpected surprise. James came into the room and whispered to Michael and me, "The rule is that no patients are allowed outside passes until they have been here for a minimum of two weeks, but Dr. Stevens is out for the rest of the day, and I think you two can handle it. If you want to go out for a nice meal or something, I can arrange for a wheelchair you can take. You just have to promise me that you won't mention it to the rest of the staff."

"Of course," I promised, as I squeezed Michael's hand and contained my desire to scream with delight. I now had been surrounded by beige or white walls with not a single breath of outside air, for two-and-a-half months. Neither of us had any idea what we would do, where we would go, or how we could celebrate our new found freedom.

Michael promised to make all the arrangements and to bring something nice from home for me to wear. When he returned that afternoon, he was dressed in dress shoes, brown corduroys, and my favorite ribbed blue sweater. It was really a spring sweater, but he had decided that being chilly was worth my smile. He helped me change and moved me into the loaner wheelchair. It was enormous. I felt like a child trying out Santa's throne at Christmas. I needed a seat belt to keep from sliding around (or out of it altogether), but there wasn't one, so Michael told me to "Hold on," and we were off.

It was mid-January, and the sidewalks were rough with snow and ice. Even though CRF was only a couple blocks off of Michigan Avenue, I really had to hang on to stay in the wheelchair. It was heavy and unwieldy, but Michael did his best to avoid jostling me. We could see the street as we approached. It glimmered with the white lights on the trees, still decorated for the holidays. I was excited.

Once we reached Michigan Avenue, I was struck by the roar of the cars and busses. Post-Christmas shoppers overflowed the sidewalks. The volume and complexity of the sound was overwhelming and surprisingly painful. I covered my ears, but it was immediately clear that I needed to use my hands to remain in the chair. As we bumped over the ice, Michael worried he would dump me, and every jerk of the chair hurt more places in my middle than I could count… But we managed to laugh at the ridiculousness of our choice to venture out under these circumstances.

All of the difficulties aside, I was beaming. We were alone! He and I against the world again. Alive. Scared, but free without all the machines and staff and intercoms and call buttons. Only the two of us.

It turned out our destination was several long blocks farther than we realized, but we eventually arrived at the Bloomingdales building, which had a high-end food court. It felt like we passed through an airlock once the outside doors closed behind us. Now I could hear just the noises around me in the lobby instead of all the heightened sounds of the voices and cars roaring on Michigan Avenue. Michael's arms were already tired as he pushed me up the steep incline of the lobby floor. Eventually we found an elevator and made it to the food court.

I was giddy with the excitement of being taken to dinner. I selected the Italian deli and restaurant, and Michael chose the Mexican. I have always loved choices, but after not having *any* for so long, I hardly knew what to do with the delicious selections. I chose a mixed green salad with balsamic dressing and a manicotti—simple, but both things I love. The seating area had wooden tables and chairs, but they were small and close together. I wasn't sure how I would get my wheelchair in there. I'd already felt self-conscious about being in the chair, and this situation made it worse. I was relieved when the people at the next table made some room for my chair.

We sat down with our meals and toasted our soda pop glasses. "To being alive and being on the outside."

I grinned at Michael more than I ate. He kept asking, "What is it?"

"I'm so happy to be with you, you and me. This is all I want."

My palate had become accustomed to bland hospital food, so I was unable to eat the salad with its intensely-flavored dressing, but the manicotti was perfect.

On the way out, we noticed a Swatch store and decided to take a look. I already had a red Swatch with a compass design on the band, but here was a new line of metal watches I had never seen. One had a band made of 5 thin chains that were held together at each end. I figured there was no harm in trying it on, knowing that all watch bands are too long for me. Surely there was no way to shorten all the tiny delicate chain links, so I could try it on for fun with no risk of being able to buy it. It was elegantly made and silver. I had never had a dressy watch before, and I thought for a moment about how time had almost stopped and then restarted for me.

To my surprise, the clerk explained that he could, in fact, adjust the length to fit me if I liked it. The watch was almost $100, which seemed quite expensive, but in that moment I became a girly-girl. "Will you buy it for me, as a present, a memento of our first day back together?" I am careful about asking for things from Michael because he has never denied me a single thing I asked for, and I knew the current situation would only amplify that dynamic.

I left with the shiny watch dangling on my wrist, a keepsake from the outside.

*

"Today is the day you have been waiting for!" Stephanie announced.

"Seriously, I get to do the stairs today? Really?"

"Okay, let's go!"

Then, a familiar face walked into the room. It was my internist, Dr. Tomas. He had been following my progress through conversations with Dr. Segel, but I hadn't seen him in person until the moment he entered.

"What are you doing here? Not that I'm not delighted to see you, but you came here all the way from Riverbank Hospital?"

"Oh, we're just around the corner, and I wanted to see for myself how you are coming along."

"Well, you picked the perfect day, because *today* is a very special day," I said, grinning. "*Today* is the day I climb the stairs!"

"One stair." Stephanie interjected.

"One stair? You are kidding me, right? I'm not climbing one stair."

Then I looked to Dr. Tomas and explained, "This is the deal. I have 32 stairs to get into my apartment. They are going to teach me three different ways to get up a step, but I have to be able to climb 32 stairs to get out of this place. Now, I have wanted to start working on the stairs since the first day I arrived, but they have made me wait nine days. You, my friend, have arrived on a most auspicious occasion. Because Stephanie, here, announced they are finally going to let me do the stairs."

"One stair," she stated flatly again.

I cocked my head and looked at her as if I was looking over a pair of invisible glasses.

Dr. Tomas laughed, "I can tell that you haven't been working with Ara for very long, or you wouldn't be insisting that she will only be doing one stair."

Stephanie tried to explain, "Dr. Tomas, I mean no disrespect, only that Ara is still extremely deconditioned. It will be physically impossible for her to even do the single stair without a tremendous amount of physical support. We are only letting her have the experience today, so that she can begin to understand the process, the concept of climbing a stair, so that next week, when she will be strong enough, she can actually try to climb a stair."

"I'm ready to do the stairs," I said matter-of-factly. "I've been ready."

"I'm sticking around for this," Dr. Tomas said, amused.

"Oh, Dr. Tomas, you won't be able to, we have a forty-five minute conditioning session that we need to do first. Then, the last thing we are going to do is that single stair."

"How is that fair? You are setting me up so that the stair will be too hard for me if you exhaust me first."

"But Ara, I explained, right now, it is about you beginning to understand the process for climbing the stairs. It isn't about you actually climbing stairs."

I glared at her. "Fine then, let's begin the conditioning."

"Like I said," Dr. Tomas said with an enormous smile on his face, "I'm definitely sticking around. This is gonna be good. I've got all my money on Ara."

Stephanie pushed my wheelchair down the hall where she gave me a number of one- and two-pound weights and instructed me to do various isometric exercises. Next, she gave me a walker, and they put one- and two-pound weights on my ankles. Then she gave me isometric exercises to do with my legs, followed by bean bag tosses into a target, throwing a spongy ball through a pretend basketball hoop, and a variety of other exercise games. I was fatigued, my arms and legs shaking with exhaustion, but I could think of nothing but the stairs.

At the forty-five-minute mark, Stephanie said, "Okay here we go. Are you ready?" She wheeled me down the hall, past the information desk where a number of staff people were always congregating, to a door. She tapped a code into a keypad.

"Where are we going?"

"These are the only stairs we have," she explained as she ushered me into the concrete stairwell in the back of the building.

She wrapped my ribs with the same strap that the physical therapist had used in the hospital to help me sit up and then stand up for the first time.

It was exhausting to stand while she was putting the strap around me and cinching it up, so I sat back down in my wheelchair and rested a moment.

Stephanie looked at me sternly. "Now I need you to listen to me, because I need to keep you safe here. The floor is concrete, and if you fall it is really gonna hurt. There are three ways to climb stairs. One is pulling. This is the one you will be doing today."

She demonstrated by putting both of her hands on the railing and then using her arms to lift her body from one step to the next.

"The next one is crawling. It is just what you would think."

She got down on all fours and showed putting both hands one stair above and then moving a right knee and a left knee up another step.

"The third is called bumping. This one is like crawling, but it is backwards."

She sat on the step. Then with her arms behind her on a step, she lifted her bum up and onto the step above.

"Are you ready now to give it a go?"

I looked over at Dr. Tomas and smiled. I was glad that there would be a witness, since it was supposedly physically impossible for me to do what I was getting ready to do.

Stephanie helped me to stand. I placed both hands on the railing. Before I tried to pull my body upward, I used my right hand to place my right foot onto the step, lifting my leg behind my right knee. Then I was in position. With both hands on the railing, I had all my weight on my shaking left leg. I focused all my attention on my arms and my right leg. I needed to pull with my arms and push with my leg.

Stephanie began the count, "On one, two, three!"

I pushed and pulled with all my might, and with a wobbling, shaking commitment, I made it up and over that stair. With my weight on my right leg, I then drew my left leg up.

I was dizzy from the strain, but I wasn't done, and I wasn't ready to cheer the victory.

"That was incredible," Stephanie exclaimed, "I was barely helping you."

"We are not done," I said, "Let's go."

I knew I needed to keep going quickly, before I collapsed from the effort.

I placed my leg on the next step and focused on my arms.

"Now!" I said.

"Wait!" she said, "I'm not with you, it isn't safe."

"Then count, go! Now!"

"One, two, three!"

And again, I pulled myself up over the step. Somehow this one was easier even though I was more exhausted. My body had done it once. It understood the motion, the feeling, the height of the step, and the amount of pressure needed to rise above it.

"Again," I proclaimed, but this time my voice cracked.

I placed my foot on the next step, but my entire body was shivering with fatigue. I hadn't said it out loud, but I had wanted to do seven steps. I knew at this point I wasn't going to get my seven. I was reassessing... maybe five?

"Ara, I think that is enough for today. You did it. You made your point, and you got more than a single step. Honestly, you are doing an amazing amount of the work yourself. Let me help you back down. You can give it another go in two days."

"I'm not done. Please count."

She sighed and adjusted her grip at my back. "One, two, three."

I struggled. I was pulling and I wasn't making it up. But I kept pulling. I alternated my attention. *Pull arms. Push foot. Pull arms. Push foot. Pull arms. Push foot.*

I was up.

YES!

Now I was smiling. I had figured out a way to overcome my own body. I had used my mind to get around my body on that one. I would do it again.

"Let's go again!"

"Come on, Ara. Your whole body is shaking uncontrollably. You need to stop. You have done plenty for today."

"I need one more." I had adjusted my goal again, from five to four, but faced the fact that it was all I had in me.

"One, two, three!"

I shuddered. I pulled. I pushed. I wasn't moving.

I screamed in my head.

COME ON ARA, THREE, GO GO GO GO PUSH, PUSSSSSH!

I began to move up and over the step, but I knew that this time she was doing more than 50% of the work. The moment my body was aligned over the fourth step, my knees buckled and I collapsed. Stephanie yanked with her strap, and quickly gripped me with her other hand. Dr. Tomas got in the mix somehow, and together they kept me from cracking my head open on the concrete.

The stairs were spinning around me like the bender on my 21st birthday. I couldn't really think straight. Stephanie was pushing my wheelchair out into the hall when I heard Dr. Tomas say, "Told you."

Now I could go home.

Realignment

I began making calls. Wendy and Michael had been exceptionally thoughtful when they communicated with people while I was in the hospital. They made two email lists: one for close family and friends who received blow-by-blow updates of my progress (albeit sanitized) and a more filtered version for colleagues and acquaintances. The different levels of censoring would permit me to decide what and how I wanted to tell people once I got out. I was extremely grateful for this, but it meant all of the subsequent conversations explaining what happened to me went something like this one with my academic advisor, Katherine Graves:

"I have some bad and some good news. I was really sick. I was in the ICU for 60 days with a necrotizing infection, and then in a rehabilitation hospital for three weeks, but I'm home now."

"My God, Ara, I don't know what to say. What happened?"

Then I would begin to share some of the specifics, and the person would rapidly become overwhelmed. In Katherine's case, I wanted to assure her that I was getting better quickly and intended to return to my studies immediately.

"I want you to know, although I'm having trouble reading right now"—I didn't tell her I could only read children's books at about a second grade level —"I will be back on track and plan to attend the seminar in June."

"Ara, that is only six months away. It seems like you need to take time to recover and maybe even consider whether or not you still want to be in the program. I think you need to take some time off."

"I don't need time off, I just need time to ramp up. I will be back up and running soon. I need a month or two, because every few days I'm able to do more than I could the day before. Soon, very soon, I should be able to start sending you the abstracts I was intending to get to you by the end of the year."

"Ara, well, let's see how you are feeling. We can check in with each other later."

*

A few weeks later, I finally felt strong enough that I could sit in my car for the long call with Devon. He was my oldest friend, and I hadn't seen or heard from him when I was in the hospital. Despite being on the blow-by-blow list, clearly he'd been bamboozled by Wendy's cleverly executed emails. I didn't want Michael to overhear our conversation. Michael had done what was necessary to protect himself from the numerous people who had been inquiring about my condition (not taking phone calls, not allowing visitors in the ICU, and so on), and I didn't want him to feel bad about it. Calling Devon from the car would give us the needed privacy.

I knew this was likely to be another long, awkward call. Since it was bitter cold outside, I took a blanket and trundled out to where the car was parked next to the video store at the corner of Belmont and Hoyne.

"So, Devon, I'm out of the hospital."

"How are you, love?"

"Much better, but it's still pretty hard. I can't really do much of anything."

"So, what happened?"

I began with the story that led up to my landing in the ICU, then the infection, and the consequences of my time in the hospital. "Ara, my God. I had no idea you were that sick. The emails didn't sound like you might *die*. I feel terrible I wasn't with you!"

"It's okay, I wasn't alone. Yvonne was by my side almost every minute, and I mean exactly that: about every four days she left to take a shower. The nursing staff would even bring her food sometimes."

"But I didn't *know*. I had no idea! I'm horrified you could be in that state, and I was living my life, oblivious to you hanging out there on the edge!"

"That's not your fault. The situation became insane the first day, and Wendy was doing the best she could to support Michael. He was completely buried, and so Wendy began managing all the communication. The first night I was in the ICU my mom called. She had seen me in the hospital a few days earlier, so she wanted to know how I was. When Michael told her I was in the ICU, she told him that she and my Dad would be there in the morning. That night Wendy spoke with Katie, Katie called Diane, Diane called Yvonne.

"Michael wanted to get to the ICU before anybody else arrived in order to talk to the doctors and get his bearings before having to deal with the onslaught of people. But he forgot about the time zone difference with Michigan, so when he arrived my parents were already there. It turned out a few friends were there too. Before he had a chance to talk to the doctors, Yvonne showed up with her suitcase. Then friends and family started calling the ICU, even ringing directly through to my room. It quickly became a zoo."

"Oh, no."

"Yeah, and to make matters worse, there wasn't anything to tell anybody. At first, the doctors didn't know which end was up. They knew the infection was severe, but they couldn't find what caused it for, like, three weeks. It turns out there was a perforation in my bladder, but they were convinced that any infection as severe as mine had to have been caused by an injury to the bowel. They looked and couldn't find anything wrong there. They also checked my bladder, but at that time the wound was swollen shut. So, when they injected this dye into my bladder to see if anything leaked out, nothing did.

"Keep in mind, the infection was progressing since this whole drama started. After I had the ectopic surgery, I was in the hospital for four days when they wouldn't listen to me. Then home for three days. Then for the three weeks in the ICU while they were cutting away at my abdomen every day or so. Eventually, at the three week mark somebody says, 'Hey, we can't find anything wrong, so let's bring in a urologist to take a look.' The urologist found what was then an 'old' injury to my bladder.

"The surgeries to take out the dead muscles and stuff were just perfunctory, sort of cleaning up the mess the bacteria left behind. The doctors kept bombarding me with several broad-spectrum antibiotics in the hopes of clobbering it, clobbering and cutting."

"Wow," Devon said quietly. "Wow."

"Anyway, like I said, for a long time there until that three week mark, it was touch and go hour by hour.

"But the whole time it was a clusterfuck of a people management situation. Friends wanted to visit, but I was in this drug-induced coma, so it wasn't possible to talk with me. So usually if someone did come by they got super freaked out, and then Wendy and Michael had to manage that person's breakdown. There were also a few crazy incidents where a random visitor would show up and a doctor would tell important information to that person, and that left Michael out of the loop. It rapidly got out of control, so Michael and Wendy had to lock down the ICU to only immediate family and a few friends they would escort."

"Sure."

"Poor Michael was in a coma of his own. The only way he got through each day was Wendy. It was all Wendy. She got him to the hospital each morning to talk to the doctors, and she sent out the emails. Honestly, the emails Wendy sent were the truth, but they gave as little information as possible, all to minimize the pressure on Michael. They designed it that way."

There was a brief pause before Devon responded. "Still, I can't believe I wasn't there for you, Ara. How are you now?"

"Well, to tell you the truth, both good and bad, I keep getting stronger, but it's really hard. You know, we live on the third floor, so it takes me about forty-five minutes to get up and about thirty minutes to get down those stairs.

Plus, I have doctors' appointments several times a week. I'm not good for much else. That's the physical part.

"But Devon, here's the thing: The medically induced coma was hell, beyond description. I had horrifying delusions nonstop. They were way more real and intense than anything I've experienced in daily life. It's like I was in an alternate reality, and all those things actually happened to me there. And now, those supposed-delusions are part of my experience. It is pretty much all I can think about. They're so *vivid*. I keep trying to tell Michael about them. I want him to understand what happened to me, to understand what I went through, what I'm going through now, but they're all so hideous. He is so fatigued and exhausted he doesn't want to hear about them. He wants to hear anything else."

"Oh, honey," he said in that warm way of his. "Have you written any of them down?"

"I have started writing them, but it's not enough. You know me, my core need is always to be understood, so I guess I want to know someone *gets* it, someone who matters to me. I guess it's just—they're too gruesome, so no one wants to hear them, much less understand them."

"It sounds like this is a job for a therapist. Are you seeing anyone?"

"I am. I'm seeing the guy I saw during the year before we started IVF. Luckily, he's a Jungian analyst, so he can appreciate the power of them, but I don't really want to rehash them to see if I can uncover any hidden meaning, like doing dream interpretation. For one thing, it would take years, and I don't have years. I want to focus on getting my life back on track. I need to figure out what I'm going to do."

"But Ara, I don't see how you can jump back into your life. It sounds like it is going to take some time."

"I told my advisor I would attend the next seminar, in June, but you're right. I'm beginning to realize there's no way that's gonna happen. I still can't read and comprehend anything more complicated than a primer. My body has gotten stronger, but it seems like my head has stopped. It's freaking me out. I'm gonna keep trying, but unless there is some kind of big leap, I think I'm going to have to accept it'll be a long time before I can go back to grad school. I was about a term away from completing the degree, but now I can't possibly do it.

"Worse still, I don't have the stamina, focus, or even close to the attention span to go back to work as a psychotherapist."

"That sucks."

"Honestly Devon, I can't follow a recipe with three steps. I can't keep track of which steps I have done and which ones I haven't. I try crossing them off, but I get so confused and angry and frustrated. I just end up in bed sobbing.

"Michael doesn't know what to do with me. He's encouraging me as best he can, but it's hard to know what to do with me. I get it. *I* don't know what to do with me."

"I hear you."

"I've never been suspended from my life like this. I don't know what to do when I'm not propelling myself forward. I flit from pushing forward, to stopped, to slumped in the chair in a daze. I honestly don't know what is next for me."

*

I was worried about our livelihood. We had bills to pay and a mortgage and Michael couldn't do it alone. I needed to come up with something I could do in my diminished state. But at this point my fatigue was so high it took tremendous will to get up from a chair or the couch to a standing position. This meant even getting up and walking the 22 steps from the living room to the bathroom was a major accomplishment. When I was in rehab, my achievements were always a "one-off." But now I was home, and I had to produce these feats of physical prowess over and over in a given day. In the case of needing to pee, the amount of energy it took was so intimidating I would put it off until it was unbearable, which only made the task more difficult.

Since it was clear, for at least the interim, that I wasn't going to be able to work, I decided to give myself a sabbatical. For a couple of months I would do whatever I wanted. Unfortunately, that meant something other than reading. My hope was that focusing on a specific activity, anything, might indirectly help to bring my cognition and stamina back online. I thought if I could choose an activity that excited me, I might be able to garner the energy to do it, at least for a little while.

While choosing among sabbatical endeavors, I lit on the piano. I'd always wanted to play the piano as a child, and as a piano was out of reach financially it wasn't an option. Michael had a keyboard in his music studio which he brought up to our apartment for me to use. Our friend Doug Corella offered to come to the house to give me lessons. He wanted the lessons to be relevant and asked me to pick some music I enjoyed. I didn't make it very easy on myself. Although I was starting from zero with no music fundamentals, what I listened to at the time was primarily world music, which was layered and complex. It was a challenging place to begin.

Corella was the perfect teacher, breaking the music down into tiny steps. He was gentle and kind, shining a light just ahead of where I stood on the path. Unfortunately, my Type-A head set was not excised along with my abdomen. Everything I had ever done, I'd always done with an intense investment. When I opened my fine art gallery, I worked 110 hours a week, took every conceivable action to create success for my artists. When I had my intern psychotherapy practice, I was devoted. I talked with colleagues and went to seminars, and was committed to holding the gate open for the psyches

Ara Lucia Ashburne

of clients to do their healing work. The same was true of my personal interests, whether learning to fly planes or jump horses... everything. I couldn't comprehend doing something casually.

Now unable to keep my thoughts straight to execute a three-step recipe, I soon realized I couldn't possibly conjure the necessary focus for learning something new, something technical, like playing the piano. I lasted two lessons.

I reevaluated. I decided the piano failure was because it was a new endeavor. Maybe I could do an activity if I had a little foundation. I decided to give drawing a try. I had vigorously complained about required drawing classes when I was a photo major in my undergrad. The truth was I longed to be more skillful, and the little moment I had in the hospital drawing a tree outside my window felt meaningful. I turned to another friend, Doug McGoldrick, now a professional photographer, who had received his Master in Fine Art in Painting and Drawing.

My reticence about drawing stemmed from an experience in first grade. Our teacher, Ms. Schmidt, gave us an assignment which at the onset seemed cool. She put a life-size piece of paper on the floor and traced an outline of each of us. We were to draw ourselves. I was absorbed by the experience. I had on a sweater, a plaid skirt, my favorite navy blue suede shoes with an embossed logo of Winnie-the-Pooh on the side. Toward the end of the exercise, she gave us a two minute warning. I quickly drew in the holes for the buttons on my sweater and then looked up.

My eyes locked onto the drawing of my classmate, David. It was incredibly detailed and accurate. I looked back and forth at him and the drawing, amazed at his accuracy. He was wearing striped pants, a buckle with a running horse, a shirt pocket with a loose stitch across the top, a collar. Everything was drawn in precise detail. I looked back at my drawing, and I was devastated. By comparison it looked like something a pre-schooler had drawn. I wanted to hide it. It was in this moment I concluded I couldn't draw, and I would go to great lengths to avoid the activity going forward.

In the early '90's when I was attending Texas Woman's University, photography majors were required to take a number of general art classes, one of which was a year of figure drawing. I ranted about this, saying that there was no situation wherein a photographer was going to need to draw a nude human. I knew that behind my rant was fear. I was petrified of the public humiliation. It was a class after all. It wasn't like I would be able to do my assignments in private. Other students and the teacher were going to see my pre-school drawings.

The figure drawing instructor, Don Radke, began the first class by having us create quick gesture drawings. Gesture drawing is an attempt to capture the basic shape or movement of the figure in a very short time frame, ten to fifteen seconds, maybe a minute. Right before we took our first break, he went around the room and said two adjectives describing each person's drawing. For mine he said, "bold and determined." It freaked me out. We hadn't gone around the room in the beginning of class and introduced ourselves. He had no information about me, and yet he had described my personality. How did he see that in the drawing? I knew only one other student in the class. He nailed her too. Did this mean it was impossible to not draw like oneself?

When we got back from lunch he explained how this was true. He described the process of drawing as unique to each artist. It's three steps. First is the seeing, what the artist observes. Next the information has to go through the body. And thirdly, the mark is made on the paper. So the observation goes through the body and is translated into the mark. And thus the result is unique to each person. I was all-in.

But I remained frustrated by what I felt to be a major distortion in my work—the drawing never looked like what I observed. Radke, as we called him, believed that was the beauty of drawing. He continued to direct me to famous artists whose work was not representational. He wanted me to let go of my insistence that my drawing look like what I wanted it to look like. He kept pushing me.

Here was my chance to try drawing again. I could attempt to pick up where Radke left off and see if I could gain more skill, increase my ability to create what I observed. Since much of my photography and performance art work had an element of self portraiture, it made sense to start there. Doug took a picture of me with a polaroid camera and then drew a grid on it. This process involved breaking down the overall image into its parts, drawing what was in each square. Then one draws one square at a time. This would eliminate the problem I had with structure and proportion. I started to work on the drawing, but I struggled. Again, I had an incredibly short attention span, maybe five or ten minutes. Then I was completely exhausted and would need to go lay down. Doug had the great idea of creating little still lifes that I could use to draw between lessons. He would wander about the house looking for objects and made small set-ups out of them. He gave me suggestions for getting started, and then I would have to send him on his way.

The second week in I wanted to create a drawing symbolic of my situation. I wanted to illustrate the concept of being trapped between my old life which felt like it was catapulting me toward success and my current life where I was standing in front of an eternal wall with no door, no magic entrance. I wanted to depict myself as a monster to represent my new wrecked body and tormented mind, the horrors my life had become. But it quickly became apparent that instead of picking up where Radke left off, all I could accomplish with my current mind and body was again drawing like a pre-schooler. I was disgusted and depressed. I ended the sabbatical after a month.

*

Given I could no longer read, I had to adjust my career goals to something that didn't include the rigors of academia. I decided to channel my original aspiration to become a therapist toward becoming a coach. This was a goal I originally had for after grad school anyway. It is a role similar to being a therapist, but I saw it as giving me the tools to support clients to be more active participants in their care and to be more goal-directed, more focused on translating their insights into action. This also didn't require a graduate degree. It seemed doable.

In the spring of 2001, at the beginning of preparations for the reconstructive surgery, I flew out to meet with my friend Katie, a marketing executive. We did a three-day intensive. She helped me create a business plan to start a coaching practice. Her tough questions allowed me to discern a mission, a target market, and an outline for a marketing plan.

As the three days progressed, the reality of what it would take to start and build a successful coaching practice become increasingly clear. I would need tremendous motivation and energy. These were qualities I had in abundance prior to getting sick, but now I couldn't string together enough momentum to get through my day. This wasn't something I was going to be able to do with a deficient mind and body in less than the maybe two hours a day that I was "operational."

Like a languid flood, creeping from the back of my psyche to slowly overtake my conscious awareness, a feeling of despair turned my mind into a swamp with no way out. I didn't say anything to Katie at the time, as I was grateful for her help. But by the time I found myself on the plane back home, I knew I had no hope of launching the plan we'd created. I was left with only one question: had the present changed so dramatically, so irrevocably, that the future might never resemble the past in any way?

On the plane heading back to Chicago, despair gathered around me like a dense cloud, and the sounds of the plane engines and other passengers' voices fell away. I was doomed. With no other creative ideas for how I could work, make a contribution financially, or do anything meaningful, I began to slide away from myself.

Before Everything Bad Happened, Michael and I had agreed I would be the one to support us, and he would be a stay-at-home Dad. Now the commercial space on the first floor which once housed my businesses (first an art gallery, then my burgeoning psychotherapy practice) sat empty and unused. Unfortunately, the hospital to which the ambulance had taken me was not a member of our HMO. Creditors were hounding us on a daily basis. Michael returned to his job as a legal assistant, mostly for the health insurance to cover my ongoing care, but the income wasn't enough to support us.

We had been counting on me.

I had to come up with some means to bridge the gap, save the building, and put us back on track with only enough wakeful life energy for about two hours a day. I spent all my time combing job websites. I couldn't work retail, because I couldn't stand or keep track of information long enough to work a register, let alone lift anything or sort stock. I couldn't work customer service because I couldn't hold three numbers in my head long enough to repeat them back to someone. Even the simplest, lowest-paying jobs were too demanding physically or cognitively or both. It became apparent that essentially all jobs required someone to perform either a physical task or a mental task. I had never viewed the world in such black and white terms before. With a busted body and a busted mind, I could do neither of these.

I considered myself to be a Manifestor. I made things happen, but manifesting took life energy. My life force had been diminished to a glimmer, enough to barely run my basic operating systems, but not enough to pursue passions or transform visions into reality. My future had become a complete blackout.

I wanted my doctors to offer some greater expectation of recovery, but they didn't. They continued to say, "You are the only one of you. You can only wait. We expect you to continue getting better, but it is a slow process. You need to be patient."

Dr. Tomas, my internist, was the only one to put a number to it when he said, "It could easily be 10 to 20 years."

"20 years! You're kidding, right? Really? What am I supposed to do during those 20 years when I can't do anything?"

He didn't have an answer.

One morning I awoke, and the darkness appeared so eternal I couldn't see out any more. My driven temperament and love of work made me ill-suited for such infinitesimal progress. I had become a person with no purpose, no point I could see, no goal I could strive toward, no future I could find, no hope I could locate, no nothing. Such despondent rumination went on for days, then weeks. The more time passed wherein I couldn't see what to do with my life, the more it began to look like one that wasn't worth living.

I began to consider suicide.

*   *   *

Whenever I embark on a project, I start by doing research. Killing myself was no exception. I used the internet to research the most effective method and was surprised at how many websites I found. These sites were morbid (in the truest sense of the word) yet oddly comforting. I felt like there was a sense of community in the fears, questions and thoroughly-researched answers posted on the various suicide forums. I wondered about the circumstances surrounding other people's lives. What had brought them to the place of no return? How were their lives destroyed? Most of the sites were technical in nature with everyone discussing the pros and cons of the various methodologies. No one was telling their stories. I was fully aware of how creepy it all was, but I also felt a growing appreciation for the right I believe everyone has: the choice to end your own life.

I do believe that a person should do everything they can for themselves. That means seeking support, and I'm a strong advocate for meds (which I know isn't the answer for everybody). I believe as a society we aren't doing anywhere near enough to make therapy and meds available to help people who have mental illness. But in the end, regardless of how regrettable it might be, I believed then and I still believe now, that only the person who is living the life, the person who has to bear the true weight of that life, can decide if that weight is too much to bear. And it is possible it's truly too much.

As I assessed my situation and evaluated my options, I decided my best chance of success—to avoid being left alive and rendered paralyzed or otherwise incapacitated—would be to use a gun. There were challenges. Identification was required to buy a gun legally, of course. To my surprise at the time, I discovered no handguns were allowed in the Chicago city limits. The old me would have had the energy and the creativity to come up with a solution to work around these obstacles, but the dark-and-devastated me didn't have the resources. I was going to have to find another, more complicated method. This meant constructing a multi-layered plan, a plan with built in back-ups, and a back-up on the back-ups. I ultimately referred to it as my Three Point Plan.

I thought about the people whose lives would be upset by my suicide. I knew "upset" was an understatement. Still, I believed it wasn't fair of anyone to expect me to live with nothing to live *for*. I also believed that, if most of my friends and family were stuck in my predicament, they would at least consider it, too. Alone, I sat in the green rocking chair and stared hollowly forward. Once or twice a day I would make half of a peanut butter sandwich. That was all I could manage. No one would wish this upon themselves.

Eventually, I believed I had sculpted a solid Three Point Plan. That in itself was a relief. I knew if a moment came when the darkness became too excruciating, I had a solid and effective strategy for departure. I began to think about my suicide note, who should receive one—Devon, Wendy, Yvonne, Diane—but I couldn't figure out what I would say to each of them. I decided I would instead leave a single note for Michael. I knew he would never forgive me, and there would be nothing I could say in the note which would bring him any comfort, but somehow it seemed more cruel to leave nothing. If our positions were reversed, I would assume there was a note hidden somewhere in a special CD or book and I would never stop looking for it. So, I had to give him something.

I considered listing some of the magical moments we had together in the hope he would be encouraged to hold on to them, but I feared those memories would then be tainted with loss. I thought about saying I was sorry, but then thought, *Well, if I got a suicide note which said the person was sorry, my response would likely be, "Fuck you! If you were sorry, you wouldn't kill yourself, so I don't think you're very sorry!"* After running through the pros and cons of every conceivable option, each considered and then discarded, I decided I would only say, "I love you." It seemed pure and true. I wanted to follow it with, "I hope someday you will understand and forgive me," but that seemed incredibly selfish and unfair. Killing oneself and then giving someone an emotional job to do in the goodbye letter? Nope. I would leave it at "I love you."

As my depression compounded, I had less and less to talk about. Michael came home every day from a monotonous job with no idea of how to wrestle me out of the dark. A routine began to form. He would come home, grab something to eat, then hide out in the bedroom, watching syndicated reruns of "Seinfeld" and "Friends" until he fell asleep and another day began. One day, though, he came into the living room, sat down next to me on the couch and said, "Ara, I need to talk to you."

I panicked. Had he deduced my plan? I hadn't documented it anywhere, hadn't told anyone the specifics.

"I need you to know I love you," he began. "I know that might not mean very much right now, but I do love you. I know if you decide to kill yourself I cannot stop you—no one can stop you—but I want you to reconsider. Consider living.

"Can you remember what it was like when we first fell in love? I know our life has turned into a nightmare, but it isn't *really* a nightmare because we still have each other. If you go, then my life will be the truest kind of nightmare. I still want a future with you. I still want to have kids with you, and even if that can't happen I want to share the rest of my days with you. There are adventures you haven't lived, places you want to go. As long as we are together, we can still have a life." For the first time I could recall, he was crying and I was not.

"I know I've asked you this before, when you didn't have any control over your situation, but now you do. Please live."

It held me. I liked the idea. It was true, I still wanted those things, to live a life with him, to travel, to have adventures. I could feel the faintest wisps, a stirring inside me, but I didn't know how to solidify them or how to act on them. Within a few days, the wisps of the words began to fade behind the pressures of a life I desired but could no longer reach. But with my reconstructive surgery a few weeks away, I decided I could hold on a little longer. I became attached to the idea, once rebuilt, I would be better than I was.

*

I had been referred to Dr. Alex Petrosian as one of the top abdominal reconstructive surgeons in the country. At my first consultation, I lay on the table as he examined my abdomen. A large skin graft taken from my left thigh, a region that ran from just above the knee all the way up to my hip, now covered my intestines, from my pubic bone to two inches below my sternum. This graft was temporary, used to close the abdominal wound so my body could continue to heal and avoid contracting any infections, but it offered no structural support for my guts. It was merely a thin layer of skin covering my intestines. You could see all the workings of my insides. Michael found this view of peristalsis fascinating. I found it disgusting.

Dr. Petrosian stared at my abdomen. I watched his eyes darting back and forth, looking carefully and intently. He did not move. His concerned and thoughtful gaze continued for several minutes, until I couldn't take it. "Please say something. The silence is killing me."

"Well, this is a really big area." This was not new information. "Normally, a flap surgery of this kind would be a free flap, where the hamstring is taken and moved to cover the abdomen, but in your case the hamstring is not big enough. I have read about the possibility of using the latissimus. I'm trying to figure out if that will work. I need to check with my colleagues, look into the research and get back with you. You don't use the latissimus for much besides archery, so it would be preferable."

"Okay, so if that's doable, how soon can we get going?"

"We would have to do a minor surgery to prepare for the major reconstruction. The minor surgery would involve an incision to prepare the area for the flap surgery. The incision cuts through a number of blood vessels leading to and from the flap—around the main vessel. This vessel, the thoracodorsal artery, would be the only inroad of nutrients to the flap. Over time this vessel would become larger and stronger. Then, when the flap was relocated to your abdomen, it would already be receiving a strong blood flow through this artery which basically keeps the muscle alive.

"Also, we would put two small balloons under the skin in your back. Each week you would come in and we would inject saline into the balloons. This would stretch the skin, so we would have enough to close your back once the latissimus has been removed."

The reconstruction would move my latissimus muscle, as well as the adjacent skin, fat, and fascia (the fibrous connective tissue which surrounds groups of muscles, blood vessels and nerves) to cover my abdomen. One end would remain attached at the lower spinal vertebra, while the rest would be threaded beneath a couple muscles on my left side, pulled across my abdomen, then anchored at a few points on my right side. Dr. Petrosian called it a "partial free flap," because the one end would remain attached at its original spot.

Part of my back would be on my front. Weird, sure, but anything would be better than my intestines hanging in front of me like a fanny pack. After a couple weeks of investigation he confirmed his proposed procedure should work. The preparatory surgery was scheduled in a month, and the major reconstruction was scheduled for June 4th.

Twice a week, I was picked up by the hospital's shuttle and my pain-ridden body bumped along the road to Dr. Petrosian's office for my saline injections. It was always the same kindly driver. After a few trips, he timidly asked my ailment and then helped me to track the number of visits as the months progressed from winter into spring toward the Big Surgery. As the months passed, the saline hump on my back grew larger and larger until I couldn't sit up straight or sleep comfortably. I had to guard the balloons against cold breezes, which would chill the saline and then my back. As the time passed, I became increasingly irritated, and I looked more and more like a hunchback.

Eventually June 4th did come. The surgery was to begin at 6:45 a.m. It lasted twelve and a half hours (most open heart surgeries are done in three and a half). Several doctors assisted. I came prepared for at least a week-long stay at the hospital. I packed my laptop for checking emails and CDs for entertainment, but there is no way to fight hospital boredom.

When I awoke in my recovery room after the surgery, there was a machine at my bedside with a microphone. This was used to monitor the single blood vessel feeding the latissimus that was now across my stomach. Nurses would come in every couple of hours and turn the machine on, place the microphone on a very specific spot on my belly, and listen for the telltale sign of blood flow. "ShroomShroomShroomShroom" went the machine. We soon became very attached to this sound. It meant blood was flowing, and the muscle was alive and viable. The after-effects of the drugs and anesthesia put me right to sleep, but this time without the horrors of the ICU.

Dr. Petrosian's reconstruction was an heroic achievement. I never heard him say this. Rather, I heard it repeatedly from those who witnessed the surgery. I asked Petrosian if I was going to end up in some journal. His response was, "No, nothing new happened. It is just that all the things that made up your surgery have never been done at the same time." As far as he knew, it was the largest abdominal reconstruction that had been done. He had done it successfully. He managed to cover the huge area and had enough skin to close my back, with only two quarter-sized pieces of skin to spare.

I appreciated that his victory was the next best thing to a medical miracle, and now all my guts were protected by a piece of synthetic mesh and muscle, with a single strong blood vessel—I was deeply grateful. But I was left with a body which was far less than the original. I was in shock, and I was struggling to grasp the reality of my new shape. I still lacked the thirty interlaced muscles that make up a normal abdomen and control an abdomen's shape.

As I looked down at the 83 staples that snaked across my abdomen, I had to face the fact that I'd been given an abdomen that protruded like I was seven months pregnant. This would be my shape. No diet or exercise would change it. This was my sentence for the rest of my life. And that was the least of my problems.

The person I thought I could become in my life was nowhere in sight. She was gone.

*

Some time later, Michael had an opportunity to visit friends and see a music event in Detroit. It would be the first chance he had to do something fun for himself in the eight months since the ICU. I assured him I would be fine, and I meant it. I had been suicidal for months and had a finalized plan for at least two of them. If I'd been ready to carry it out, I would already have done so. Every day looked like every other whether he was home or not. I couldn't see any reason for him not to go. I took him to Union Station, kissed him, told him I loved him, and drove home.

When I entered our apartment and shut the door, I took a single step—and felt a shift, a realization: the main reason I hadn't initiated the Three Point Plan was because it needed a lot of time to execute. It required a big chunk of time as well as privacy, and now I had both. Although I wasn't sure on an intellectual level that I had eliminated all possibilities for a future in my lessened state, I knew if I were going to do it, now would be the time. I paced the apartment. I was relaxed because I had all the freedom I needed, but at the same time I started feeling stressed because I wanted to be absolutely sure. Even with the spark of hope long ago snuffed out, my brain wasn't yet convinced there was truly no way out. I was 98% sure, but not 100%.

I considered whom I could call. Was there anyone with whom I could process this final decision? A phone call wouldn't do. Yvonne had stayed up many nights talking this through with me. At this point, I felt I needed contact with a live person. I became worried if I didn't find someone to be present with me, I might impulsively take the opportunity to kill myself before I had finished exploring all of the options for life. If I did it, I wanted to do it because I had decided for certain.

My sister, Julie, who lived in Detroit, was visiting my parents on the west side of Michigan for the weekend. This meant she was only a couple of hours away. Although she had small children, my parents might be willing to watch them for a while if she told them she had to see me. So, I called. For whatever reason, I felt embarrassed to tell her my situation. "Julie, I need to discuss something with you privately." She agreed, and went into a separate room, away from family.

I calmly explained I was suicidal and had realized the only thing keeping me from doing the deed was privacy and time, and Michael was gone for the weekend. With her background in speech pathology, Julie had extensive clinical experience, so it was no surprise when she asked me standard suicide hotline questions.

Did I have a plan? "Yes."

Would I tell her the plan? "No."

She made me promise not to do anything until she arrived. It would likely take her at least three hours to get to Chicago, which was not enough time to carry out my plan, so I agreed.

I had barely hung up the phone when she called back to ask if she could bring Dad. I was horrified. "You told Dad?"

"Ara, this is important. The family discussed—"

"The *family* discussed it? Who discussed it? Julie," I said, "that was a private conversation."

"You know I can't keep suicidal intentions private. Mom, John, Melissa, Dad, and I discussed it. We decided it would be good if Dad and I came together." I was confused. The situation had become complicated. "Would that be okay?"

I didn't know what to say, so I agreed. I was fitful until they arrived.

We went across the street to the Beat Kitchen for a bite to eat. Julie and Dad sat across from me at one of the outdoor tables. I hoped they would start the conversation, entertain me with stories about my siblings or what Julie's kids were up to. Instead, they stared back at me. After a while, I realized they weren't going to say anything. I was going to have to do the talking. What could I say?

My sister and I had shared deep secrets and the agony of broken hearts before, so I figured I might be able to find the words to tell her how I came to this place. But my *father*? How was I to look into the eyes of the man who raised me and tell him I was prepared to take myself out? I was afraid to try to explain.

My whole life, my father had been a pragmatic man. We frequently argued about controversial topics during the years I was growing up. Also, he often said he thought both Julie and I were too emotional.

Nevertheless, I idolized my father. While we were very different in some ways, we had much in common. He was the model of driven temperament, and his love of work shaped me growing up. That aspect of him, one I had internalized in my own personality, played a part in my predicament. I owed him some kind of explanation, so I slowly laid out how the situation had evolved. They both watched me with rapt attention.

When I was finished, my dad nodded, "I can see how you would feel that way." This was not a calculated response. He meant it. "I've always tended toward being a little down myself, but it's never gone that far for me. I've always been able to pick myself up. Given your situation, I can see how you wouldn't know how to get yourself back up."

I couldn't believe my ears. It was the first time I'd had a conversation with my father where I went in feeling stressed, and he responded to me with compassion and empathy. There was no fight. I felt embraced by his words.

The three of us talked some more, and they told me they loved me. Neither of them argued with me about my plans. I had been prepared for a fight, and was met with none. I was even more confused now.

We finished our meal and returned home. Julie and Dad were still quiet, letting me set the pace. Having spent months either trying to come up with a life I could live or fine-tuning my plans for not-living, I had nothing left to talk about. After sitting in uneasy silence for a while, we wound up playing a board game for several hours.

At one point, when Julie was whipping us both, I said, "Hey, I can't believe you are playing so hard. You aren't even going to let the suicidal sister win?"

"Of course not!" she said, and we all instantly understood the double meaning implied by our exchange and burst out laughing. In the end, they spent the night. The next morning, the three of us went to breakfast, and then they departed. I was so baffled by the encounter, deconstructing it had me occupied until Michael returned that evening.

Although we had spoken on the phone several times while Michael was in Detroit, I had avoided telling him the impetus for Julie and Dad's visit. When Michael arrived, I 'fessed up about what had transpired while he was away. He was furious. "You lied to me!" he said, referring to my assurances that I was fine before he left.

"I didn't lie. I didn't know having you gone would make a difference," I proclaimed. But at the moment, the subtleties didn't matter to him. He held on to his belief that I had broken a promise. He was exhausted from the weekend and the train ride home and had to get up for work on Monday.

"I don't know what to do here. I feel trapped," he said.

"What do you mean?"

"Well, I can't go on like this. *We* can't go on like this. I know I can't possibly comprehend what you are going through right now, but both of our lives are hanging in the balance here. I have to go to work tomorrow, but I don't feel like I can leave you alone. I get you're suicidal, and I get *why* you're suicidal, and I don't blame you. But at the same time, you can't expect me to take off to work tomorrow like it's just another day, right?"

"I can see how you would feel that way."

"You are calling Segel in the morning. *Promise me* you'll call him first thing. If you don't, I will." I had to admit, his insistence surprised me.

"He's my doctor, it's not appropriate for you to call—"

"I don't want to call him," Michael said, cutting me off. "I want *you* to call him, but if you don't, I will. I guarantee. We're in this together."

In the end, I agreed.

*

Both my psychiatrist, Dr. Segel, and therapist, Dr. Modoro, had ongoing knowledge of my status, but it had been a while since I had seen either of them. Amid the various other appointments I'd had in order to prepare for the reconstructive surgery, I was too exhausted to see them, too. Besides, as is often the case with depression, I was convinced no one could help me anyway. Still, I complied with Michael's demands, and Dr. Segel insisted on seeing me that day.

"Why would you want to kill yourself?" Dr. Segel challenged me as soon as I sat down.

"Why wouldn't I? I've had a miserable life, and now it's worse than miserable. I'm done."

"It has been several years since you had your initial consultation, when we went over your history. Why don't you remind me of what was so miserable about your life."

I looked at him, incredulous. "That would take hours."

"It's okay, I have hours."

I thought he might have had a little extra time, as I was his last appointment for the day, but assumed he would need to move on to deal with his own life. "Don't you have to walk your dog?" I asked him. A picture of his wife and their dog sat on his bookshelf in his office. It had been there for years.

"No," he said, as he looked at his pager and pushed a few buttons. "I've got all night." I wondered if he had sent a message to his wife saying he was going to be late.

Oh, fuck, I thought to myself.

"Well," I began, "I've had a miserable life. I was abandoned by my birth mother at two months." I had been asked to write timelines of my life for several therapists, so I was accustomed to succinctly rattling off my misfortunes. I went on, describing my childhood with a strict father and mother, the religious conflict that caused me to leave home at the age of twelve, followed by the challenges I faced as an undiagnosed bipolar teenager.

My late teen years were not better. I lived in a series of run-down apartments in Chicago, barely scraping by financially. At that time, I endured abuse at the hands of a trusted adult, my boxing instructor, who I'd come to know during the runaway years. I continued training with him, and he brutally assaulted and raped me. I recounted the lesser hardships that followed, up to when Everything Bad Happened. I finished with a brief recap of my despair about not having anything to live for.

"And that is why I want to kill myself. Why wouldn't I?" I asked proudly. The telling had lasted more than a half hour, during which he listened intently and with the occasional nod.

He said he hadn't realized the extent of the sexual abuse I had suffered and wanted to know more. He asked me a series of questions. Having been a patient of his for several years, I could feel each of the "if–then" control flow moments. He was following a mental flowchart, a tool of his medical training. We discussed some of the specifics, like the time my instructor locked me in a room for four days passing food and water under the door, and the time he penetrated me with objects for his own amusement.

After this telling, a tiny bit of darkness seemed to move over Dr. Segel's face. "The person that abused you is a sociopath, the worst kind," he added ominously. "What he did to you qualifies as torture. He is dangerous."

"The nature of the torture inflicted on you creates a kind of Post Traumatic Stress Disorder that was likely activated by your stay in the ICU."

I blinked repeatedly. "Are you saying the sexually violent nature of so many of my hallucinations was caused by this?"

"The nightmares you had in the ICU could have been terrifying regardless of this personal experience, but it is likely that these images and feelings were already in your psyche and took shape in your delusions." He interlaced his fingers as he continued, "Also, when a person is held captive, it can create a dynamic called Stockholm Syndrome. It's been well-documented and can develop in a very short period of time, sometimes as short as forty-eight hours. This means as a captive, you come to care for your captor, as they are the one who chooses not only when to give you pain but also when to lessen your pain. At times, this can make the victim feel grateful for the supposed 'restraint' offered by the captor. This dynamic would have been amplified by the fact he was a trusted person when you were so young."

"What does this mean for me?" I said, trying to wrap my mind around what Dr. Segel had told me.

He leaned forward in his chair. "Your depression, this deep depression you are experiencing is highly aggravated by PTSD. PTSD isn't curable, but it *is* treatable. If we treat the PTSD, we can more effectively treat the depression, and we can pull you out of this. I can see it now, and I'm sure we can get you the help you need."

Huh, I thought.

"You need to talk to your therapist about this immediately. Are you still seeing Dr. Modoro?"

"I happen to have an appointment with him tomorrow."

"I'll call and leave a message for him so he is apprised of your situation."

I left Segel's office feeling conflicted. I truly believed I was over what had happened. It had been decades, and I thought I had moved on with my life since then. Yet, at the same time, I was aware on some level I was holding back. There were parts of the story I didn't tell Dr. Segel.

*

When I arrived at Dr. Modoro's office the next day, my apprehension had swelled to consume me. Despite believing I was "over it," I wasn't looking forward to reliving the experiences. I'd always been shy when it came to talking about sex in general, so having to be explicit about being raped repeatedly seemed impossible. Previously, I had tried to talk with two different therapists about this trauma. Each of them wound up crying before I had said much of anything. Both times they referred me to someone "more qualified" to handle my "complicated case." I never went to the referrals. In the first situation, I didn't believe the referral could handle it either. In the other, I couldn't afford the hourly rate. I wasn't sure Dr. Modoro was the guy for the job either, but Dr. Segel was convinced he could help.

As we began, in an effort to get the experience over and done with, I stared at the floor and rapidly recounted the atrocities. There were inappropriate teasings during my preteen years ("Your pussy is so tight! You should stretch yourself out with a soda bottle!"). As I got older my instructor used inappropriately aggressive training techniques, sometimes knocking me unconscious. Then he would kick me until I woke up, and the training would resume as if nothing had happened. Eventually, I tried to quit training with him, only to have him break down the locked door of my apartment in the middle of the night, physically drag me outside, and force me to work out in the alley. He had imprisoned me, starved me, raped me, all under the pretense of training. I took a job in another state in order to escape.

Dr. Modoro listened all the while with a clinical reserve, yet with enough warmth to make me feel understood. As he perceived it, I had found myself hooked into an abusive relationship. Because this man had been my instructor starting when I was a pre-teen, I never thought of it as a "relationship." But applying that lens allowed me to understand, in a critical and honest way, what part I played in the dynamic and to recognize that I was too frightened to see my way out of the entrapment.

*

After a few months of working with Modoro, I began a treatment for PTSD with Dr. Segel called Prolonged Exposure.[*] It involved describing the traumatic experiences as accurately as possible in excruciating detail. The retellings were recorded and I listened to them over and over until I was basically numbed out and the experiences no longer had a triggering impact.

PE isn't a "cure" and it doesn't erase whatever happened, but it can dial back a person's reaction enough so they can go on living without the former

---

[*] The method of Prolonged Exposure Dr. Segel used with me was developed by Edna Foa, PhD, Director of the Center for the Treatment and Study of Anxiety and her group at the University of Pennsylvania. It involves vividly describing the traumatic encounters, with coaching by the therapist, to describe the entire episode using present tense language, with eyes closed, describing what was seen, heard, felt, smelled, and tasted (this allows for a more complete recall of known events). The traumatic episode is described in great detail, and as much as is possible to resemble a linear story, with the ordinary events surrounding the experience embedded within it. Recalling the ordinary elements has a way of triggering more complete recall of the painful, traumatic ones. Relaxation exercises are used many times during the retelling to break up the pain and distress triggered by recalling the trauma. These recountings are recorded by the patient (just for their own use), and taken home. The patient listens to the recordings repeatedly—the exposure—until they no longer have a "charge," or the patient's reaction to the experience is diminished. It produces clinically significant improvement in about 80% of patients with chronic PTSD and related depression, anxiety, and anger.

encounters intruding on daily life. Although recounting everything in detail was horrifying, I accepted it as necessary pain in the short term to try to find lasting relief.

Dr. Segel had me make a long list of the various experiences, and we went through them one at a time. Once we reached the end there were just three minor items left. I thought they were small and insignificant. As the process was beyond exhausting and I wanted it to be over, I suggested we quit and not do the remaining two or three. Segel said, "Hmm, well why don't you tell me briefly what they are."

I looked down at the first one and as I got ready to explain, I froze. I couldn't move. I locked.

Dr. Segel was gentle. For over a half hour he kindly asked the question in different ways to see if he could get me to say what had happened. Finally, he said, "Could you tell me not from your point of view, but as a judge or an outside observer?"

I shook my head no.

Then he asked if I would be willing to write down what happened.

I nodded.

He handed me a yellow pad and a pen.

The pen felt heavy. The tears poured down my face as I wrote out the first of the three incidents. It was an extended torture—a humiliation.

I understood now. These were *not* the little ones. I had thought that raping me was a big deal, but it turned out, in my case, raping me was the least of it. I was able to manage that, I just took my mind to another place. But during *these* tortures, my instructor had engaged me verbally. He kept my attention so I couldn't tune out what was happening. There was no escape.

The next session, Dr. Segel was able to get me to read that first incident I had written down. It turned out all of the remaining episodes had to do with humiliation. It would be several weeks before I was able to process all of those incidents, let alone begin Prolonged Exposure for them, but I had finally begun the quest to heal.

I would find relief. The power of all those layered traumas were eventually diminished by the PE. After I finished the run of treatments, the next time I encountered people from my life, the first thing they would say was, "Oh my God, Ara—you're back!" The creepy, Thousand-Mile Stare, as Michael called it, would come to be replaced by a sparkle in my eye that let people know I was "in there" again.

Together with Dr. Segel and Dr. Modoro, I began to see the connections between the series of entrapments in my life. I had been trapped and tortured by my instructor; I had been trapped and tortured in the coma; and I had then become trapped by my life, or lack of it.

Dr. Segel was right. I knew the PTSD had played a role in the delusions during my time in the ICU, but I hadn't realized it continued to affect me afterward, fueling my depression and suicidal ideation. Better than being right, he gave me a task to focus on: healing, instead of dying.

*

Sessions with Dr. Modoro continued for several months during which time we slowly processed my gruesome past. Meanwhile, appointments with Dr. Segel every couple of weeks were spent in pursuit of the right combination of medications to keep me from feeling suicidal but would still allow me to function. Many psychotropic medications take time to build up to effective concentrations. So when he would add or remove a drug, or modify a dose of an existing medication, it usually took several days or weeks before we could effectively evaluate how the cocktail was working. For the most part though, this would be a game of inches played out over several months.

In addition to treating the ongoing depression, we were grappling with a complication. My anxiety was on the upswing. Sleep issues, a symptom of my Bipolar Disorder, had been an issue throughout my life. This problem was made dramatically worse after the ICU. And over the last couple of months, as I was facing the reality that I could not work, it was escalating further still. Dr. Segel supported me in every way he could. He recommended every conceivable strategy: reading boring books (I tried reading about the mathematics of frequency), hot baths, warm beverages, gentle music… but the nights always ended with me pacing. I'd call Yvonne and she would talk to me for an hour or so to keep me from crying from frustration and loneliness.

Dr. Segel increased my bedtime medications in an effort to knock me out. I began seeing him daily, and at each visit he would inquire hopefully, and I responded, "Nope!" He would shake his head in shock and dismay, as the doses of the medication he was giving me were considerable. It got to the point where giving me anything stronger would require medical supervision. That meant he would have to check me into the hospital, the dreaded psychiatric ward—my deepest, darkest fear (aside from snakes).

When I had been awake for more than a week straight, going on two, the previously punchy nature of sleep deprivation gave way to impulsive ideas, like driving to St. Louis. Or going for a walk at 3:30 a.m. along the North Avenue beach. Or catching a train going west and using dice to choose the city. At first, I promised I wouldn't kill myself or go on adventures for a specific increment of time, two days, a day.

I knew these weren't good ideas. By the eleventh night with no sleep at all, my agitation was intensifying. I didn't know for sure if there were any promises I could make and keep that were more than a few hours long. By day thirteen, the impulse to act was overwhelming. I knew there was no alternative. I called Dr. Segel and agreed to check myself in.

*   *   *

It was strange to pack for the psych ward. What to take? I packed as if I were going into the hospital for another surgery and brought my laptop, my CD player, my day planner, and my cell phone. Once I arrived it was all taken from me. I was left with the Proust book I still dragged around, just to read a sentence or two and wallow around in the language a bit.

I was immediately given a heavy dose of olanzapine which had me sleeping the first afternoon. Unfortunately, every few hours I was awakened by the staff who cajoled and bullied me into attending various group classes on self-esteem, goal setting, creating support, and other topics, most of which seemed to be directed toward patients with drug addiction and eating disorders. I repeatedly reminded them I was in the psych ward because I had not slept for 13 days and I *needed* to sleep. "Policy is policy," they would say, and so I was forced to attend. Dr. Segel later explained insurance companies need documentation that something is happening while I am in there, or they would think I might as well be at home and save them the cost.

My second day, I was seen by Dr. Grant, the physician covering for Dr. Segel. He had success balancing compounding issues with Bipolar Disorder using oxcarbazepine. Dr. Grant was interested in trying it with me. He started me on a low daily dose and increased it over the next few days until I was up to 2400 milligrams. It worked. Although I was still quite depressed, the suicidal ideation disappeared. Even the subtlest inclination to kill myself slid away. I was amazed with this side benefit, since I had only been admitted to resolve the sleep issue. It was hard to believe the answer was truly that simple, a single drug, but the evidence was plain.

Once it was clear I no longer needed daily monitoring, I was sent home. Many of my doctors have said we can never know or fully understand the effects the ICU trauma had on my body. It certainly diminished my higher reasoning capability and amplified my Bipolar Disorder. In the case of my executive brain function (concentration, memory, and the ability to organize data), there was still nothing anyone could do. But in the case of my Bipolar Disorder, oxcarbazepine became more critical than lithium. It was the key to keeping me alive.

*

A few weeks after coming home from the psych ward, I came up with a way to demonstrate my new outlook, my ability to see a life looking forward. I decided I would get a dog. The dog would be my proof I planned to live. The problem was Michael didn't like messiness or a disruption of his routine, so I knew he was going to protest on the grounds of dog hair. But, as it was the only choice I could come up with, one afternoon I told him.

"I've decided to get a dog."

Our marriage of eight years hadn't had many unilaterally determined decisions.

"You what? When were you planning on telling me?"

"I'm telling you now."

"When did you think this was going to happen?"

"Well, today is Monday, so I was thinking either tomorrow or Wednesday, since Thursday is the Fourth of July holiday."

Michael knew me well enough. I rarely shared a plan with anyone that wasn't already fully-formed in my mind. "And where is this dog going to come from?" he asked, knowing I would already have decided.

"The pound." I said simply. "It's on the south side."

"Well," he said, "at least there's that."

We went on Wednesday, July 3rd, 2002. The Chicago Pound on South Western Avenue was a gigantic facility. Both of us were shocked by how many dogs were there. There had to be a couple of hundred. Each cage had an index card with a name and any health information available for the dog inside. Most of the dogs found their way to the pound without any information, so those dogs were given names by the volunteers. If one wanted to meet a dog, the system required the prospective adopter to find a staff person or volunteer who would take the dog out of its cage and then lead it to an enclosed area for an introduction to the person. Since quite a few people roamed the aisles and the facility was grossly understaffed, I became concerned someone else might snag the dog I wanted in the time it would take us to locate a staff person. I decided to collect the cards of the dogs we were interested in. I kept the cards ordered in my hands in the sequence I went through the aisles so I could keep track of which card came from what cage. Michael wanted to take home all of the dogs with severe injuries. He believed no one else would adopt them and we knew the alternative. I was looking for a spunky personality that would make a good companion for me during my long road back from hell.

There was an adorable, black, mid-sized retriever mix with the pound name of "Barney." He was hyper and bounded about his cage, but I saw in him the spirit I was trying to regain. That name wouldn't do, however. He barked and pounced up and down as we stood outside his cage, and Michael said, "No, not him? Really?"

I stuck the four other cards in my back pocket and took the "Barney" card to the front desk. "I want to meet this guy!" I declared.

The woman put a leash on the furry fellow and led him to a play area outside the room with the rows of cages. He skipped along beside her the entire way. She put him in one end of the play area. I went to the other and called him over to me, "Come here, buddy, come here!"

Without hesitation, he bounded in my direction and then flopped over onto his back for a belly rub. I was enchanted.

"We'll take him."

"We will?" Michael said, "Just like that? Are you sure?"

"What else do you need to know? I love him. He's terrific!"

Ara Lucia Ashburne

The facility was closed the next day, so it would be two more days before we were allowed to take him home. To prepare, we left the facility and went straight to the nearest pet supply store to buy dog equipment. We spent the driving time to and from the store coming up with names. We decided on Calder, after the artist who made playful sculptures and mobiles.

Now we had to learn how to take care of a dog.

It only took about three more days before Michael became even more enchanted than I had been. His love for Calder grew into a love of all dogs, everywhere. I should have seen this coming, after he said he wanted to bring home all of the injured ones. "I never knew!" he would say. "I never had a dog before! I can't believe what I've been missing!"

More importantly, now I had a buddy, someone to be with me during the long wait back to my life.

The Fairy Spark

On January 11, 2004, notable writer, actor, monologist and performance artist Spalding Gray died. He committed suicide. Just the summer before, we finally saw him perform live at Ravinia, an outdoor performance venue outside Chicago. Before that, Michael and I had followed much of his career via books and videos. He was a remarkable storyteller.

At the Ravinia performance he recounted the story of a devastating car accident he, his wife, and two friends had experienced the summer before in Ireland. Like my time in the ICU, his time in the Irish hospital included multiple surgeries, ongoing pain, and a recovery which began with rapid improvements but soon slowed to a near stop. Spalding seemed okay at the time. He was making fun of his situation, which was of course his gift.

His injury and the chronic pain he suffered afterward, however, clearly added to his mental and emotional challenges. He had never been able to get a satisfactory diagnosis or treatment for the high anxiety from which he'd suffered for years. Maybe it was due to Obsessive-Compulsive Disorder, maybe Bipolar Disorder, maybe another issue or a combination. Whatever was going on was now compounded by physical pain and management of the physical injury from the accident. The fact that he killed himself demonstrated clearly he hadn't been okay. When I heard the news, I couldn't stop crying.

At one point Michael said, "I don't understand why this has captivated you so. You didn't know him personally. Why is it you can't stop crying?" Though in hindsight it seems rather obvious, it wasn't until that moment I realized that like Spalding, my injury had become a total obstruction to the reality I once lived and was a crevasse in the core of my identity. All the newspaper articles were saying how horrible it was that he killed himself. I thought it was horrible too. I couldn't believe I would never hear another story told in the way only Spalding could tell it. But there wasn't any article talking about why he might have done it. I couldn't know for sure what his final reasons were, but I had walked a tightrope just this side of death for over a year.

I knew the difference between being alive and living. When I was in the hospital, Yvonne was the one person who respected my right to say, "I'm done, I want out." I don't know if Spalding had anyone. I believed our situations were close enough that, maybe, if I could speak from my own experience, I could provide some deeper understanding of his pain and his final choice.

I decided I would write an essay in his honor and try to get it published. There was a deadline, due to the nature of the news cycle for his story. There would only be a week or two at the most where there would be public interest in it. I started by tracking down every article and tribute I could find. Next, I went back over all my journaling on my own depression and suicidal feelings. I started to see relationships. I pasted all the news articles on the wall, and spliced my story amongst them. Then I began to write.

It was published in a journal that focused on the work of people living with mental illness. Shortly thereafter, I received a letter from a journalist in Canada. Her boyfriend, also a journalist, had committed suicide two years prior. She'd read my essay and shared it with her boyfriend's family. She told me they'd never come to terms with his death. They'd been in agony, but after reading my essay they were now at peace. She wanted me to know what a difference it made.

This drove home the idea that we can never know the impact we have, as moments like this one were rare. This led me to consider the possibility of writing a book. Maybe writing about my experience in the hospital could someday influence a medical student or doctor. My hope was that sharing my experience of the delusions would heighten awareness about the possible consequences of having patients in medically-induced comas and the subsequent trauma. Encouraged by the journalist's letter, I started trying to write a little each day.

* * *

"I think you should take a trip to Brussels or Paris. I think that's what you need," Michael said during another drive from Chicago to Detroit. Many of our best conversations occurred in this isolated, interruption-free environment.

"Uh," I began to protest.

"No, I know what you are going to say, and I want you to hear me out," he insisted. "I know you can't carry anything, and I know you can't stand for long, and you can't walk very far, but listen. You wouldn't need to take anything but a small backpack. These are real cities, they would have everything you would need. You could make that part of the adventure when you got there. Go with the clothes on your back and a toothbrush. Then buy clothes and whatever small items you need once you're there. They're big cities. There would be plenty of places you could go despite your limitations.

"If anyone can figure out how to make it happen, it's you. I know you could say we don't have the money, but life is short, and I think you should do it. Make figuring out how to do it cost-effectively part of the challenge too."

I was thinking as he was describing it. There was no way I wanted to go with only a small backpack and then try to find clothes for this over-sized, misshapen body in Europe. I suspected one of my friends, however, would be open to the adventure, and she could help me manage the luggage and my environment. The most likely candidate was Yvonne. Later, when I asked her about it, she said she would do it.

As a long time lover of all things French, I'd wanted my first trip to Paris to be as a French-speaker, so it pained me that I had no language skills. I learned how to say, "I'm truly sorry I don't speak French" (*Je suis vraiment désolé, je ne parle pas Français*"), and vowed I would say this expression as I greeted any person or inquired about anything, whether in bad French or in English. I also created a series of flashcards, one of which said in French, "I have an injury and cannot lift my bag, could you please assist me?"

I knew I had an overly romanticized view of the French and of Paris, so I was prepared to come home with my bubble burst by reality. We would have ten days and would need a considerable part of each day for me to rest, but I would do everything I could to get off the beaten path and see the real Paris. We would visit the smaller museums and chapels and avoid many of the obvious attractions. This would help to keep me out of the large crowds or lines and away from locations where finding a place to sit would be difficult. This meant skipping Notre-Dame and the Louvre, and I figured I would save the Eiffel Tower for when, if ever, I returned with Michael. We would go to one of the smaller chapels, such as La Saint-Chapelle, and we could go to the Rodin Garden and the contemporary art museum, the Centre Pompidou, and the Picasso Museum. I would figure out a way to go to Musée d'Orsay even if I had to sit on the floor, because Winslow Homer's *Summer Night*, one of my favorite paintings of all time, was there.

Other than these major markers, we would wander about the city and languish in her little shops, bookstores, cafés, boutiques, and galleries, and reveled in watching all the people on the streets. If I held up physically, we would make the train trip down to Chartres Cathedral toward the end.

Yvonne and I flew on separate flights, she from Boston and I from Chicago, to arrive at Charles De Gaulle Airport around the same time. We shared the long cab ride to our hotel in the city. As we began our journey and gazed out the window, I was eager to capture the moment but anxious about being perceived as a tourist—or worse, as an ugly American—so I planned to keep my camera out of sight while exploring. Here in the cab, however, I felt safe from the public eye and pulled my camera out.

After about a thirty minute drive with no views, we were suddenly approaching the Arc de Triomphe. I couldn't believe it! My careful planning hadn't taken into account the way historic landmarks would pop up unannounced as we drove around. I couldn't get the window down fast enough and snapped my only photograph of it with the window only halfway down… and then we were past it. I hoped my whole experience of Paris wouldn't feel like that last moment, a flash before my eyes.

At the first stoplight, I saw a server at a corner café resetting a table for the next set of customers. I noticed him take time to carefully straighten the fresh flowers on the table. I've never seen anyone reset a floral arrangement on a table at a café between customers—not unless it was toppled. I was dazzled. This was the Paris I had romanticized and dreamt about. She was real.

When we were stuck in traffic and at stoplights, I was able to look out the window and observe the city life. Things looked like a James Bond movie with foreign-language road signs, and foreign cars, and the multitude of cafés on every block. Some of it, though, was surprisingly familiar and looked like the cities I knew: people on their way from the shop with a few items in a plastic grocery bag, or business people with briefcases, or young people that could be picked up and dropped into any urban environment.

Once Yvonne and I got to the hotel, she settled in for a little nap, so I decided to go out for snacks and beverages. At the nearest corner store, I picked up grapes from the crates outside the door and entered a surprisingly tiny space. The entire shop was maybe ten feet square. I grabbed a bottle of white wine, soda, two French chocolate bars, and bread. I would have to find cheese elsewhere.

I tried out my sentence. *"Je suis vraiment désolé, je ne parle pas Français."*

The shopkeeper paused for a second as he put together what I was saying, then he grinned from ear to ear.

It worked! He understood and didn't scoff at me. He chuckled slightly and replied in French, which, of course, I didn't understand. I paid for my purchase with my Euros, the shopkeeper smiling all the while.

I stepped out of the shop and headed toward our hotel. When I heard the shop door open behind me, I thought I must have forgotten something.

Turning around to see, the shopkeeper waved to me, still smiling. He then turned his attention to rearranging the grapes in the crate outside since my purchase had disrupted his display.

Seriously? I thought. *Oh my God, the display in the crate? Outside? At the corner store?*

A simultaneous mixture of emotions came over me like a wave. First wonder, then excitement, then a moment of recognition: *The ordinary person in*

France truly does see and care about beauty. It was part of daily life. I was in heaven. I was home.

Yvonne and I wanted to try to fight the jet lag and get on a regular schedule as quickly as possible, so upon my return we decided we needed to keep moving. We proceeded by taxi to the Rodin Garden with enough time to enjoy a couple hours there before it closed. We chose to forgo the museum area and walked through the serene gardens to see the sculptures. It was surreal to view sculptures I had only seen in textbooks, on television, or from a slide projector during an art history seminar. Standing in front of *The Thinker*, I realized why my art history teacher made us memorize the size or scale of a work of art. I didn't get it at the time, as it was just another detail to cram into my head. While all the slides projected on the screen were the same size, my professor wanted us to understand the various works give different impressions based on whether they are small or large. As I stood there in front of *The Thinker*, all six-feet two-inches of him, I got it.

We walked toward the back of the gardens. There was a large, ivy-covered structure with three arches. Beyond the arches were benches and wooden lounge chairs. All were being used except for two chairs, right in the middle. We wanted to run for them but walked calmly over and sat down, facing the ivy archway. A wooded grove was to our right, and a truly blue sky, with stereotypical puffy white clouds, was overhead. It only took moments of drinking in the view before the jet lag sent both of us to sleep. About a half hour later, I awoke. Like in a magical tale waking up from a dream, I was in the Rodin Garden, in Paris. Appreciating the silliness of the feeling, I still couldn't help sharing it with Yvonne, "I woke up and I'm in Paris, and I'm not still dreaming!"

That night we went to hear a concert at La Sainte-Chapelle. It was classical, a group called Les Solistes Français. We didn't know what we were in for, but we thought, *Classical music at La Sainte-Chapelle? How could we go wrong?*

The concierge at the hotel assisted us in buying tickets in advance but explained we would need to go about a half hour early in order to be seated. A queue of people had already formed when we arrived, and there was no place to sit. I pulled out one of my flashcards and approached one of the guards monitoring the line. My message read, "I have an illness. I'm not feeling well. Can you direct me to the toilet?" With kindness, he shuttled me through a hallway and to a restroom. I could hear that he was standing outside the door. The toilet was a seat, and I knew if I sat down for even a few minutes I would have enough stamina to make it until the doors opened for the performance.

La Sainte-Chapelle was built in the early 1200's, a true medieval chapel, and is now situated inside the Administration of Finance. It struck me with its simplicity and its size. The Rodin sculpture was so much bigger than I had expected, and this chapel was so much smaller. The paint on the walls seemed primitive yet sophisticated with incredible golden arches and stained glass windows.

We nestled into seats in the fourth row at the end of the aisle. There were nine different musicians, mostly violins, a couple cellos, and a bass. Everyone was dressed in black in a mix of modern and turn of the century garments, with women in bustled skirts and the men in tuxedo shirts. They played with the kind of passion I had only heard rock music played. We had so many questions. Who were these people? Did they play all over the world or only in Paris? How long had they been together? As the program was in French, we couldn't get any answers. All we could do was submerge ourselves in the simultaneously delicate and powerful sound of the strings. When they finished, the entire audience leapt to their feet in applause. I had heard Europeans were more reserved than Americans with respect to standing ovations, so I figured the euphoria wasn't me and my elevated emotional haze of finally being in Paris—what I experienced was found to be extraordinary by everyone in the room.

That was our first night in Paris.

*

It was still extremely difficult for me to get to sleep, despite taking several medications. At home, I watched certain kinds of television to distract my brain as I waited for the drugs to knock me out. French television likely wasn't going to work, so Michael put a number of audiobooks on a digital music player I could listen to instead of watching TV. It took a little practice but eventually I made the transition. In Paris, I listened to Bill Clinton's *My Life* each night as I drifted off to sleep.

I would be lucky to get to sleep around 1:00 a.m. or so. Due to the heavy med hangover, I would sleep until around noon, sometimes later. I made a deal with Yvonne, an early riser, to wake me at 11:00 a.m. She spent mornings going to see the things my body wouldn't let me, like the Louvre and Sacré-Cœur Basilica. She would have a whole day's worth of adventures on her own. When she returned to our room, she would work vigorously to bring me to consciousness from the stupor of the medications. Once awake, I would ask her where she had been, and I would decide whether I wanted to hear all about it, like the Louvre, or when I couldn't, as in the case of Sacré-Cœur Basilica. Truth be told, the Basilica of the Sacred Heart was the place I most wanted to see in all of Paris, but as it was located at the summit of the butte Montmartre, the highest point in the city with an untold number of steps, there was no possible way. Being airlifted by helicopter was the only way I would ever see that sacred site up close.

As her explorations usually included the market, she would have cheese, salami, or hard boiled eggs for me to eat while she reported in. In the afternoon, I would choose the outing, and afterward, we would have dinner. Every day was filled with magical moments, but just walking down the street was fascinating enough. All the pastry shops had such glorious, elaborate cakes and desserts. I couldn't believe how exotic they all were. Other than a croissant, there seemed to be no such thing as an ordinary pastry.

One evening, we stumbled upon an establishment where everything inside was made of rose petals. Everything. It appeared as if they made displays for jewelry stores or fancy parties. In the window was a three-dimensional bodice of a woman made of rose petals. It was so exquisite and alive and real. These creations couldn't possibly last more than a day. At the hour of our encountering it, the shop was closed. With English as our only language, there was no way to ask more about it.

I loved walking down the Seine and seeing the postcard vendors and the people selling things: used books, paintings, caricatures, chestnuts. I thought the only place chestnuts existed was in a Dickens novel. I was disappointed when I tried them and didn't care for the taste or texture.

Our time was coming to a close. I decided I needed to go to the Musée d'Orsay, while Yvonne wanted to see something else. We planned to attend two separate events and agreed to meet later at the Odeon Theater, an easy landmark near our hotel. I knew going to a museum was going to be a challenge physically, but I had done my research and knew there would be benches where I could rest. If I could have gone in the morning, it would have been less crowded, but that wasn't feasible. Even if I had to resort to my French apology and my cards, I would make it through the museum somehow.

I took a taxi to the museum. Upon arrival, I obtained a map and directory and made a plan to go through it methodically. Normally that isn't my style, but I didn't know when I would get back here again, and I didn't want to miss anything. As a semi-regular museum-goer in the States, I usually take things in fairly quickly—only hovering if a work captivates me—so I figured I could take it all in if I didn't linger at any one piece too long.

I went from room to room, resting on the benches along the way. It felt like I was walking through the pages of an art history book. This time, instead of being struck by the scales of pieces, I was blown away by all the different textures of the paint. Some artists had a light touch, and others used big bold pushes of paint as if it weren't just color, but also shape being laid on the canvas. In the case of one of the Chagall pieces, however, I was startled by the scale, as it was about twice as tall as me. Once again, I had not taken in the data I was supposed to memorize in art history class.

Room after room, I explored, but I did not see Homer's *Summer Night*. I went through every gallery, so I thought it must have been lent to another museum or was out on tour. I was leaving, disappointed. I was just outside when I thought I heard someone call my name. Since I know no one in Paris, I kept walking. But then I heard it again and turned to see Yvonne heading toward me from inside.

"What are you doing here?" I asked.

"I finished at the other place and wanted to see if I could find you here."

"Seriously, you thought you were going to find me in the d'Orsay?" She chuckled in that hearty way of hers and said, "Well, I did find you."

I laughed then too, because I knew Yvonne could find me anywhere. I don't know why I was questioning her.

"So, how was it?"

"It isn't here."

"What do you mean, 'It isn't here'—the Winslow?"

"I went through every gallery in the museum one by one, and it isn't here. It must be out on loan."

"Did you ask someone?"

"No. It seemed too hard to ask, and they're about six people deep at the information desk."

Yvonne marched toward the desk.

"No," I called out, "Yvonne, it's okay. Let's just go," but she kept walking.

While she waited in the line, I sat. Once she made her way to the front of the queue, Yvonne asked about the painting.

The person at the help desk opened a brochure and made a circle around one of the galleries and handed it to her. She returned to me and said, pointing at the map, "It's here."

"It can't be. I went through every room."

"Well, we're here now, so we might as well go see."

"Yvonne, I'm exhausted and I don't think it's there. Besides, that's upstairs. I can't do another set of stairs."

She was undeterred. "Then we'll find an elevator."

She did. It turned out they had several, and access ramps, too, none of which I'd seen earlier. We went directly to the gallery which supposedly held the painting.

There were about eight people in the room. A few were looking at *Summer Night* and the rest at whatever else was in the room. I don't know what else was there. I didn't see. I walked into the middle of the room and drank in Homer's painting. This time, I wasn't struck by the paint or the scale, but by the image itself. I was drawn in, an invisible observer, a ghost standing just behind the two women dancing. I felt their intimacy, their world, apart from all others who were talking and laughing on the rocks by the water's edge. The two women dancing weren't aware of the stormy water, the darkness of the night, or even that there wasn't any music playing. They simply danced together in their own reality.

Without a gasp of breath or a single sound, tears began to run down my face. When the couple in front of me turned around and saw me crying, they quickly gathered the others in the room and left Yvonne and me alone with the painting. I don't know how long I stood there transfixed, held in the moment between those two women. Eventually, a new group entered, and the spell was broken. I looked over to Yvonne and she had been crying, too. We held hands and walked quietly out of the gallery to sit on the bench outside the door.

"I don't understand what just happened to me," I said, as I tried to make sense of it all. "I knew I was drawn to the painting. That's why I wanted to see it, but I've never been so moved by any work of art before now. No play, no piece of music, no artistic vision, or creation took me so far out of my own head and into its world."

"You don't have to understand it," she replied quietly.

"I know," I said as I squeezed her hand.

"Do you want to go back in?" she asked.

"No, I've had my experience. I'm ready to go now."

*

As Yvonne had to leave a day earlier than me, I was on my own for my last twenty-four hours. On my departure morning I walked two blocks with my wheeled suitcase to catch a taxi. Without a word between us, the driver leaped out of the taxi and put my suitcase in the trunk. Once we were both in the taxi, he turned around and looked to me for directions.

I simply said, *"La Gare,"* indicating my destination was Gare du Nord Train Station.

He nodded, and off we went through the busy city streets, passing through neighborhoods I hadn't seen. My eyes filled with tears. It hit me all at once. I was leaving my Paris.

The taxi driver must have noticed I was crying and said something to me in French. When I replied with my usual expression, his response was, "You are sad to leave home."

"Oui," I said. "I am sad to leave home."

* * *

Late in the summer of 2006, Michael and I attended a wedding in the Detroit area, and we decided to stop by and see my sister Julie and her family before driving home. Her husband, Jeff, was at work, but Julie and her two kids, Adam (then age 3) and Olivia (age 5) were there. Olivia was excited and wanted to show us the book *Fairyopolis,* which we had given her for Christmas. Its story was written from the vantage point of a researcher, Cecily Emily Barker, who has a little girl come to stay with her in England. When a photograph is taken of the little girl in the garden, they notice fairies in the picture and begin documenting the different fairies and their lives. It is a beautiful and elaborately illustrated encyclopedia of fairies.

Olivia excitedly showed us how she carried it in her backpack to school every day and wanted us to see many of the pages where she had memorized the information about the different kinds of fairies, their habitats and lifestyles. I was enchanted by her enthusiasm but confused as she was behaving almost as if we had never seen the book. Regardless, it was clear that she wanted us to know how incredibly cool it was. Her passion was infectious, and I couldn't help but remember when I had become obsessed with unicorns as a child.

On the drive home, I felt an overwhelming urge to respond to her. I remembered when I was all-about-unicorns, Yvonne helped me expand my collection of unicorn greeting cards until I had over a hundred. I was so proud of my collection, using transparent tape to create a growing mosaic of wallpaper in my bedroom. My mind raced—what could I do to let Olivia know I appreciated her immersion in the world of fairies? By the time we exited M-14 onto I-94, the pressure to act compounded in me, and the stress of not knowing what action I would take intensified. I couldn't think straight and finally asked Michael to pull over.

"What do you mean, 'Pull over?' Do we need to go back for something?"

"I just need to think. I can't think while we are speeding away. I need you to stop. Please, just pull over."

He obliged, and in moments we were idling at the side of the freeway. The cars and semi-trucks blowing past us shook our car.

I began thinking aloud.

"I need to give her something. What can I give her? It needs to be something that acknowledges the realness of the fairies to her. To her, these fairies are as real as her breakfast cereal. What could I do that would be *real*?

"What if I made her a pair of wings, fairy wings? Not like a bad ballet costume, but something real fairies would make? Wings made from natural objects—leaves and flowers. That's it! That is what I'm going to do. I don't know how, but I am going to do it.

"Okay, you can go ahead and drive now."

Over the next couple weeks, I researched fairies. At this point, Olivia was an expert, so if I screwed this up by not adhering to the folklore in *Fairyopolis*, I was going to be busted. We checked a copy out of the local library for reference.

I began experimenting with leaves. As summer moved into autumn, the only leaf I could find which still had color was the Purple Shiso. The only flower I found that survived the drying process and still seemed sturdy enough to handle was the Black-Eyed Susan. Then I had to perfect the lengthy process of drying and pressing leaves and flowers. I strung twine from the dining room across to the living room in order to hang them. Soon, pressed leaves were lying on every available flat surface in the kitchen, the living room, and the dining room. Piles sat on the dining table, on the tops of the books on bookshelves, on the desk, even the backs of the couch and easy chairs. The flowers were even more trouble, as the petals were fragile, and many were lost in the process. Luckily, they were growing wild outside, so I had a bountiful supply to replace all the ones I destroyed until I had enough for my purpose.

Finally, the assemblage process began. It turned out making wings proportionate to Olivia's size out of natural objects, instead of just some chiffon fabric, made them heavy. The wings began to droop. I had to use wire to create an armature for the leaves and other natural objects to hang from. Now there was the problem of how she might wear them without the wire stabbing her or the wings dangling from her tiny back. Michael came on board, reluctantly at first, to help with the engineering aspect. After several days of wrestling, we came up with a way to attach the wings to a block of wood which would serve as a central support piece. We covered the block with leather from an old backpack-style purse and positioned the adjustable straps for her arms to go through.

As we wrapped up the construction, Michael and I began discussing the problem of delivering the wings to Olivia. Since, according to *Fairyopolis*, fairies don't read and write, leaving a note was not an option. Part of what made the original tome so endearing to us was how the reader could uncover and peruse its various inserts—notes, envelopes, and the like. It had been designed as a sort of elaborate scrapbook, assembled long ago. Michael got the idea that we could create a companion volume in the form of a journal which was written by the daughter of the original author. Perhaps she was in the United States to study fairies. We would position it as the author had come across these wings, had to figure out to which little girl they belonged, and then had to find a way to deliver them to her.

As always seems to happen with my creative endeavors, we were at the scope creep stage. Michael may have been reticent to climb on board when he was being asked to figure out an engineering solution to the heavy wing conundrum, but now that we were creating the research diary, he was invested. It became a fully collaborative effort. We wanted to mimic the concept and style of the original book and include pictures and handwritten notes. We wrote the text together and searched for images to include in the book, including two sketches of fairies Michael drew, one for the Purple Shiso leaves and one for the Black-Eyed Susans.

As the elaborate nature of our ruse began to snowball, we had the idea that the journal should have a photograph of the wings at the moment the author stumbles across them. We enlisted the help of a dear friend, Michael Madill, to manipulate some images for us. He drove to the wooded area by Olivia's subdivision, secured a suitable location where the wings could have been found, took a digital photo, and then added the wings to the image. Cleverly, he also took a picture of her house from across the street from down in the grass, a fairy-eye-view of their home. Once the wings and book were finished, we drove them to Olivia's house (when we knew no one would be home) and left them on the front porch.

We stopped over at Madill's place in Ann Arbor on our way home. We didn't know for sure, but we thought Olivia might want to tell us, as the givers of *Fairyopolis*, about the mysterious delivery. Sure enough, about fifteen minutes after she arrived home from dance class, my cell phone rang, and it was her, all right. I answered, nervous I might slip and say something that could possibly break the magic, but for naught, as I couldn't get in a word after "Hello?"

Olivia was in a state of ecstatic fervor. She screamed, "THE CRAZIEST THING HAPPENED TO ME TODAY!!!!" She went on to describe the wings and the book, the circumstances under which they arrived, and the fact the fairies were coming "to measure her" tonight. I wasn't sure how she had extrapolated that from the cover letter or the journal, but no matter. She insisted I must "Come now, now, NOW, NOW, *NOW!*" to see the wings the fairies left for her. I reminded her I lived on the other side of the state, but promised I would come within a month's time to see them. "I promise!" I said.

Although we were relieved to have completed this project, Michael and I were also a bit sad it was over.

There could be no doubt that Olivia and her fairies reignited a spark in my heart.

*   *   *

It all began with a dress. With the assistance of a seamstress, I created a unique garment. I had purchased unusual plastic fabric, taupe with splashes of black on it, and chose an antique pattern to give the piece a 1950's silhouette. I loved the contrast of this edgy, contemporary fabric with the classic style. Once it was assembled and I was able to see it on a dress form, I sat and looked at it for a while.

This dress would look interesting next to a big, floofy, 17th-century gown.

Unbidden, an image popped into my head. I contemplated the edgy and the soft, and thought of a woman's take on "Little Red Riding Hood." Maybe they met periodically in the woods for a game of cards. Maybe it was a sort of duel, a perpetual melee. I imagined an ongoing back-and-forth between the two, like fencing, a stalemate, this story without end. In my mind, it soon became a series of photographs.

I enlisted a costume designer to make the second dress—a 17th century ball gown. I already had the fabric I would use, a cotton candy pink. I would position two women on the level branch of a tree and have the train of the ball gown trail down the tree all the way to the ground. Once the images were created, I wouldn't put them in a brick and mortar gallery but would post them as a short narrative on the internet. I called upon Michael Madill once again, to create a means of visually displaying the images on the web. I needed help sculpting the language for the site to get the right flavor, and my friend Diane suggested her friend, the poet Elizabeth Cross. Liz created the term "photo-fable."

There are not many times in our adult lives when someone new comes along and is able to find her place among the ranks of old friends and kindred spirits, but Liz did just that. Instantly, we snapped into place. Our creative time working together often moved into the terrain of a spiritual experience. I named the characters: Tala would be the wolf in the plastic '50's dress, and Louison would be my "little pink Riding Hood." *Tala & Louison*. Liz came up with the subtitle, *The Woods Opened and Through*.

Since Michael and I lived, at that time, in Southwest Michigan, I worked hard to contract local people for the project. I asked around and got the name of a photographer. Although I had never been a professional photographer myself, I had experience in the field. I majored in photography at one point and had worked as a photo assistant. Although I've always had a strong visual sense, my technical skills were weak. I needed a photographer I could trust to handle the technical aspects of things—whatever was required to create the images I wanted.

When we met in person, he seemed excited by the job. He was relaxed and would clearly be easy to work with. We emailed back and forth as the project progressed. I found a location with a tree, auditioned and selected local models, and oversaw the construction of Louison's dress. As the shooting date grew closer, I contacted the photographer again because he hadn't responded to my inquiries about equipment costs. Ten days before the shoot he revealed he intended to use natural light, which had never been part of my plan.

I called him to explain I needed different light on each of the models. Tala needed a harsh, sharp light, and Louison needed soft lighting. "I need the lighting to emphasize the difference between the two characters."

"That would mean you would need scaffolding to get the lights above them."

"Okay," I said.

"It can't be done," he said, matter-of-factly.

"What do you mean, 'It can't be done?' You just told me what we need to do in order to make it happen."

"It can't be done. It's too expensive."

"I want to do it. If you need scaffolding, than we can get scaffolding."

"It isn't possible."

"I don't understand. You just told me you need scaffolding to get the lights above the models. Why can't we do this? Is it that you don't *want* to do it?"

"No," he said simply, "you can't do it."

What? "Can't?" What is with this guy? I tried to remain calm. "But this is the lighting I need in order to make the shot work. Please, can you price out what you would need to do it?"

"There is just no way to do it."

Oh my God, he's refusing to do it, and I can't figure out why!

"Okay," I said, "I can see you don't want to do this. I'll get back with you."

I had no intention of using this guy.

The second I hung up, I called my friend Marc Sirinsky, one of the artists I featured in my art gallery in Chicago. We had developed and maintained a close, personal friendship over the years. Fortunately for me, this close friend was also an experienced photographer and professional photo editor. Prayerfully, he would have a referral that could get me out of this fix. I relayed my earlier conversation with the previous fellow, and Marc was as perplexed as I.

"Yep, he just *refused* to do it," I said, pacing as I spoke. "I can't figure it out. I don't know if he's afraid of heights or if he doesn't have enough experience with lighting to feel confident—I can't explain it. Regardless, he flat out refused, and now, here I am, ten days out with no photographer. Who do you know that would get what I'm trying to do?"

"I know the perfect person in New York. I'll get back to you."

The next day, I was in the grocery store parking lot, getting ready to leave my car, when I got a call from a New York area code. I stopped, one leg out the door of the car, and answered the call, saying, "You must be the referral from Marc Sirinsky."

"Yes," came the reply. It was a woman. *Cool.* "My name is Danelle Manthey. Tell me what you are trying to do."

"Well, it is sort of a riff on 'Little Red Riding Hood.' The set is an enormous tree. There are two models. One is sort of punk, edgy and in a fifties-style dress. She represents a wolf. The other woman is in a 17th-century dress with the train tumbling down the tree. She represents Little Red Riding Hood. They're playing a game of cards."

"Oh, I get it. Like Gregory Crewdson."

Two weeks before, I woke up in the middle of the night and the television was still on, showing a PBS program about a photographer I didn't recognize. I tried to discern, through squinted eyes, who he was while the program followed his creative process. With the help of a crew, he created a set for a scene with an actor, props, and set pieces. In this photograph, it was winter in front of a movie theater with a single guy walking down the street. I had never before seen anything like it. It was exactly like what I wanted to do! It was very legitimizing; I wasn't the only one. His name was Gregory Crewdson.

I tried to wake Michael up. I shook him roughly—as waking a sleeping Michael is nearly impossible—saying, "Michael! Michael, you have to see this!"

"What?" he said, bolting upright in a panic, ready for an emergency.

"You have to see this guy! He's doing what I wanna do! Or, I want to do what he is doing."

We both watched, mesmerized.

"Wow," Michael said finally. "How does that feel? This guy is a big deal."

"Well, this guy has technical skills I don't have."

"Well, he has a lighting guy and other technical people too."

"Yeah, but he knows how to use a camera properly. Still, it's so cool to see someone doing what I'm doing. On PBS, no less."

So when Danelle said, "Oh, I get it. Like Gregory Crewdson," my response was, "Yep, you get it."

"I need to light it with contrasting lighting," I told her. "Can you do that fifteen feet up a tree?"

"Absolutely, but it will take several people to do it. You need scaffolding, and ideally you need two cherry pickers. I would like to come out and see the location, so I can make sure I know how many people I need and be certain I'll have all the right equipment with me. I'm actually going to be in Chicago next weekend. Would you be available for me to come out and scout the location with you?"

"That would be fantastic!"

I couldn't wait to tell Michael she'd said, "Like Gregory Crewdson."

*

Two days before the shoot, I was in a state of panic. Suddenly the production was dominated by technicians: Danelle the photographer, multiple photo assistants, a videographer and his two assistants, a half-dozen lighting people, and general production assistants. There was also a creative team to make sure everything had the right look: costume designer, prop master, set dresser, and hair and makeup people. But I had no one there to make sure I didn't lose the story I wanted to tell while I was responding to all the technical demands.

Devon would have been my first choice to help me, but he was working on a movie in New Mexico. My next thought was my cousin Orion who was living in New York City. He knew stories. He has read more than anyone I have ever met. I begged for him to come to help me. I was ready to fly him in, but he was taking the Law School Admission Test in a few days, so there was no way he could come. But he did calmly talk me through the problem.

He crystallized it. "I get it," he said. "What you need is a guardian of the narrative."

"Yes, that is it, exactly."

"Well, now you are clear about what you need, you just need to think about who you know that could do that for you."

"It is you, Orion. You are the one."

But he couldn't do it.

I got off the phone dejected and crying.

That night, Michael built a fire in the fire pit out behind the house. I walked over and sat in a lawn chair and sobbed. I had done all this work, a year of preparation. I had all these people ready to create this shoot, and I was terrified I would become consumed with technical details and have no support for the real reason I was there: the story. I didn't know anyone who could come and be my Guardian of the Narrative.

Then it came to me: Liz! Of course, Liz the poet! I called her immediately.

"Liz, I likely have the oddest request you may ever receive..." I began. It turned out she loved the idea, but not the call time. The shoot began at 3:00 a.m.

But she would be there.

When Danelle and I met the previous week, she explained my shot list of 12 images would normally be a two-day shoot. This was the first time I had ever art directed a project of this scale, so I hadn't realized. No matter, I didn't have the budget to make it a two-day shoot. The photography crew had already committed to a long day, as they all were driving two-plus hours from Chicago to Michigan and back again.

Right on schedule, the trucks started rolling in to the location. These were big trucks, and when their headlights shot directly at me in the pitch dark, I suddenly realized the scope of what I was about to do. I had worked as a photo assistant in Dallas more than a decade before, but on small shoots. What I had created here was a medium-sized shoot with about 30 people on the set. When they opened the back of the lighting truck and I saw what was inside, I felt a wave of nausea. The first truck had the generator. I knew we needed one, but I hadn't pictured a model the size of a commercial refrigerator. The second truck had the lighting gear. I had seen trucks just like these in Chicago on the periphery of movie sets.

Immediately, Joe introduced himself to me as the lead lighting guy, then asked to meet the photographer. He and Danelle had a brief conversation, then, instantly, six guys were working furiously, pulling metal pipes and wooden planks out of the truck and assembling the scaffolding. I didn't know how to run any of the equipment or do what they were doing, but it only took me a couple minutes to realize my only job was to make sure Danelle understood what I needed. These were not my guys, they were her guys. She knew what direction to give them based on the requests I would make of her. And in that moment, I could feel the ground under my feet again.

The video crew was already rolling. I had hired them, at Michael's urging, to make a documentary video of all the behind-the-scenes activity. A battery pack and wireless microphone were attached to me. At first I felt self-conscious, but then realized, *It's okay. This is my audio, being recorded for me. It's okay. I get to decide what gets used. I can speak freely.*

My sister, Melissa, a middle school math teacher by day, was my assistant. She was going to keep us on-time. Trying to get 12 shots done in a single day without going overtime meant we only had 45 minutes for each shot. This included set-up, shooting and break-down. It meant solving any problems that arose as quickly as possible. It also meant I might have to let certain technical problems go, or be okay if I could not get exactly what I wanted from my models. The schedule was intense, maybe impossible. I was going to make creative decisions, Danelle would coordinate her technical crew, and Melissa would keep all the people on the set when they needed to be there. Her job included getting people to me or away from me when we were trying to solve a problem (depending on what the circumstance dictated).

Even though I had been out of the ICU for more than six years by this time, the truth was my health was still shaky. Michael and I didn't actually know if I would have the endurance to make it through an entire day of shooting. We figured I could do it if I was careful, but we couldn't be completely certain.

A few years before, we had gone to an outdoor dog training seminar in the spring. I had just been hanging out the first day, sitting most of the time, but at one point I got cold. The next day I couldn't get out of bed. It wouldn't have mattered if it were my wedding day, I couldn't get up. Over time my stamina improved, but this autumn day in 2007 was going to require standing a fair amount, and though it was supposed to warm up later, it would be cold in the morning. I hadn't yet done anything even remotely as challenging as what this day would require.

I was only on the set for a half hour before Liz arrived, which was a tremendous relief. If I collapsed, the plan was for Danelle and Liz to continue without me. Liz knew the story and Danelle knew what things were supposed to look like. Without me on the set, they would have to speculate, sure, but at least all of the time, energy, and resources wouldn't have been for nothing. A large computer monitor was set up so I could see the shots as Danelle took them. We got a number of director's chairs so there would be places to sit. It was soon clear I was needed all over the set. I didn't get much of a chance to sit.

We set up the first shot. The two women sitting in the tree open up the book, which becomes the table they use to play cards. We were supposed to shoot this scene as the sun was rising. The technical crew had everything ready, but one of the members of my creative team didn't wrap up his efforts in time, and we missed the sunrise. I would have to change the lighting in post. This was not how I wanted to start the day. This sent me a strong message: "You might be the director. You might have a vision. You may have people here to support this vision, but you can't actually control people. You may not be in control today." I realized then I was going to have to ride this experience like a surfer riding a wave. I couldn't control the environment (like the sun) or the people I brought together to realize this project.

Next up were shots eleven and twelve, which took place on the ground. As often happens on a movie set, we were shooting out of sequence for logistical reasons. For shot twelve, Tala was positioned near the tree, brandishing the cards she had taken from Louison, and Louison was in the background, with the metal box which held Tala's cards, grasping it tightly. In this shot, Tala was to appear smug and clever because she hasn't yet realized Louison has made off with the box that holds her cards. I directed the model playing Louison to appear frightened because she has never dared to do something so brazen as to steal from Tala before. She was supposed to run away, into the woods in the distance, but take one quick look back, fearing, in a single leap, Tala could pounce on her and end her life.

Liz and I watched the computer monitor as Brian Eaves, the digital photo technician, displayed Danelle's various test shots. Danelle's camera was attached to his laptop, instead of using a memory card, and the computer was connected to external storage and monitors. Brian managed the files as the shots were taken. He made note of which images I liked and what I did or didn't like, so they could be recalled and evaluated throughout the day or at any point in the post-production process.

As the shots were set up out of sequence, our second shot of the day was actually the last photograph of the sequence, photograph 12. While Danelle, Brian, and the lighting crew were working out technical details, Liz and I were talking about the story, and I was preparing to tweak the model's position. Liz and I were looking at the monitor while talking when we suddenly froze. We stared at the monitor without saying a word. I was afraid to say what I saw—I didn't want to put ideas in Liz's head—so I asked, "Are you seeing what I'm seeing?"

Liz didn't take her eyes off the screen, "Yes."

Then, in complete unison, as if rehearsed, we said, "It looks like she's in love with her."

We were referring to the expression on Louison's face. She was looking at Tala as if their long love affair had just crumbled, as if her heart would never mend. Her longing was an echo that would go unanswered, and the pain would leave her forever lost in the woods.

My mind raced. Had Liz and I already worked together too long? Were we now caught up in our own private, creative world? I had to have verification, so I called out to Danelle to come over when she had a moment.

Danelle was talking to Joe, but stopped what she was doing and came over to look at the monitor.

"Danelle, I need to know: how does this image read to you?"

Without hesitation, she replied, "It looks like she's in love with her."

Liz and I looked at each other, wide smiles bursting across our faces, and spontaneously high-fived each other. Maybe we had worked together too long already—but in a good way.

"What is going on?" Danelle asked.

"Well, I didn't exactly plan this. In the conceptual phase, I considered this storyline, but thought it would seem too contrived, so I abandoned it. But now it has happened anyway, and I could not be happier. So we are going to go with it. I'm going to have to make a couple changes to the shot list, but I promise I won't do anything that will add time or shots."

Then, three different people interrupted, needing me to answer questions. I turned to Liz and said, "Okay, Liz, I guess that means *you* are going to have to take a look at the shot list, and you are going to have to figure it out. Whatever you come up with, it can't mean more shots."

"Got it," she said, still wearing her huge grin.

When we were finally ready to take shot twelve, I said, "I sure wish I could have a little pop of light on the metal box that Louison is holding. She is so far away, it's disappearing in her arms." Brian relayed my comment to Danelle, Danelle said something to Joe, Joe said something into his sleeve like a CIA agent, and suddenly there were a half-dozen guys running—and I mean running. Equipment flew out of the truck, a light was set up twenty feet away from Louison, and in about 40 seconds there was a sparkly glint on the metal box. I couldn't believe what I just witnessed.

Wow, so this is what this day is gonna be like.

Unfortunately, not every problem was solved so quickly. The biggest one with my models. I realized on the set that I never should have hired models in the first place, but I'd only ever heard of models being used for still photography. What I didn't think through was that I was trying to tell a story. I needed actresses. I explained in rehearsal I would need to move them into specific poses and they would have to hold those poses for extended periods while conveying the feelings needed for each shot. We had rehearsed the scenes for four weeks, but I wasn't able to give them an entire acting workshop in that time. I tried to use a loose method acting approach, drawing on their personal experiences in the hope they could convey what was needed in each of the shots. I got what I was aiming for in almost half the shots, but in the remainder I didn't.

Still, I had created something. With the help of a team, I had found something creative I could do. It didn't matter that most of the year-long prep had been done from bed on a laptop. I made it happen. I was ready to do another one.

My body held up through the day of the shoot. Sure, I was in bed for several days after, but we knew that was going to happen. And something else, something deeper, happened.

Melissa and I were the last two people to leave at the end of the day. We scoured the site to make sure we didn't leave anything, not a single gum wrapper. Once we were satisfied, we climbed into my car to head home, and she said, "You know, I never understood about you and your friends. I have family and I have friends, but not long after high school I stopped hanging out with my friends and just hung out with family." I knew this was true. By and large, it was true of most of my family.

"With you," she continued, "your friends have always been your life. I knew that, but I never understood it before today. You guys understand each other—or at least, you can communicate with each other—in a deeper way than anything I've ever seen before. More magical. I've never seen anything like it, never. It amazed me. You guys all know each other's minds. I've never witnessed that kind of creative collaboration. I can see now, how your work, your friends, your life—it's all one and the same. I'm kind of high from it all."

"Yeah," I said, "and now you have crossed over. Used to be, Yvonne and Orion were the only family members who were part of my friend-life. To be part of my work is to be in my life. It *is* my life. I can't begin to tell you how happy it makes me to share it with you."

Months later, I reviewed the video footage with David Wittenstein, the documentary video editor. Since David hadn't shot the footage, we had to watch everything so he knew what he did and didn't have to work with. We came across Melissa and me high five-ing, right after I said, "It's a wrap." David used this bit toward the end of the final short documentary piece, amid a bunch of fast cuts of various people laughing or having a good time at the set. I've watched the video a ridiculous number of times while we were editing, and that one moment brings tears to my eyes, every time.

After completing *Tala & Louison* I began work on my next photo-fable. This one would involve two women, a lovers' quarrel, a man on a horse, intrigue, a secret letter hidden in the woods...

* * *

It was 2008. Michael and I had become quite active in supporting Barack Obama for the general election. Although now we were living in Michigan, when we lived in Chicago we had been rather evangelical about Obama when he made his run for senate. Like many of his "fans," we waited with anticipation for word he would, in fact, make a run for the presidency.

Once Senator Obama announced his intention to run for President, our involvement was sudden and thick. Here was a chance for the predominantly African-American community of Benton Harbor, Michigan to vote for an African-American candidate in the presidential primary. Not just any candidate, either, but one we thought could conceivably go all the way to the White House, maybe even be one of the best presidents of all time. We decided we would have to do whatever we could.

The idea of going door-to-door made both of us very uncomfortable. It was twelve degrees outside and I had a sinus infection. Yet, with the primary now only ten days away, we felt we couldn't wait. Michael and I formed a tandem operation.

Seeing as Michael was rather tall, bald, pale, and awkward, we had a feeling that, between the two of us, he wouldn't be as well-received as I, so I did the knocking. I'd go four or five doors and then warm up in the car for a few minutes, and then do four or five more. Michael drove, and rolled and rubber-banded flyers for the doorknobs of houses where no one was home. We met a number of other organizers and were in too deep to stop at the primary, so we continued contributing to the Obama campaign until the November election.

Obama won the general election. I still have the image from the front page of *The Chicago Tribune* of Barack, Michelle, and their two daughters as they stood in front of the throngs of elated citizens in Grant Park, Chicago. I had never been a part of a movement before and certainly never part of such an enormous victory. Although I was deeply moved, I couldn't yet celebrate. Throughout the campaign process I was also deeply concerned about Proposition 8 in California, an initiative to take away the rights of gay and lesbian people to marry. I had made financial contributions to fight it and sent letters to various California politicians, but there was only so much I could do from Michigan.

I wouldn't know until morning what would happen. California was still counting votes into the night, and they were three hours behind us. I watched all through the night. By dawn it was clear Prop 8 had passed. I was numb. I knew the vote would be close, the level of organization and resources provided by the Mormon Church were great, but I had hoped and prayed California would defeat this hate-based bill. I couldn't stop thinking about it, and I couldn't stop crying.

Although I self-identified as bisexual, the most tragic part of it, for me, was about marriage itself. My marriage to Michael has helped me grow more as a human being than any other factor in my life. There had been only a six-month period when same-sex marriage had been legal in California. When Prop 8 passed, though it only stopped new couples from getting married, it felt to me like those once-legal couples had their marriages ripped away. As if the weddings never happened, their wedding gowns, tuxedos, and wedding albums were stripped from them. All the blessings, emotional and spiritual, the struggles and the joys of these committed unions were erased. I couldn't imagine losing the one thing I most valued, the most sacred thing I had, my marriage.

*

By the end of the second week of crying, I decided to do something the only way I knew how: create art. My next photo-fable would be about two women, lovers going into the woods to marry, and a man who followed them in an attempt to stop them. This time I already had a title, *We Vow*.

As before, I began with the garments. For me, the conjuring of the characters happens as I conceive of what they will wear. I searched to find the right costume designer who could make clothes to represent my vision of dresses inspired by 1890, with a slight modern twist. I couldn't believe how many competent, nationally-recognized costume designers responded to my Craigslist ad. I asked one of the hopefuls, Helene Siebrits, "Do you prefer to work for a director who leaves you free to work on your own, or do you prefer to work for a director who micro-manages every detail of your work?"

"They are two completely different ways of working," she replied. "One is an opportunity for me to stretch my creative muscles, which I enjoy." She gave me an example of a project when she had a successful relationship with a director who had given her little direction. "But then," she continued, "there are directors who have a very clear vision. "In those cases, it is a matter of understanding that vision intimately and completely, so that my work can serve the project." She said, "I don't feel like I'm being micro-managed, because then the process is about serving the vision." I needed both.

Helene got the job.

We first met at a hotel in Chicago. She brought about 15 costume history books with illustrations of costumes from the period I had chosen, around 1890. I opened one and began to page through it.

I pointed to a sleeve in one, then a bustle in another, then in a few more pages a neckline I liked, then a different bustle. After I had chosen four or five elements, she completely zeroed in on my aesthetic. She opened other books and showed *me* what I liked! It was wonderful, and we were both giddy and laughed like school girls. The process had begun in earnest.

My next trip to Chicago was for casting. I learned my lesson with *Tala & Louison*, so this time I was determined to use professional actors. I put an ad in several Chicago theatre publications, and about 150 people showed up at the audition. It was exciting and terrifying.

Part of me thought, *This is a great turn out!* Another part thought, *What if the specific actors I need aren't here?*

Devon, in his role as a producer, and Danelle, the photographer from the first shoot, were on hand. This time, I would know for certain they could not only act but they could act with a camera in their face. Devon kept things organized for me at the audition. He tracked which actors I had seen, who I wanted to see again, who I was done with, and everyone's head shots, resumes, and potential availability. His most crucial role, though, would be as my sounding board, to keep me from losing my mind from the anxiety of the experience.

Looking through head shots the night before, I had already made up my mind to cast a fellow named Matt Devine as the military character. I called Devon and said, "Unless this guy sucks, he's got the job." Matt turned out to be every bit as intense as his head shot suggested, and he took direction brilliantly! Now I needed to find his oppositional character, the minister. Throughout the day, after someone auditioned, I would let Devon know if I wanted them to wait in the theater's lobby or to send them home. One man I kept was Kyle Rehder. Periodically, Devon would ask, "Can't Kyle go now?" Each time, I said, "Nope." After 28 years of friendship, we were usually completely inside each other's heads, but in this case he couldn't understand why I kept Kyle around.

When I saw Kyle initially, I worried he wouldn't be strong enough to hold his own against Matt, but intuitively, I thought he had it in him. As I went through the remaining men, the ones that could have played the minister all had a peculiar quality. I wanted the minister to be accessible and warm, not a weirdo. I wanted the viewer to be able to feel connected to the minister. Then, when he pulls out his gun, it would have a much stronger impact.

After I rejected the rest of the men, I put Kyle and Matt together. I asked them to walk across from opposite sides of the stage, and pass as if they didn't know each other. Then walk across the stage and pass as if they knew each other and didn't trust each other, but didn't want anyone to know. I was delighted. Each time, they both showed a range of subtle expressiveness. I saw everything I needed to see. With an, "Okay, thanks, we will get back to you," Devon sent them home, but now he agreed with me about Kyle.

I wasn't finished, though. I was also auditioning for two female characters, Josie and Cora. Josie was a fiery, strong, and more dynamic type, while Cora was the more fragile, sensitive, and emotional of the two. At the very beginning of the day, I became fixated on a beautiful young actress named Aimee Bello. She would be perfect to play Josie. I used Aimee to play against potential Coras for most of the day and kept watch for the more subtle character. I tried to keep an open mind, but I hadn't seen someone who would be a better Josie than Aimee. Several women were Cora-maybes, but there were still no Cora-yeses. It was getting toward the end of a long day.

In the last round were five new people, four men and one woman, Ari Khatib, who was intriguing. I didn't know what I could do with her, because she was clearly another Josie, and I had my heart set on Aimee. I asked Devon if I could see the last three women I'd held out in my mind as possible Coras.

"Can I see that red-head again?"

"No, remember, she left for another audition."

Well, she was too melodramatic anyway.

"What about the one in the yoga pants that had the great physicality?"

"No, remember she had a show, she had to leave."

She just didn't have any chemistry with Aimee anyway.

"And that tall one, the one who was too quiet?"

"Ara, everyone has left. Only Aimee and Ari are still here."

"Oh my God, no!"

"Seriously, you sent everyone away because they weren't right for one reason or another. You only have those two left."

"But they are both Josies! What am I supposed to do?"

"Well, we could come back for another round of auditions, or you could arrange to see the women you rejected at another time."

"No, no, you're right. I rejected them because they didn't work. They weren't right." I paused a moment, and sighed. "Oh my God, what have I done? Okay, bring Aimee and Ari out."

Devon looked at me, confused. "What are you going to do?"

"I don't know yet."

Devon rose to summon the Josies from the lobby.

I thought about all the times I auditioned for shows throughout my life and how terrified I had been. It had never occurred to me that the director might be more terrified than I could ever be. This was so important to me. Whichever women I chose, they would forever be the characters in the story I created. They would become the voices of the story with their bodies, their eyes, their gestures, their energy. They would be the life force of *We Vow*.

I looked up to see Ari and Aimee waiting. I got up and joined them on the stage with no idea what was going to happen next.

I asked them to face each other.

I took a deep breath to buy myself a moment.

And then I thought to myself about what I had here.

I put one hand on each of their shoulders. I took a breath and exhaled with a prayer, and the answer came.

Aimee has a broader range, but Ari has more intensity.

I have to let go of Aimee as Josie.

"Aimee, I'm going to ask you do something I haven't asked you to do all day. I'm going to ask you to play Cora."

She was clearly surprised. Even though she had frequently been present when I gave directions to the other women who had played Cora, she bought herself a little time asking, "Tell me about the character, as I haven't played that character." I described her again.

I told them I wanted to see the moment when the two of them reunite in the forest after being separated for a long time. I told them to hold on to the excitement, the tenderness, the sacredness, the intimacy—but not to kiss. As I walked back into the audience, I let them know they would have a moment to think about it, and that Danelle would be photographing them.

I declared, "Action."

The moment was electrifying! They held each other's gaze. I believed the ache and longing of lovers pulled apart, called away by war or tragedy. Then it shifted into a deliciousness that bubbled up from inside both of them. Then, they ignored my direction, and they were kissing. Under normal circumstances I would have yelled, "Cut," but I was so captivated by the intimacy they had just invited us into, I was lost in the moment with them. It took me a minute to get my bearings, to catch my breath, to call out, "Okay, okay, cut, cut. Thank you. You can wait outside for a moment."

When I heard the lobby door close, I looked over at Devon and said, "Holy shit!"

"Yeah, no kidding!"

"Okay, so, can all four of them rehearse at the same time?" My heart was racing. Yep, they were all available evenings. It was a done deal.

I went into the lobby and told them, "You both have the part!"

Aimee asked, "But how is that? We were just sitting here saying, 'It could only be one of us,' because we are, well, we're both ethnic. We were sure you'd think we looked too alike, you would only pick one of us."

"No, you two were brilliant together. The 'looking different' is my problem and the costume designers' problem, not your problem."

They both leapt up and hugged me with tears in their eyes. I couldn't believe how much they wanted to do this project! They were all-in.

*

The next few months were a flurry of costume design and fittings. I wanted the women's dresses and men's tailored suits to be historically accurate (even down to the jacket buttons, in Matt's case), but with my own little twist. We sought out additional designers to make original props, a milliner and corset maker. We shot video of each stage of the development process and edited and posted it on the web as quickly as possible while construction and rehearsals went forward.

After my experiences on the first shoot, I knew the single most important person on the set and the one most crucial for my basic survival was Brian, the digital technician Danelle had hired for *Tala & Louison*. He was like a personal assistant inside my brain. He noticed even my subtlest reaction to a shot, and used my reactions to create a rating system to organize over 2,500 images as we were shooting. I would be able to determine when we had the shots we needed on the fly and had proper notes during post production. Not only was he supremely facile at his job, he was a relaxed and positive person, no matter what stress was happening on the set. He was an infusion of chill. (After the first shoot, Danelle told me that when she called to secure the equipment, she explained she had a highly technical, fine art shoot and wanted "the best digital tech in the city." They said, "Oh that's easy: Brian Eaves!")

When I was ready to schedule my new shoot, he was the first person I called.

After I briefly described the situation, he said, "Ara, let me guess. You're going to do it outside again, right?"

"Well, yes," I said, sheepishly.

"What are the dates you're considering?"

"Well, I was thinking either the second weekend in October, the first weekend in November or the first weekend in December."

I secretly wished for snow, so I hoped he would pick the December date, but he said, "Then I will take the earliest date, in hope that it will be the warmest." I immediately called Danelle, the photographer, to confirm she could do the same date.

As October bore down on us, additional crew were brought on board. When we reviewed my shot list, Danelle was relieved to hear I intended to schedule two days this time. I needed someone capable of doing period hairstyles, a fairly sophisticated task, so I decided I would rely on a professional booking service. Danelle wisely recommended Ford Modeling. Gianluca Mandelli was chosen for hair and Alfred Lester would do makeup.

Liz returned to serve as Guardian of the Narrative. I also brought on Marc Sirinsky in an official capacity, to oversee post-production image processing. He would also be on set, to help me make decisions about when I should keep shooting and when it would be easier to solve the problem in post.

Scouting the location revealed serious challenges, and after several exasperating months, I turned to David Wittenstein. He was already documenting the pre-production process with video, and was slated to supervise a video crew the day of the photo shoot as well. He was a seasoned producer in his own right, and had repeatedly asked for more responsibility on the project. At one point, he had revealed to me that he had experience with permits and licensing, so I brought him on as a producer to help me scout locations and wrestle with the required paperwork.

Our first choice of location was a state park about an hour north of Chicago, but authorities with the Illinois park district weren't returning our calls. David and I were in his north side Chicago office on phones non-stop for two-and-a-half weeks trying to find alternatives, right up until two days before the shoot. I had several people flying in from different cities by this point. They were asking about rental cars and hotels, and I still didn't have a location confirmed.

Additionally, we had to determine how we would get the equipment we needed to the site. We would have to haul it in over difficult terrain. On the flip side of that issue, every potential location wanted assurance our crew and their gear would not harm the environment. These issues were complicated enough that Wittenstein consulted Danial A. Miller, a film industry veteran with thirty years of experience in location logistics, to recommend solutions.

Eventually, two days before the scheduled shoot, we received word our contact at the State of Illinois, the one who was supposed to approve our application, had been gravely ill and this was why our calls had not been returned. Finally, her supervisor approved our application, just thirty-six hours out.

Again, my health was a big question. Would I be able to sustain, not for a single day of shooting this time, but for two days? If I got too cold on the first day, I would be completely immobile and unable to direct the second day of the shoot. Michael tracked down the company that designed coats used by Arctic explorers and expeditionists, Canada Goose. We were banking on this being the coat that would get me through the two-day shoot.

A small entourage of people knew the risk this time. Marc would be there. He knew the capable person I was before Everything Bad Happened and had also seen me in my most fragile state shortly afterward. Whether I wanted him to or not, he would be watching me like a mother hen for any indication I wasn't going to make it. Devon would be there too, on the periphery, ready to serve as wise counsel. He could read me from a distance and know exactly what was going on in my head. If I were to fall apart, not just physically but emotionally, he would be the first to notice.

Liz would be there again as Narrative Guardian if I needed her, but we both agreed that I had come a long way as an artist and a director in the two years since the previous shoot. I wasn't trembling in fear of being the sole person responsible for making the story happen amongst all the interlinking technical components. I would have her as a back-up if there were a crisis, but I had learned to ride the waves of chaos and know the center of my self, my art, my work, my story. I was holding *We Vow* steadfast in my heart.

My brother Dan ran security. My longtime friend, Deborah Hanson, whom I had known since graduating high school, flew in from Boston to be the photographic documentarian of the event. My sister, Melissa, would be there to keep this operation, far more complex than the last, tracking on time. I had a posse.

They knew the gory details of the last decade, and would support me physically. They did their best to make sure I was fed and was sitting whenever possible. Someone must have told Danial about my problem with the cold, because every time I held my position for more than a minute, he repositioned one of the heaters to be near me.

Because of the Park District's time restrictions, we had even less flexibility for error than the first shoot. The grounds wouldn't open until 5:00 a.m., and they closed at 5:00 p.m. sharp. We couldn't leave anything on the grounds and had to have everyone and all of our gear out before closing time. To compensate, we began our 3:00 a.m. calls in the trailers in the hotel parking lot, and then the trailers, trucks, and personnel caravanned over to the location parking lot.

For this shoot, we had a half a dozen director chairs. I didn't want to look like a queen on the set. If my crew sat on them, then I wouldn't look so ridiculous. It was all wishful thinking. I didn't end up sitting this time either. The majority of the time I was either huddled up next to Brian (with Marc hovering over my shoulder), or in the tent that served as a makeshift backstage, looking at the large screen monitor. After each shot, Brian put my favorites on a 27-inch display in a tent, so I could see them better and make assessments. I went back and forth all day.

We were all feeling the crush of the shooting schedule, but using trained actors and a month of rehearsal paid off with incredibly dynamic shots. Additionally, Danelle was no longer confined to the scaffolding around a single tree limb, and as such her lighting brilliance was unleashed. Her assistants doubled as stand-ins for the actors. She would create her lighting scheme, then bring me a test shot to see what I thought of it. We had a total of 11 shots and only one of them was slightly "less than genius." In that instance, when she showed me her test shot, I paused for just an instant, and she read my hesitation.

She said, "She hates it!" and took off with the test shot and her camera.

"But wait," I said to her departing back, "No, I didn't—" but it was too late. She didn't care. Anything less than extraordinary wasn't enough for her. Of course, her next light painting blew me away. There was no break for her or her crew, as they were either shooting or setting up for the next shot. I was so blessed to have her, because she took my story and brought it to life with light.

In the middle of day two, we were ready for Shot Four. Not a lovely name for what needed to be the most poignant photo in the series. I was far more terrified than I had been during the auditions. Despite working this scene to the bone during the month of rehearsals with Aimee and Ari, they hadn't actually given me what I wanted. Their chemistry was so strong they weren't able to produce the tension of the separation, the space I wanted in order to show the suspended moment before the kiss. I needed the viewer to see what Josie and Cora couldn't have, what they were waiting for, wanting, needing, longing, hoping, desiring, but *not* having. They had come close, but they never got it quite right. The night of the final rehearsal, I lied and said they had, because I thought it would be bad mojo to say, "Yeah, you guys don't have it. I sure hope you can pull this off when we are on the set." Now we were finally going to do the almost-kiss shot. I asked for the set to be cleared to help create the intimacy of the moment.

Before we began, I walked up to the women and gave them the same simple instruction: "There is just one thing to think about here. This is about the space between you. You cannot let your faces touch." I knew if I over-directed them now, I would make a mess of it. As I walked back to Brian and the monitor, I said a prayer. *Please God, there is nothing more I can do. Please, if this is meant to be, please make this happen, please, God!*

I looked over at Danelle whose camera was poised close to their faces.

I called out, "Action," and time was suspended.

Their eyes met, and in that instant, all of the past moments between the two characters narrowed to a single point.

All the innocent times they played together at the edge of the lake as children were in that moment: The time when Josie tried to teach Cora how to shoot a rifle; the hundreds of notes they wrote to one another, all left hidden in the earth by the tree; the first time Cora reached over and touched Josie's face; the first time they swam together in the moonlight; their meeting with the minister, just the week before when they asked him to marry them; the letter to Cora's brother sent in the hope he would come in time to support their marriage; and now, the moment before this kiss merged with all their other kisses; all of those moments became one.

I wiped the tears off my cheeks as I watched them. I wanted to call "Cut," but I couldn't catch my breath. They had me captivated—again. I had to push myself to get through the whirlwind of love the two of them created. I quietly said, "Okay, we got it," something I had never said after a single take.

Ari said, "Seriously, you got it?"

I nodded, wiping the tears from my face. As the director, I was supposed to be the person who had it together, so I turned away from my actors to gather myself. When I turned around, I realized no one had cleared the set as I had asked. People had just backed up about ten feet. Everyone had seen it all. One of the two hundred pound-plus lightning crew guys was wiping tears from his eyes, too.

Danelle and Devon walked over to me. Devon was shaking his head, speechless, and Danelle said, "That was magic."

Scooting

It was an unremarkable winter day in December, 2008. Michael and I were driving from one errand to the next when I got a call from Diane.

"I have a question for you."

"Okay, whaddya got?"

"Would you be willing to co-sponsor a ball for the inauguration with me?"

"What do you mean?"

"There's the big White House ball, but then there are these smaller balls of varying levels of importance all around the city. I would like to have a ball to raise money for City Blossoms. It would be fairly small. We would split the costs between us."

I looked over at Michael. He had heard Diane's request. City Blossoms is a non-profit organization in Washington DC that builds community garden projects with inner city youth. He knew Diane had given me tremendous and steadfast support over the years in the form of well-timed advice or poetic gestures of support—like the poster of Morocco I hung in my room at Cooper Rehabilitation Facility, or a care package of Indian food when I was emotionally hurting. While I thanked her with words every time, it never felt like enough. Michael and I both nodded to each other without a word, and I said, "I'm in."

"Don't you want to talk to Michael about it?"

"I did. He's right here."

*

Diane was going to host 14 people in her house for the duration of the events in the capital. Orion, Yvonne, and Devon were attending as well as a number of old friends of Diane. I forget who coined the term, but leading up to the weekend, people began referring to the event as "Obama Camp." I was to be tucked into the garden apartment she rented out, as her tenants would be out of town for the weekend. This way, I would have the best odds of getting to sleep, which still required an arsenal of meds, as well as getting the requisite amount of sleep, which remained 11 to 12 hours. The morning med hangover was always slow going. I also would need to get away to rest during the day to manage my overbearing fatigue.

Diane and I worked through a number of scenarios that might allow me to attend the inauguration ceremony, but I didn't think any of them were genuinely feasible. There would be no place for me to rest, and the minimum duration of the outing—including transportation to the event, time there, then travel back—would be at least five hours. I still could hardly stand for more than ten minutes, fifteen at a push. Diane urged me to go in a wheelchair, but I didn't want the drama. Neither did I want the event to become about me or managing me, so I decided to stay behind and watch it on television. It was a bit peculiar to travel to D.C. to attend the festivities up to the inauguration, but not the inauguration itself. The event everyone would remember and talk about I would experience alone.

One day before I was to leave for Obama Camp, I received another call from Diane.

"Are you in your car again?"

"Yes."

"Then you need to pull over."

"Oh my God, what's happened?"

I could tell by the tone of her voice she was excited. She had something big to share.

"I have tickets for you and me to attend a party at the French Ambassador's residence two nights before the inauguration!"

"What? What does that mean?"

"Well, this is one of the special events which precedes the inauguration. It's hosted by the French Ambassador. It'll be attended mostly by Washington people, but it's a way for the Ambassador to extend a warm welcome to many of Obama's friends."

"Oh my God, Diane, what the hell does one wear to the French Ambassador's residence? It sounds like a little black dress affair and I don't have a little black dress! Diane, what the hell? I'm flattered and excited, but terrified! Wow! Thank you! This is crazy! Seriously?"

"Yes, seriously!"

"Oh, how I wish I spoke French! Damn! Okay, well, I'm already on US-31. I guess I'll keep driving straight to South Bend, hit the mall to see what I can find. I'm excited, but I don't know how I could find something I could have altered to fit my body in a *single day*, but I'll figure it out."

I eventually found a 1920's style, sleeveless black cocktail dress with a sheer beaded neckline and a layered flapper-type silhouette. I wished it wasn't sleeveless, as I was still considerably overweight. Given I had one night to find a dress, it was the best I could do to hide my seven-months-pregnant-looking profile. It was certainly serviceable. I found a delightful pair of Marc Jacobs red patent leather pumps for a spark of color.

*

When I arrived at O'Hare Airport, I entered the craziest scene. I was walking toward my gate and noticed a dozen women carrying extremely long garment bags up over their heads. We were all carrying ball gowns on board, too scared to check them! We looked at each other smiling and laughing. None of us knew each other, but shared the funniest sense of community—all of us heading out of Chicago to the inauguration in D.C.

When I arrived at Diane's, the energy was infectious. Everyone was receiving house keys with an Obama image, coordinating who was going to cook what meals and what the schedule would be for the next few days. There was volunteering in the community on Martin Luther King Day, preparations for the ball, dresses that needed altering. Her house was bustling.

Diane only had two tickets to the French Ambassador's party, so we both tried to keep a low profile the day of the event. I was self-conscious about her choosing me, among all her gal-pals, to go to this event. I suspected some of them may have thought it was a consolation prize for not being able to go to the inauguration. If so, it was one hell of a prize! Diane wore a smashing little black affair with a fitted bodice with an elegant sheer black overlay, satin stripes, and a satin black neckline. She was striking.

Once we arrived, I was completely overwhelmed. I had been so excited to go I hadn't thought about how many of the political people there Diane would know, since she had worked "on the hill" for more than twenty years. Her charm and effortless grace allowed her to hold court like an experienced master of ceremonies. Dozens of people wanted her attention to share insider gossip or ask her opinion on a piece of legislation which was moving through the political machine. I knew she was a woman of influence, but I had always pictured her doing it on the phone. These were the people of her daily life. Some she hadn't seen in person in a long time, and some she talked to on a daily basis. They were all about her, the Queen Bee. Clearly, her colleagues adored her, men and women, young and old. Diane was so unassuming and humble about it all, as if they were her brothers, or uncles, or friends. She made it all look so easy, but you would have to know her well to have any idea that these social events took a great deal out of her.

After standing by her side for a mere five minutes, I quickly became aware of my limitations. Now I remembered *standing* was far more fatiguing than walking. I didn't want to interrupt her conversation to excuse myself, but an appropriate break in the conversation wasn't coming. I felt the muscles in my legs twitching. My knees were going to buckle. I had to find a place to sit quickly or I was going to collapse and create an embarrassing scene. I touched

Diane's arm briefly and slipped away. I went to the sitting room and found a comfortable chaise by the fire.

About fifteen minutes later, Diane found me.

"Are you okay?" she asked quietly.

"Of course," I explained. "I couldn't stand any longer."

"Have you seen the room where they are serving the desserts?"

"No, not yet."

"Well, you must come. Here, let me take your arm."

Diane took my arm like I was her grandmother, and we made our way into the dessert room. I was immediately transported in time. The table closest to the door bore a 12-foot-high display covered with candelabras and cascading pieces of bread, cheese, and honey. Another table was laden with three-tiered trays loaded with tiny delicacies. I could hear a number of different languages being spoken. I looked around the room. Among the honored guests there were a half a dozen people dressed in Louis XIV-style costumes. Diane used the positions on the clock to point out various European politicians and Obama's closest friends from Chicago. There was also an exquisite woman from Ghana in African dress and women who had to be top models from New York, Paris, Milan. It was like a dream-world on the other side of a wormhole.

As the evening continued, I soaked it all in from my vantage point as a people-watcher on the outer edges of the action. Around 11:30 p.m., I heard loud voices in the next room where the French pop band was playing. I got up to see what all the fuss was about. The band was playing American cover songs from every era, each tune true enough to form to get everyone into the spirit but with enough of a twist to make it their own. The floor was hopping all night, a wild mass of bodies dancing over a twenty-foot-wide emblem of the Napoleonic Consulate. When the band played "Electric Boogie" (originally by Marcia Griffiths), the crowd transformed into coordinated rows of dancers doing the Electric Slide.

This wasn't an ordinary group of line dancers. African American men in colorful suits and women in elegant dresses wearing incredible hats, white guys in black-and-grey suits with their dates in little black dresses, folks in traditional African dress, Asians, Latin people, Indian people, and eight people that had leapt through time from the court of Louis XIV... all doing the Electric Slide. I so wished I could join them. It was a strange feeling. The joy on the floor was so contagious I couldn't possibly feel sorry for myself. All of us watching were laughing, clapping, cheering, and sharing in our jubilant hope for tomorrow.

*

The morning of the inauguration, it was no surprise Yvonne was the first one out of the house. She left at 4:30 a.m. to find her spot in front of the

Washington Monument. Two others seeking good places to take photographs left a couple of hours later, and the rest of the gang left by 8:30 a.m. Diane's entire neighborhood was silent. No cars, no people, no kids playing outside, nobody. Diane set up a television for me in front of a comfortable chair. I went and found a box of tissues.

Brian Williams began, "On a cold, but glorious day in Washington, there is no way to estimate the crowds…" I watched as the camera pulled back from the White House to reveal a sea of dots. Thousands upon thousands of heads were crammed into the area in front of the National Monument and spilled out beyond, all there to witness this remarkable day. Memories came flooding back: waiting years to see if Obama would actually run for president; being busted for handing out flyers explaining the confusing Michigan primary (at the grocery store, then at the movies, then at the community center, the shopping center, and apartment complexes); my car fish-tailing seven different times in a snowstorm while on my way to meet the press at a straw poll. Now here I was, in Washington D.C., on *the day*, moments before Barack Obama would become the 44th President.

"My fellow citizens," he began, "we remain a young nation, but in the words of Scripture, the time has come to set aside childish things. The time has come to reaffirm our enduring spirit, to choose our better history, to carry forward that precious gift, that noble idea, passed on from generation to generation: the God-given promise that all are equal, all are free, and all deserve a chance to pursue their full measure of happiness."

Only three sentences in and I grabbed my first tissue.

Barack would be the first American president that I believed in my heart would speak for all people. This included LGBT people and under-represented people in other lands. I held on to this hope and this prayer as I listened.

That evening we all dressed up in our finery for the City Blossoms Ball. Diane and I wore the dresses I had designed for us. Orion wore a tux, and I couldn't wait to try and have a dance with him. It ended up lasting a mere single verse and half of a chorus, and then I took a seat by Jo, a close friend of Diane's I had come to know.

She said, "It sure was fun to see you dance, Ara." Jo knew what I had been through. She was getting up there in years, and by this time her Multiple Sclerosis had progressed. She appreciated what it meant to do even a little.

* * *

Being insanely goal-driven, I loved the opportunity New Year's resolutions presented. January 2010 was no different. My favorite challenges are those just out of reach. I made a vow, again, to reduce my weight and increase my endurance. I had managed to get my weight down from the bloated all-time high of 187 pounds to a still-way-too-high 170-ish pounds. Right out of the

ICU my clothes were falling off of me. I was tiny, a bit over 100 pounds, well below my "dancer weight." The ideal would be 135 to 140 or a place where my view of my body felt like that number.

After the abdominal reconstructive surgery, I was shocked to realize my repaired body doomed me to a perpetually pregnant silhouette. The social awkwardness of strangers or new acquaintances mistakenly assuming I was pregnant was an endless hell. I routinely had to decide how I might get out of the situation fastest—would I go through the uncomfortable explanation that I wasn't pregnant, or lie by nodding and playing along? The latter choice was often followed by "When are you due?" and other invested questions. After trying this tactic a few times, I chose the truth as my standard answer. This would be followed by an apology and potent silence. I would be the one to change the subject and try to trudge through the weird air that hung over us.

These encounters weren't always verbal. Sometimes they were "knowing glances" from women, looking at my abdomen and then at me with a gooey-sweet grin. It sucked. I wondered whether if I were a little heavier, I would look fat instead, which I was convinced would be preferable. When my weight climbed as the result of one of my medications, I discovered it made absolutely no difference. I looked like a pregnant heavy person.

Being out in the world meant I had to figure out ways to dress and make the best of the situation. If I learned anything from my mother, it was how to put together an outfit. Although her style is more classic than mine, over the years she taught me the basic fashion rules and the importance of making a good impression with one's apparel. The problem was, at my size and shape, there were no clothes that allowed me to express my personal style. I even tried maternity clothes, but the fashion was to aggressively own and embrace the pregnant body. That works well for the proud mother-to-be, but not so much for me. I dressed in layers whenever possible and worked to create looks that would draw attention anywhere else.

This just wasn't a body I could identify with. Although I had always been conscious of my tummy, it was from the vantage point of the dancer's body I'd once had. In retrospect, my previous little problem was nothing. This currently overweight, highly fatigued, misshapen body was one I was used to but not one I had come to terms with. Exercise was difficult. Every few months I would try again to walk more than 12 minutes to see if I could get past the overwhelming fatigue that left me bedridden for days.

During the first quarter of 2010, I made another attempt to break the fatigue barrier with a concerted effort at an exercise program. It had been 40 quarters since this all began, and I still hoped I could create some semblance of a real life. Despite the concerns of my surgeon who would not permit me to use a treadmill because I might fall, I decided it was time to try.

His concerns about injury weren't imaginary. For ten years, I had operated within the constraints given to me by Dr. Petrosian and avoided anything that would create intra-abdominal pressure—anything that could rip out part of the mesh or the latissimus in my abdomen. This meant not lifting anything over 15 pounds or so (he admitted he didn't know what the weight restriction should be), no jogging, and no bike riding. There was very little I could do. Even sneezing hurt since it yanked on the point where the mesh was attached. The truth is I did fall occasionally, especially outside, in winter. Without an abdomen, balance was an issue. Petrosian made it clear if I tore his reconstruction out in any significant way, he didn't know if it could be repaired or what the consequence would be. I heard repeatedly, "There is only one of you."

Because of this, Michael angrily insisted on doing everything he could for me. According to him, I was not allowed to open the door of a business because business doors were heavy. "It's a matter of wear and tear over time," he repeatedly said. He would always do the lifting, pulling, pushing even if it was within my limits. I, of course, felt smothered by this.

Over time, I learned what tearing scar tissue felt like, and what I could and couldn't lift without causing strain. I figured out how to use my body to leverage things, or the momentum of an object to move it, and how to pivot objects to get them through space when their weight was too much. Often, I shuttled the contents of a suitcase piecemeal, or loaded a car full of groceries using two or four times as many trips because things were too heavy.

Sometimes though, I had to do what I had to do, so I decided to be careful and took a calculated risk. That's what I did with the treadmill. My plan was to make it past the fatigue wall—the 12-minute mark—but gently and carefully. I created a Sean Paul playlist on an internet streaming radio service and began slowly. I hoped to keep a casual pace for five minutes the first day. I would then take at least one day off before returning. I wound up remaining at five minutes for a week, but at least I wasn't bedridden afterward. It felt like progress. I was determined not to rush it, to stay focused, and to proceed carefully.

After a successful first week, I bumped my time up to seven minutes and walked the treadmill four times the next week. So far, so good. The next week I went for four days at nine minutes each. It all felt so ridiculous. Nine minutes? Really? I wasn't pushing hard. I didn't break a sweat or anything. I walked a wee bit quicker, which easily pushed my deconditioned body into an aerobic heart rate.

The next week I went for 11 minutes. I was getting nervous because this was very close to the point when my body usually fell apart, but I had never built up to it this slowly before. I stayed at 11 minutes for an additional week and increased my pace a little.

It was getting exciting. I began to think about the things I could do if I were able to become fit. *Could I walk a marathon? What else could I do? Could I climb a mountain? No, plenty of intra-abdominal pressure there.* I kept pushing along and dreaming to my homemade reggae-rock radio station.

By week six, I'd lost five pounds and was stronger. I was eager to break the 12-minute wall, but I'd felt good all the previous times when I wound up in bed. I decided to go for 13 minutes but slow the pace, take it easy, and only use the treadmill three times that week.

All systems were go.

Week seven, I stayed at 13 minutes but walked four times and increased the pre-programmed intensity—still only walking, but a teeny bit faster. Still moving forward.

Week eight, I went for 15 minutes four times with a variable intensity. I got more excited. I was losing about 1.5 pounds a week—not fast, but by then I was down 13 pounds total. I could see the difference in how my clothes fit (or didn't). As winter moved toward spring, I'd been at it for two months. I stared out into the woods, thinking, *What would it mean to travel?*

I started dreaming of Paris. *What if I could travel alone?*

Week nine: 20 minutes, variable effort, five times.

Week ten: 25 minutes each time, and I even sneaked in a 27-minute day for one of those. I was approaching a half-hour and still going strong. Had I merely delayed the breaking point, soon to spend twice as long in bed, or had I broken the seal? Watching the snow melt away in the marsh, longing for the green shoots of spring, I couldn't help but wonder if this was going to be the spring of my life too.

On week eleven I decided to go for the 30-minute mark.

I did it!

Elated, I made proclamations about having "beaten the beast" and "busted the barrier" and "walloped the wall," but Michael was not so sure. He asked a lot of questions. He always wanted more proof, but I *felt* different this time. I was stronger. Unlike in the past, I wasn't being willful, pressing on regardless of feeling frail. I felt physically bolder. Plus, I was twenty-two pounds lighter.

Then I started to get cocky, and mid-week I pushed up to 40 minutes—only once, to see if I could.

No problem.

The next week I did 45 minutes. There was a little voice of doubt inside my head which persuaded me to hold there for a bit. So, for two more weeks I hung on at 45 minutes, variable speed, walking, but a little faster.

Then, I tried doing an hour.

I couldn't.

I was okay, though. I didn't crash and burn.

I felt fatigued, so I stopped at 52 minutes. I was fine with that. I thought about how originally I was trying to get past *12* minutes, so having to hang on at 50 was okay.

I backed off to 45 minutes again, hung there for a couple more weeks, then aimed for an hour again. I varied the intensity to see if I took it a bit easier, maybe this time I could make it past 60 minutes.

I DID IT!

I was ecstatic, my mind whirring, thinking about the implications. What else would I be able to do if I could stand longer, walk longer, do anything longer? My mind went back to traveling again, to Paris and the idea of going by myself. I thought about how I might do it alone. Maybe on a scooter?

I will tour France on a scooter, I thought. That way, I'd be able to carry my luggage on the bike and the scooter would do the labor. With a more fit body, I could see and experience the country instead of spending half of my time resting in a hotel room! I thought about how badly I'd wanted to see Basilique du Sacré-Cœur in Paris.

A fantastical idea began to brew in my imagination: maybe this time I could take a scooter from Western France down to the Chagall Museum in Southern France, then travel up through the Arc de Triomphe as I had in the taxicab, but this time under my own power. Now, I believed I could climb the three-hundred steps of Sacré-Cœur.

*

In 2009, on my forty-fourth birthday, I got my first scooter, a Vespa LX-150. Ever since I lived in San Francisco, I'd wanted one of my own. Out there, parking was a major problem, not to mention expensive, so there were tons of them. A couple of times I rented one to show friends the sights. I loved riding them, and the Vespa was the quintessential brand. To me it was the only *real* scooter.

While researching getting a scooter for my post-ICU body, I learned that although the weight of the scooter was a factor in its maneuverability, it was more important where the bike's center of gravity was located. Based on this selection criterion, Michael and I chose the Vespa LX-150 over a much lighter scooter I couldn't push because of its awkwardly-placed center of gravity.

When I began riding my scooter I found I could only go for about 20 minutes. Afterward I would pass out completely for three to four hours. The only other experience that caused this level of fatigue was getting too cold or seriously over-exerting myself. I decided to consult Dr. Tomas about it.

"You know what," he began, "I don't think the fatigue you're experiencing is general. Rather, it's the strain of balancing while riding, made extraordinarily difficult by the fact that you have no abdominal support. What you need to do is ditch that Vespa and get yourself a three-wheeled scooter."

I frowned, "I don't want to ride a three-wheeled scooter. I have this vision of myself riding a classic Vespa across France. A three-wheeled scooter doesn't fit that vision."

Tomas replied warmly, but with his usual frankness, "You're going to have to change your vision. You aren't going to get an abdomen any time soon, and if you are determined to ride a scooter without one, you're going to need more support to balance." This was one of those moments when I didn't want to admit it, but I knew I would have to face the facts. We would have to at least investigate a three-wheeler.

I was anxious that my whole dream might be falling apart. There were two kinds of three-wheeled scooters, ones with two wheels in the front and ones with two wheels in the back. From my reading, the ones with two wheels in the front were safer. Given a number of other factors, this meant the only option for me would be the Piaggio MP3. But even the smallest MP3 was a monster at 450 pounds, twice the weight of my LX-150. I couldn't imagine how I would be able to push it without intra-abdominal pressure.

It was a couple of more weeks before the ice was off the pavement and the dealer in Grand Rapids was willing to show us the MP3. Once in the showroom, I was able to paddle it with my toes almost effortlessly. I pushed the scooter ahead quickly, rolling about four feet. Michael yelled out, "Woah! Hey! Hey, *wooooah!*"

I looked at him with a huge grin on my face.

"It wasn't hard. I swear. We've found a match."

Even so, Michael was anxious about the added bulk and, justifiably, he was still concerned about me even riding a scooter. I had a minor wipe-out with the 150 the previous summer. He was sure Petrosian would lose his mind if he knew I was getting on any scooter. I asserted Petrosian would be happy to hear I was now going to be riding a three-wheeler. Michael was sure it wouldn't make him any happier. I knew he was right, but I didn't care. It was better than Christmas. Now I only had to adjust my attitude about this roboscooter being "my ride." I would have to come up with a name for her.

I posted a video online asking for suggestions. A few recommendations came through back to back, and together they inspired me to name the scooter Michi, which means "friend" in Japanese. Michi was also the name of my first supervisor when I had my private psychotherapy practice. She encouraged me to trust myself. Trust (and Michi) was what I needed to find my way on this big adventure.

*

Devon and Michael hovered like mother hens while I did the final safety checks on my scooter. 2010 was unseasonably hot, and it was another 96 degree day. I had on what would become my summer uniform: riding boots with heavy socks to prevent chafing, armor–reinforced riding jeans, a tank top, my white Corazzo jacket, black leather gloves, and a helmet. As I started off down the driveway, I thought how, if I were driving a car (or was perhaps a more experienced cyclist), I could have turned around to wave goodbye. Even though I finally had my "scooter legs," I was still a newbie, and I had to keep my hands on the grips and my eyes on the road.

After months of physical preparation, my scooter tour adventure had begun. As I traveled down our bumpy, dirt driveway, I knew I was moving out

Reconstruction

into the world alone with this reconstructed but emboldened body. I prayed this wouldn't turn out to be one of those "be careful what you wish for" moments.

I'd had to face the fact that I lacked the experience and the resources for a trip across France by myself. Instead, I now planned to travel across the Midwest, intending to cover 3,400 miles and 26 towns in 50 days.

On my trial run up to Muskegon, about 130 miles north of our home, I realized I had a problem. The previous scooter wipe-outs have given me a PTSD response to riding. I had a screaming voice in my head, not a hearing-voices-kind-of-voice, but a part of me that said, "You're gonna wipe out! You're gonna wipe out! DON'T WIPE OUT! DON'T WIPE OUT!" It was a part that wanted to keep me safe, one that preferred I didn't ride a scooter at all. I still clearly remembered flying over the handlebars of my Vespa the year before, and I couldn't stop picturing it.

The "voice" had solid grounds to dislike riding—evidence was on her side. I had to explain to her that screaming about how I was going to wipe out was more likely to *make* me wipe out than keep me safe. During that trial run I realized I had to direct my concentration toward something more constructive. I would be better served if I could get the freaked-out part to be vigilant by focusing on tasks which contributed to my safety, like going over my pre-ride checklist, keeping an eye on my GPS navigation, monitoring my speed, tracking the condition of the road, and so on. There was plenty for her to do. Slowly, I was able to make this shift, and I replaced her hysteria with the more positive mantra, "I am held by the light." In a way, my mantra had a kind of literal meaning, too: "held" was sort of like "held up," upright, on all three wheels—safe!

*

I spent the night on the *USS Silversides* at The Great Lakes Naval Memorial & Museum. When I plotted out the journey, it was my plan to stay at interesting places and see if I could discover a Midwest I hadn't experienced before. I was giddy to spend the night in a submarine, a real one!

When I made the reservation, the receptionist couldn't contain her laughter when I revealed it was for me alone. I had no children and wasn't the chaperone for a class trip or club.

"Nope, it's just me," became a kind of slogan for the whole escapade.

She burst out laughing, then quickly apologized and tried to get it together as she went over the specifics, but she continued to lose it and kept laughing. It didn't bother me. Then, she told me it was critical I arrive by 6:30 p.m. That worried me.

Everyone had to be on time for the briefing about the rules of conduct on the sub. If I wasn't on time, I wouldn't be permitted aboard. She also explained there would be a group of young scouts, all boys, staying the same night as me. I thought this was charming. Talk about feeling safe—I would be on the sub with a ship full of potential sailors! It was perfect.

I did a trial run three days before my excursion began in earnest, to make sure I'd worked out the system of packing up my gear. Things looked sketchy as it took more than four hours to load up and that was with both Michael and Devon helping. It was five hours ride time to get to Muskegon. If I could get the load-in time down to a couple of hours, and as long as there were no mishaps, I might make it to the site by the designated time.

I made it, and I was warmly greeted by Gary Reynolds, the tour guide. As sundown approached, the fluttering flags were lowered in a solemn and stately ceremony. The scouts lowered each flag, folded it appropriately, and handed it off to Gary with a salute. I was moved. I couldn't help but think about my grandfather who had fought in World War II on the *USS Concord*.

Under the direction of the parent chaperones, the scouts created a "bucket brigade" to pass all my gear from off-board to on-board, then down the steps to my quarters. Being the only woman spending the night on the sub, I was given the Captain's quarters for privacy. I hadn't thought much of it prior, but now that I was there with all those young boys, bunking up with them did seem a bit weird.

As I stepped down the steep ladder into the sub, a wave of reality ran through my body. There were long torpedoes, bombs, inside the sub, and the sailors' bunks lay up against them. They had to work and even sleep by them. Never for a moment were they able to forget where they were or the risk. Gary took us through each compartment and explained the workings of the ship. It was fascinating. I was impressed by the boys. Either they were all into this kind of thing or their troop leaders had given them an intense overview on the *Silversides* prior to their arrival because they exuberantly answered all of Gary's questions about the ship, its crew, and its battles.

After the tour, the boys were given several hours to explore the ship and have a pizza dinner outside the museum to which they invited me. I joined them for dinner and then set about writing my first blog post for the journey.

Before I left, we created a web site so people could follow my adventure online. Not only could I post blogs, videos, and photos there, and it had an embedded map that displayed real-time location data from a geo-tracker I wore. I also set up a Twitter account for the trip, for shorter, more frequent updates.

There was only one working electrical outlet on the ship, in the galley. A small group of boys were playing cards there, but they assured me they didn't mind me sitting there with my laptop. Soon it became clear they didn't mind, because they were excited to ask me questions.

"How far are you going?"

"What kind of a motorcycle is that?"

"Where are you going next?"

"Why are you riding by yourself?"

"Do you believe in ghosts?" (During the tour Gary suggested a crewman who died on the *Silversides* still haunted the ship.)

"Can we watch you ride your scooter?"

On and on the questions went. I thought they were all adorable, so I answered each one with a big smile until one of the older boys interrupted, "Hey you guys, she is trying to write her blog. Let's leave her be."

And so they returned to their game. Within moments, another group of boys from another part of the ship entered the galley and began their own round of questions.

Eventually, I was able to write and even employed the boys to help me, as they knew all the details about the ship's history. This turned out to be the first in a series of challenges I would face, attempting to conduct my adventure in full view of a curious, watching public. The next one I encountered in the morning.

I began that day as I would each on my tour. I suited up and went to the nearest gas station, where I began to run down my extensive pre-flight checklist (so called as it was a procedure I had adopted from my flying-lesson days). Verifying oil levels, tire pressure, getting enough water for the day's ride, and so forth. I figured this would take about ten minutes, but soon learned to allow at least 45 minutes for the process.

My unusual scooter, although a blessing for my body, was also a curse. Whenever I stopped for gas, to buy water, to pee, to eat, to rest, anything, a crowd would quickly gather. At the first gas station, I was elated, thinking, as an extrovert on a solo journey, maybe I wouldn't be so lonely after all. But by my third stop on the second day, I realized I was in trouble. With so many people wanting to talk to me about my scooter or the adventure I was having, I needed an assistant, someone who could say, "Ara, you are going to be late for your next appointment. Sorry people, we have to go." I tried to do this myself, with tremendous urgency, but it wasn't working and it added to my fatigue.

*

We knew from the onset I might not make it through the whole tour, but I was determined to finish or at least see how far I could get. The plan was to ride for a few days and then rest in one location for two or three days before picking up again. Throughout the trip I set up a few big challenges, such as a double mileage day or riding for five days straight. It was also part of the plan to get massages throughout the journey. Not having an abdomen puts a tremendous strain on all the remaining muscular systems. I needed to have body work in my normal daily life. We knew I would certainly need it on the ride, we just didn't know how often.

When my morning wake-up alarm went off during the first few days of the tour, my stiff and achy body cried out in agony. But on the fourth day, I was so stiff I could hardly move to hit the snooze. I wondered if I would be able to ride. I didn't go back to sleep, but carefully moved my arms and legs in an attempt to discern whether or not I would even be able to get out of bed to pee. If I could do that, maybe then I could assess whether or not I could ride. When the alarm went off a second time I was still unsure, but peeing had become a necessity. I overrode the pain and forced my body out of the bed. Maybe a shower would help.

I moved a little better. I knew I only needed to get to a bed and breakfast in Cheboygan, about 75 miles from my current location. This was the shortest mileage of the entire trip. I figured I could rally and push myself to do that much.

I took my time and carefully packed up my gear, a process I now had down to a 90 minute procedure. In order to open the seat for loading, I put the key in the ignition, but when I tried to turn the key it wouldn't move at all. It was as if the ignition was jammed or frozen.

Great.

As far as I understood, there were only two Vespa-Piaggio dealerships in Michigan: the one in Grand Rapids where I had purchased my scooter, and another in Detroit. I called the Grand Rapids dealer. Fortunately, Bob, the mechanic who had tuned my bike up for the journey, was available.

"What do you think this could be?"

"Well, it sounds like some kind of electrical problem. Honestly, I've never heard of this happening."

What have I gotten myself into with this MP3? Is this one of those finicky models of scooter where I'm going to spend half of my summer waiting while my ride is in the shop?

"Well, here is my situation. I'm in Gaylord, Michigan. If you were me, and you had this scooter with an electrical problem, and you were on a 3,400 mile ride on a schedule, would you have yourself towed to Grand Rapids or Detroit to fix the problem? Or would you trust a local motorcycle shop to fix it?"

"You want to know what *I* would do?"

"Yes, that's what I'm asking."

"Well, Ara, to be honest, if my bike had an electrical problem, I would take it to a dealer."

"Okay, I'm going to use my phone to try and figure out which is closer, you guys or Detroit. Thanks for being honest—"

Bob cut me off, saying, "Ara, hang on a second."

I could hear voices in the background, but I couldn't hear what they were saying.

After a moment or two, Bob returned, clearly excited. "You are not going to believe this, Ara. There is a third Vespa dealer! Did you say you were in Gaylord?"

"Yes."

"Well, it's in Gaylord!"

"No way!"

"Jan, in the office, called to make sure."

I wrote down the name and number of the Gaylord dealer.

I couldn't believe my luck. "Wow," I sighed. "Thank you so much. I hope I don't need this kind of help again, but thank you so very much!"

I called the local dealer and spoke to Chris, their sales manager. When I explained my situation he responded, "We will roll out the red carpet for you! We'll be there in fifteen minutes!"

He arrived in ten, driving a pickup truck with a trailer. He loaded up my scooter and me, and off we went. Once at the dealer, Mike began taking my information, and one of their techs, another guy named Chris, got to work on my scooter. I could see there were quite a number of bikes in the shop, so they clearly decided to bump me up the line to get me back on the road as soon as possible. Mike wasn't even finished taking my info when Chris, the tech, appeared to explain what had happened.

"The Piaggio has two 'off' key positions. If you take the key out in the 'half-off' position, rather than the 'full-off' position, the engine is actually still on."

"You mean my engine was on all night until my battery went dead."

"Exactly. We got her a power-jump for you. You're going to need to ride her straight to your next destination without stopping. We see you are set up to plug in the bike to charge it. You definitely need to do that tonight to get the battery fully charged or you're going to be in this same predicament tomorrow."

They didn't charge me a penny for anything—the tow, the jump, nothing —and sent me on my way. I thanked them profusely, took a couple photos for posterity, and I was off.

Unfortunately, all the drama around the scooter didn't distract me from how much my body hurt. By the second hour on the road, my right forearm and wrist were screaming from holding the twist grip accelerator in the down position. This pain creeped its way up my arm into my neck and shoulders. Then there was my back, which was doing all the work of balancing without an abdomen. I reached Cheboygan, relieved I would be stopped for a couple of days and eager to find a bodyworker.

Trying to find a deep-tissue massage therapist who can handle my complex situation was nearly impossible. It is rare to find a therapist with the confidence and skill to be as aggressive as necessary in the places that compensate for the missing abdomen, and also have the necessary sensitivity to avoid hurting the places with residual nerve damage. I attempted to find bodyworkers in advance of departing, but since there was no way to know for sure *when* I would need the work, I had to do the best I could to find someone once I was already desperate.

I stepped into Alice's Restaurant and ordered lunch, as I'd only had my usual light breakfast: a bag of Power Bar® Oatmeal Raisin Energy Bites™. When my grilled cheese sandwich and salad were delivered, I started my search with the server. She mentioned several places, but her recommendation was to call the local chiropractor who supposedly had a massage therapist on staff.

I was stunned that their massage therapist, Shellie Davis Charboneau, picked up my call. It turned out she had a cancellation. Next I found out her office was literally next door to the B&B where I was staying. I would have enough time to finish my lunch, take a shower, and walk over for the appointment.

Upon meeting Shellie, I found out she raced motocross. Before I had a chance to describe my aches, she said, "I imagine your wrist and forearms are hurting up into your neck," as she mimed the position of riding the bike, "and without an abdomen, your lower back and hamstrings are a wreck."

I couldn't believe my luck.

When I walked out of her office, I wasn't hurting anywhere! I knew that riding was going to re-invite those pains, but for the time being I had a clean slate. Synchronicity had provided a Vespa-Piaggio dealer in the very place my scooter had broken down, and then the universe had offered me up a biker/massage therapist at the point when my body couldn't go any more. Perfection. Now I needed rest.

*

Before I left on my tour, I had occasion to talk to various people about the journey I had planned. Inevitably, the men wanted to know what vehicle I intended to ride. This was followed by a desire to compare makes and models of bikes and stories about people they knew who had been in the most horrible accident and walked away either unharmed or were still riding maimed. In contrast, the women mostly wanted to know what I would do if it rained. I was surprised they weren't more concerned about my general safety. I'm not sure if it was because more women felt safe in the world these days, if the danger was too scary to even think about, or if they couldn't get past the rain to get to any safety issues. I couldn't figure out why they were all so worried about the rain.

Because I had lost weight while training for the ride, I needed to buy new clothes, including new underwear. I was at Victoria's Secret looking at bras when the saleswoman who was helping me asked if they were for a special occasion. I told her I was riding solo for 3,400 miles on a scooter.

"You mean you're going with three thousand people?"

"No, I'm going by myself."

"Will there be a van behind you or something?" she asked, as a horrified look made its way across her face.

"Nope, just me. But I will have more than one communication device and an emergency button that will contact people if I get into trouble," I said, trying to reassure her.

"How long is it going to take you?"

"Well, the whole trip will take fifty days, but some of those days are rest days."

"Oh, I could never do that. What will you do if it rains?"

Here I was, in the Upper Peninsula of Michigan and more than two weeks into my journey, finally forced to face the rain. At first it didn't bother me. Managing wet surfaces was easy with the MP3, but after four days of constant rain, I was worn down. Though I left well prepared with extreme weather gear to keep me dry, its bulk made riding awkward, so eventually I skipped it and just accepted being wet for hours. Unfortunately, that made it miserable when I had to stop for gas or to pee, since I had to wriggle out of and into wet jeans and soggy gloves every time.

But the real albatross was my damned goggles. Not because they were goggles (sun glasses would have had the same problem), but because they would fog up. At times, I rode with only 5 or 10% visibility. Before my departure, I tried to find a pair of sunglasses that would fit my small head and would tuck neatly into my size XS helmet. After about nine purchases and returns, I gave up and went with goggles: a tinted pair for day and a clear pair for night. Their elastic headbands made them an automatic fit.

It had rained during the return leg of my trial run to Muskegon. I discovered then that the goggles fogged up and no amount of wiping, rubbing, spitting, squinting, or praying would restore visibility. I gave up at one point, pushed the goggles up onto my forehead, and switched to my helmet visor in various configurations: closed, partially open, open more, open less. Either the visor fogged up, or my face was pelted with rain painful enough to make me close my eyes—not a good idea.

Once I got home from the trial run, I only had two days before I left on the tour, so I scoured the internet to see what everyone thought was the best solution. It seemed most people used a product called Cat Crap Anti-Fog Lens Cleaner. It's a green putty-like substance that is rubbed on lenses or a helmet visor. It got great reviews. It was worthless.

On days six and seven of the rain, I stopped at a number of truck stops and ATV dealers. I tried and rejected a number of products they offered to solve the problem. After more than a week of struggling with rain blindness and navigating by the glimmer of red and white lights from other vehicles, I banked all my hopes on a new product I read about on the internet called Rain-X® Wipes. It didn't have as many reviews, but since it was more expensive, I hoped that was the reason it wasn't more popular. Michael sent it ahead in a care package to my next stop in Oshkosh, Wisconsin.

It didn't rain another day of my tour.

*

Before loading gear in the morning, I took a quick peek out the window of the hotel's breakfast nook to check on my scooter. I saw a group of five Harley riders getting ready to leave, and one of them was eyeing my Michi.

I was told before starting this trip to be wary, to steer clear of the Harley riders in general, but in Wisconsin in particular. I was in Iron Mountain, Michigan, a few miles from the northern border of Wisconsin, and Harley-Davidson originated in southern Wisconsin. I was also warned that I might find parking lots designated specifically for American-made cars and motorcycles in southern Wisconsin, and there would likely be little tolerance for me and my Italian-made Piaggio MP3.

It was time for me to go, so I tried to brush off my hesitation as ridiculous urban legend. I crossed the lobby to my room, grabbed one of the side bags to load, and headed outside. When I got out to Michi, I was approached by the woman who had been looking at her. She was soon followed by the others. They asked about my three-wheeler, and I ended up telling them about my physical challenge. I mentioned the toughest part of my day was bending over the scooter and wrangling my saddlebags onto their frames. Since I don't have any abdominal musculature, lifting puts a lot of strain on my back, and it already hurt from riding so many hours, day after day. This led to talking more generally about the challenges people with hidden disabilities face and how the general public isn't aware something might be going on if, for example, the person isn't in a wheelchair, using a walker, or wearing a giant sandwich board which says, "I HAVE A DISABILITY!"

It's hard for me to discuss my own hidden disabilities without touching on my time in and after the Intensive Care Unit. The group shared a story about someone close to them who'd also been in the ICU and faced similar challenges afterward. We had a lengthy, engaging conversation—nothing like the animosity I had been warned about. Later, they offered to put my saddlebags on my bike.

Not one to turn down much-needed help, I took them up on their offer. They waited for me to fetch my other saddlebag from my hotel room and kindly put the saddlebags on. We said our goodbyes. I stopped back into the hotel's breakfast area to slam a glass of apple juice and a banana. Then I was ready to hit the road.

As I stepped into the lobby on my way out to my scooter, all five of the Harley riders walked toward me with this serious air of determination. I thought to myself, *My God, what have I done?* They encircled me, and the biggest of the men stepped squarely in front of me.

He paused and opened his huge hand, revealing a tiny, black velvet pouch.

"You see," he confided, "you may not know this, but evil spirits are known to chase motorcycles."

He took the pouch between his giant fingers and emptied it into his open hand. Out tumbled a miniature silver bell. I looked up at all of them.

I held my breath, and tried to not cry. I was stunned to be considered a big-girl motorcycle-rider, despite the fact that I know I'm just a little MP3 scooter chick. I looked into their faces determined to meet their gazes.

"With this, the evil spirits get caught in the bell. They spin around and fall to the ground, and make a pothole," he explained. "It works better if someone *gives* you the bell, so we want you to have this. We want you to be safe."

Somehow, I managed to keep the tears inside my eyes. I held my heart with my right hand and carefully took the bell with my left.

"I don't even know your names," I said, astonished by their generosity. "Does one of you have a card?" I couldn't imagine leaving this experience behind, not being able to acknowledge them or ever thank them more formally later.

"We aren't business people," said one of the others.

"Well, at least tell me where you are from," I asked.

"Beaver Dam, about forty miles north of Milwaukee," said another.

I felt like a character in a fantasy novel, being given a magical object from the High King and his Wise Advisors.

And then they disappeared, and I was left to continue my way.

*

Good fortune was with me throughout, because there was a series of mishaps from which I emerged unscathed. The first came when I was supposed to take a short jog from Cheboygan to the Mackinac Bridge and then on to Sault Ste. Marie. What I thought should have been a half-hour or maybe a forty-five minute ride to the bridge stretched out into several hours. My instincts told me something was wrong, but I had this ingrained training from my flying days to "trust your instruments," and the nav indicated to continue. Then I got a call from Jeff Kott. He explained he knew from my tweet I was supposed to be headed north to the bridge, but he had been watching my geo-tracking progress on the web site, and I was now close to 40 miles *south* of where I started.

It turned out, unbeknownst to me, there was a Sault Saint Marie, Michigan *and* a Sault Sainte-Marie, Canada (both of which are abbreviated "Sault Ste. Marie"). I had inadvertently programmed the Canadian destination. So, the nav established a route to Canada that ran South toward Detroit and then back North. I was so grateful for Jeff's call. I don't know how much farther I would have gone without it.

Another one of challenges had happened before I even left. I originally planned to camp for a third of the stops. But two days prior to departure, we realized the volume of the tent and camping gear would mean leaving behind too many critical things, so the plan and itinerary needed to change. The biggest impact of this decision was where to stay at the Oshkosh, Wisconsin AirVenture event which 800,000 people were attending. This close to the event there were no hotels available. I would have to find a person renting out space.

I called a woman who had llamas. My intuition was this llama farmer wasn't married to an ax murderer and didn't have a rapist cousin who stopped over for visits. But her space was filled. She suggested a neighbor woman who turned out to be one half of a lesbian couple. During my stay, I didn't say anything about my work with *We Vow* or being bi. So, I was surprised my last night when, before I left, one of them shared that they'd Googled me, knew about the project, and were tickled to have hosted me. It was pretty sweet as I was equally enchanted to have stayed with them.

Trying to get from Iron Mountain down to Oshkosh turned out to be the most maddening. There were many miles of construction on Southbound US-141. Repeatedly, I would leave it for ten miles or so and come back, assuming I would have passed the construction, only to discover I hadn't. The farm roads in this area weren't square, and I repeatedly went miles and miles out of my way in incredible heat only to wend my way to 141 and still not be able to get back on it.

Finally, I pulled over to call a friend to ask him to get on the internet and suss out the problem. In the few minutes it took for me to explain my situation, I lost the benefit of the wind to offset the extreme heat. Suddenly I was dripping with sweat. Then, a young surfer-looking kid in an old sedan pulled over and asked if I was in trouble. He drew involved, but clear directions for me. He explained I would travel on several different backroads, rights and lefts, back and around, and eventually I would have to drive for one block—one way, the *wrong* way—through the construction. Then I would find this little town a few blocks long, and from there I would be able to get back on 141. I was reticent about his plan, but he was right. There was a line of cars driving through the construction, through the town, and onto the highway, just as he described. I was saved yet again.

There were little troubles, too. My trunk broke, and I repeatedly had to get it fixed. One of my pairs of riding jeans split. I dropped Michi at a sharp turn on a steep downward incline, and it was over an hour before I saw anyone who could help me get her upright again. In the end, though, someone always showed up to help.

*

Before leaving on the trip I joined an online scooter forum to collect information. Another member, Maggie Madonia, contacted me. As the head of the Saint Louis Scooter Club, she told me how excited they were about my endeavor and offered their support, resources, including parts for my bike, whatever I needed. Maggie also strongly encouraged me to make St. Louis part of my journey. She was enthusiastic and wanted to take me on a special ride, one of her club's favorite routes. She described it as a "little twisty ride" on the Mark Twain Trail, from St. Louis to an old-fashioned general store in Bixby. This was outside my original itinerary, but she charmed me, and I was grateful for the generosity her club extended. She explained the ride would probably be a little more challenging than what I was used to, but assured me they would take it at my pace and we would all have a great time. I was in. Maggie and another member, Pete, would meet me about ten miles outside St. Louis, and we would ride into town together. The next day I would meet the club at Maplewood Scooter Shop, and the following day we would all ride to Bixby.

This meant I needed to learn to ride with a group. Other than my initial training classes with Michigan's Safest Riders, I always rode alone. I hoped I would have an opportunity to ride with a club prior to the tour, but the scooter modifications to hold luggage took longer than planned, and Michi wasn't ready until about a week before my scheduled departure.

Dan Cone, a motorcyclist who knew the riders of the Saint Louis club, offered to meet me in Madison, Wisconsin a few days before my first meeting with Maggie and Pete, then ride down to Milwaukee with me. I was grateful to Dan, as I saw this as preparation for riding with others, but I was also excited and scared. I'd done plenty of reading about the rules, etiquette, and safety of riding with others, but I was fully cognizant that skill and comfort would only come from experience.

When Dan pulled up on his 1984 Honda CB650 Nighthawk wearing a fitted red and black leather motorcycle jacket, I thought, *He must be a tough-guy motorcycle racer-dude.* After he took off his helmet, however, he immediately reached out and gave me a big, warm hug! I anticipated during my ride with Dan that he, as the more experienced rider, would lead. But he said he would follow *me*. He wanted me to set the pace and make all the decisions. "This is your ride. I'm tagging along."

I was terrified! I explained my concerns and he assured me, "We get to decide the rules. No worries."

Oh my God, he is going to be watching me ride, EVALUATING me!

We started off on back roads, and after about twenty miles he pulled up next to me at a stop and said, "Don't signal so far in advance. It makes me think you're going to turn before you're actually going to."

I knew this. I hadn't signaled that way before. Now that I was riding with him, I was behaving all weird. I had a reason, but it didn't make any sense.

There wasn't time or a way for me to explain my behavior. I needed to cut it out. I was also aware that I was having a hard time maintaining a constant speed. I was doing a worse job than usual.

When we stopped for fuel, I got up the courage to ask him how I was doing.

"You need to be careful about putting your foot down too soon at stops. It's called dragging, and you can get hurt."

I had learned about this in my safety course. I knew better. I didn't know if I developed this habit on the tour or if it was another aberration which manifested because I was being observed, but I needed to stop that too.

"Other than that you're doing pretty well." I didn't know if he was saying this to be kind or if I was doing okay. I was clearly freaked out riding with him, but I didn't know what I could do to get a grip.

Just as I was putting my helmet on to get back on the road, Dan yelled, "Wait!"

I froze. He walked over to me and said, "I've never seen anyone wear goggles! I have to get a shot of that!"

I felt silly, but I let him take a picture. I wanted to explain I couldn't find any sunglasses small enough to fit my head and inside my helmet, but I knew he didn't care. I hated their overly dramatic, "I'm from the '20's" look, but I had come to like how I could use them as a headband to keep my hair out of my face at the end of the day.

Once we hit Wauwatosa, a suburb of Milwaukee, Dan pulled up next to me at a light and asked, "Do you eat burgers?"

"That's what I was dreaming about for lunch!"

"Then I know the perfect place. Okay, now you follow me."

He carefully guided me through downtown traffic, past an industrial area, through a residential area, and into a small downtown to the DayMaker Cafe. This would be my first meal with a biker. It might have seemed ordinary to him, but I had no idea what this would be like. I feared it would be more of the makes and models of various bikes and scooters like all the other casual conversations I had with other bikers. Having only completed about 1200 miles of my journey on the same scooter, I wasn't any wiser to the gear talk. I feared this would be an awkward conversation.

The inside of the place didn't look particularly special, a diner-style burger joint, but the menu was impressive. This was a *gourmet* burger joint, and I had a hard time choosing what to eat. It was a welcome problem, a relief from the roadside diners and truck stops I had frequented thus far.

After we placed our orders, I asked Dan what he did for a living. He was an art director! He does the same thing I had when I created *Tala & Louison* and *We Vow*, except he does it every day for advertising companies. We immediately had a common language, and it was thrilling to talk about the challenges of having a vision and then translating the idea into form, while wrestling with the limits of human capacity, budget, and time. All of these realities throw wrenches into the process. We were both amused to have discovered this about each other and to have the opportunity for such an engaging conversation. It was another serendipitous happening.

I explained to him how nervous I was about riding with the group from St. Louis to Bixby. "When I left on the tour, I still wasn't even comfortable riding faster than 45 miles an hour, but I managed to get comfortable at 55 within about a week."

I wasn't sure that my progress, during what amounted to half of the 3,400 miles, was enough to prepare me for the ride with the club.

I didn't tell him about the voice in my head which started out screaming, "You're gonna wipe out! You're gonna wipe out! DON'T WIPE OUT! DON'T WIPE OUT!" And that I had finally managed her with a mantra, "I'm being held by the light."

He assured me I would be fine, that I was in good hands with Maggie and Pete. He reiterated that I was riding solidly and I was ready to handle the ride with the club.

After lunch, Dan rode with me to my hotel in downtown Milwaukee.

As we parted, Dan gave me a hug and said, "Maggie and Pete will take good care of you. It's gonna be a really fun ride. Take care!"

*

I needed to get some sleep. Tomorrow was the big day. Despite Dan's encouraging words telling me I was ready, I wouldn't know for sure until I'd done it.

Devon and I had discussed the possibility of my parlaying this adventure into a documentary once I returned home. We figured that my meet up with the Saint Louis Scooter Club was likely to be the most visually interesting event in my tour, and we made plans to video part of the ride. I created a production crew that included my favorites. I asked Devon to produce, and Brian Eaves would head up the video team. Brian recommended a couple of assistants: Damien Thompson and a woman known as Flynn, who was perfect for this because she was not only a professional photographer but a lifetime motorcycle rider. She would be able to ride a second scooter and wear a video camera for an action point of view.

The plan was to meet with Devon and crew about twenty miles north of the rendezvous point with Maggie and Pete. The meeting place turned out to be a gorgeous little park with a pond. When Devon arrived we hugged each other like a military spouse and a sailor who had been out to sea for a couple of years. Perhaps we were being rude, as our embrace carried on a bit long in front of the crew, but I couldn't let go until I felt I had enough of a dose of home, friendship, a piece of balance restored. There was so much I could say to Devon by just looking at him without speaking. He once said he thought there were two kinds of friends: ones with kinship and ones with history. But when one has a friendship with both kinship and history, there is nothing like it. At this point, we had 32 years of both.

"I can't believe how hot it is," Devon said as he wiped the sweat off his forehead. "I'm dying, and I've only been standing out here a few minutes."

"Yeah, the entire summer has been high temps like this, my friend. Imagine this stupid heat, and then in these double-layered jeans, boots with two pairs of socks, and a long-sleeved armored jacket, gloves and a helmet."

"Yeah, you're nuts, that's all there is to it. I seriously don't get how you didn't pass out by the side of the road. You're seriously crazy. I would've turned around after the first day and said, 'Forget this shit. It's too damn hot.'"

"Well, there is a little relief when I'm moving on the bike, but it has been rough."

Our excitement from seeing one another quickly shifted to the task at hand. We only had about an hour and a half before we were to meet Maggie and Pete, and we had to make sure all systems were go. Devon introduced me to Damien and Flynn, and we got to work.

Before long, it was time to take off to meet Maggie and Pete. As Devon and his crew climbed into my air conditioned Chevy Tahoe, I was supposed to get back on my scooter again, by myself. This time, I didn't want to get on Michi. I was hit with deep pangs of loneliness.

But I got on and began to lead the way. Now I truly was being watched because there was a camera. I needed to focus. In another 20 miles I would be riding with additional bikes.

Maggie and Pete met me outside of St. Louis at Silver Lake Park in Highland, Illinois. From there they would guide me to my hotel. Their scooters looked intense: Maggie rode a Suzuki Burgman 650, and Pete was on a motorcycle cross-over, the DN-01 HFT (short for "human-friendly transmission"). His bike could be automatic, like most scooters, or shifted like a motorcycle—the first of its kind with that design. Maggie stood firm with few words. She had command of her bike and the world around her, yet there was a Mama Bear quality to her as well. I knew immediately I would be protected under her care. The warmth Pete showed made him a perfect counterpart to Maggie.

We were on freeways for a short stretch. I had only ridden briefly on the freeways around Minneapolis, and I was still terrified of them, but now I felt protected like the President in a motorcade. Maggie was ahead of me and Pete behind. She traveled the speed limit, so I didn't feel pressured in this new environment. But when she signaled, indicating we would be changing lanes, I felt my heart leap.

Oh my God, am I ready for this?

When I looked back to see if it was clear, Pete had already moved over and held the space for me. I felt an overwhelming sense of relief and of being tenderly nestled in a pocket between them. I still had to control my scooter, but they created a zone of safety around me. It was an amazing feeling—finally, I had the training wheels I'd wished for at the start of my journey.

We crossed over the Eads Bridge, and I could see the St. Louis Arch to my left. The dusk light glistened a brilliant orange on the metal. It seemed enormous in real life. It was so much larger than I had imagined from postcards and pictures in books. My grandmother had taken an incredible photograph of an airplane flying through it at an air show. I hadn't imagined that was possible, but from this vantage point, I could envision it. An airplane could fly through it.

We continued to the hotel where we made plans to meet up with the gang the next day at Maplewood Scooter Shop. For the big trek, the day afterward, there would be about a dozen riders, a mix of motorcycles and scooters. We would leave from my hotel and ride across town to the Sandy Creek Covered Bridge which should take about 30 minutes. From Sandy Creek to the Potosi BP station was about an hour, then from Potosi to Bixby was about 90 more minutes.

That didn't sound like a big deal. That was a light day for me.

Surprisingly, the night before our trek to Bixby, I got a decent night's sleep. I rose early, since I needed to fuel up before everyone arrived. As this was the first day on my journey that I would be riding without all my gear, I was concerned how it would impact my sense of balance, even though it might be less fatiguing. So, I took advantage of the time to acclimate myself as much as possible, even if only for a few miles.

It turned out the Saint Louis Scooter Club is actually misnamed. Motorcycles and scooters of all different styles, kinds, and sizes began to show up. The scooter gang was a collection of characters, women and men. They were a mix of ages, a few people in their twenties and a couple in their fifties, all friendly faces. Although, one guy looked intimidating despite the smile on his face. He was introduced to me as Freak. He was a beefy-looking guy and clearly spent a considerable amount of time in a gym. He had a serious tattoo on his arm, his head was bald, and he had a Van Dyke. He wore a sleeveless Harley shirt and, of course, he rode one. Throughout my experience on the road, the Harley guys had been nothing but generous and helpful, but I wanted to do my best to not screw up this guy's day.

Everyone formed a semicircle and Maggie gave a short safety speech. I wondered if she did this every time or only when a new rider rode with them. Someone teased Maggie about not wearing shorts like she usually did.

"If I'm gonna end up on the Discovery Channel, I don't want to be seen wearing shorts while riding!" she said with a big grin.

I told Maggie I wanted to explain my limitations to the group.

"First, I want to thank you guys for being willing to ride with me. As you know, I'm a rookie rider. I only had about a thousand miles under my belt before I left, and another nineteen hundred on this tour. At this point, I've ridden completely alone with the exception of Madison to Milwaukee, which I did with Dan Cone.

"I have a physical limitation in that I don't have an abdominal structure, so I'm more susceptible to wind gusts pushing me around. As a result, I don't feel comfortable riding on the inside position. Now I know usually, when riding with a group, one needs to be comfortable enough to alternate from inside to outside depending on where one is in the line, but I need to hold the outside position regardless of where I am at any point."

"So, feel free to give me feedback, as I know I have a lot to learn. Again, thanks a lot. I'm grateful for this opportunity.

"I guess I'm ready to go."

I tried to speak with a degree of confidence or authority as I told them about my concerns, but I was aware that I had my legs crossed as I stood there, which sent the message, *Hey, don't listen to my voice. It's lying to you. I'm scared, and I'm pretty sure I have no idea what the hell I'm doing.*

Maggie let me know I would again ride between Pete and her. I was relieved I would get the motorcade treatment I received the previous day. We headed out. My nerves weren't too bad. There wasn't much traffic, and somehow it was comforting that the highway seemed to lay in a huge gulch between two large mountains. We rode out of town at the speed limit, 55 mph, and it wasn't too different from the back roads. With Maggie parting the seas and making all the decisions, and Pete at my back, I felt comfortable and coddled. I was held in a zone of safety, followed by the rest of the gang.

After the highway, we went a few miles on a back road and made a few turns. Without warning, the road became a roller coaster with no tracks. We were climbing a curve. It wasn't straight up, but an incline for sure. I was on the scooter, not a comfortable bench on a roller coaster with sides and a seat belt. It was me and my exposed body. To my right there were a few inches of gravel and then a drop off with a depth I didn't have time to evaluate. We went up and up, and before I could even process the grade, we made a sharp turn.

I don't have time to slow down, I have to drop into this turn NOW!

Then I was headed back up, then another sharp turn. We were in a constantly-climbing S-curve.

Once, thirteen years before, Michael's father let me drive his Mustang Cobra on the hilly and winding roads in Tennessee, but that was in a car. When I first considered riding through France, I wondered if I would be able to ride part of the French Alps if I practiced beforehand. I talked to a fellow who gave motorcycle tours of the Alps, and he explained I would have to learn how to make repeated 90-degree turns for about eight hours a day. I would've wanted to practice in a parking lot first, to learn to make these turns on the flat. But I was in it now, without the practice. I had to act.

Maggie was one curve ahead of me, like a pace car, although she managed to follow my lead and held steady at my speed. I couldn't look at my speedometer, but I knew from the miles I had already traveled we were doing about 30 mph. Any slower and I wouldn't have the momentum to stay upright. Any faster and I wouldn't be able to control the bike. I had to stay at this optimum speed, yet drop down just a bit as I moved into the turns so I could accelerate out of the turn. The margins were tight.

Although I knew my speed only fluctuated between 30 and 35 mph, it felt like I took those turns at 78 mph. It wasn't like the movies. There was no slow motion, no soundtrack, no montage, only the ever-crisp visual of the environment. A version of tunnel vision: Maggie, the road, Michi, and me. I could hear the bits of gravel on the pavement and the engine, and I could feel my body as it dipped and bobbed in and out of each turn, but there was no room for my mind to wander, no room for error.

When we first discussed this ride, Maggie had said, "This is going to be more elevation than you are used to." I know a fair piece about geography, so I was the guilty one there for not connecting the dots. I thought about the St. Louis area as a little higher altitude, maybe I needed to work harder because of a subtle oxygen ratio shift. She said, "There will be twists and turns, but we'll take it at your pace, and you'll be fine." I had ridden some turns back home on the hills in Berrien County. I had even called my brother Dan, who at one time had a hard-core crotch-rocket, and asked him where I could find the more hilly terrain. It was fun. I wanted more of that. What I hadn't grasped was the *degree* of the turns and that they would keep coming. I pictured riding for ten minutes or so, a few turns, then riding for another ten minutes or so before a few more turns—not TURNS, ENDLESS TURNS! By the sixth or seventh one I was feeling the stress and had to buck up. I had to get in the swing of it.

Before then, my fear was that my scooter and I might hit the ground. Hitting the ground should seem like no big deal, like when we rode horses in the summer as kids. We did all kinds of hijinks, like trying to ride standing up, or hooking our feet onto the top of the saddle and hanging off the side. These unsupervised and untrained stunts usually dropped our bodies in the dirt and knocked the wind out of us. We weren't wearing helmets or jackets with backplates and elbow pads. We landed, paused for a second to assess for broken bones, and got back up to do it again.

I knew what it was like to hit the ground at 35 miles an hour. The scooter accident I had the year before was at that fateful speed. I got out of it with a temporarily wonky knee and a fractured sternum which still hurts every time the cat decides to rest on my chest.

If I hit the ground now, it would only be the beginning. If I fell off the bike here I wouldn't be on the road, I would be over the cliff. The real deal would be the cliff. This new terror changed my perspective about impact. My speed would only determine how hard I would hit the first tree. Afterward, I would be wrapped around the next tree on my way down or broken again and again by multiple trees until my body no longer had any more momentum. Only a second to consider that vision—my body playing pinball on the trees, then hanging limply on a limb of an evergreen, with Michi mangled and strewn into bits off in the distance—and then came the next corner. No more time for imagining. I had to stay to task. I didn't even have time for the expression that allowed me to create a moving meditation. No time for "I am held by the light," not even time to get a message from my head to my lips. Only time to scream a single word in my mind: *Liiiiiiiiiiight!*

The roller coaster changed its incline from up to DOWN. I pulled my left hand closed on the back brake with all the force I could gather, but it was not enough. My brother John, a motocross rider, and I discussed this before I left. We made a rule, because a scooter like mine can lock up if the front brake is applied, causing the bike to tumble back over front. There would be NO FRONT BRAKE! NONE. I called out to my brother John in my mind: *I know what we agreed John, but I don't have a choice. I'm gonna launch this thing if I don't do something now! I'm gonna go easy!*

I squeezed both, gently at first and then harder.

The brakes didn't lock up.

Oh my God, I MADE IT!

So, it was possible—clearly, in this instance, necessary—to use both brakes. The key was to go easy at first and then increase pressure. It felt like a miracle. I couldn't understand how I made that turn, but before I could process what happened I made three more. I was braking and leaning, braking and leaning, holding a constant rhythm and pace. Maggie remained a single curve ahead, pace car distance, and held the space between us. I used this as a focal point, a guide, while my heart raced.

This mere half-hour exercise felt like a half-marathon. It ended at Sandy Creek Covered Bridge. Maggie drove into the adjacent parking lot and stopped. I pulled up a couple of spots over and Devon, in my Tahoe, parked next to me. I was so relieved to see him, but with everyone around I didn't feel like I could tell him, *"Holy hell, I was completely freaked out!"* I looked at him with wide eyes.

He asked, "You okay?" I gave him a look, a combination of *Sure!* and *Absolutely not!* I could tell he was worried.

I tried to act normally, but felt like a freshman at a high school dance, almost an out-of-body experience watching and listening to myself from behind me. Everything had a hollow sound, as if I was listening through a very long tube. People were standing around in groups of two or three, catching up on life and talking about the ride. I made a comment here and there, but I felt like a robot, smiling and talking on autopilot. Then, Maggie mentioned this was the wind-up.

"Now we're getting ready to do the real ride. The next section will be more challenging."

What?! I'm already at the edge of my ability! I don't know how I can handle anything else.

I tried to figure out what my options were. I felt like the bride who realized the day of the wedding she had made a mistake. Once everyone is there for the ceremony, it seems much easier to go through with it and get a divorce afterward. But this wasn't a walk down the aisle with "I do" at the end. This was a situation where if I'm in over my head, I'm going to end up dead.

Maggie interrupted my introspection to say, "We need to get a picture of everyone by the covered bridge." As we posed for the picture, my mind was still racing.

Should I bail? Or should I try the next leg and then decide about the last section?

After the group shot, Devon said, "Hold on a sec," and gestured to Freak. "Would you mind repeating what you said to me, but to Ara? On camera?"

Devon was going to put me on the spot, but then I remembered Devon was on my team. He wouldn't do this unless it was positive, right?

Freak said, "Sure." He looked at me and waited.

My heart was pounding. *What is this guy gonna say about me? Oh God!*

"I've ridden with a lot of newbies," he began, "and you are, by far, the best I've ever ridden with, as far as *riding your own ride* and taking your time in the turns. You're doing the right stuff. I watched you through all those turns. You handled yourself marvelously. I've taught a lot of people how to ride and by far, you are number one." He had a warm grin on his face as he pointed his finger at me. "Keep riding the way you're riding, and you'll become a professional."

I shook my head in surprise. "Wow, that means a lot to me."

He made my decision for me. If he, the experienced Harley dude, had that much confidence in me, I should at least give the next leg a shot. I figured I would get back in the groove, maintain focus, and continue holding the light.

Maggie was right —the next leg was harder. The turns were tighter, the grade steeper, and it seemed the inclines varied every couple of turns. I pressed my own edge, kept my eye on Maggie, and managed to follow the rhythm on the outer boundary of where Michi, the mountain, and I could keep it together. Then, as I came out of a turn, I realized I had miscalculated. The turn wasn't over. In less than an instant, my body and mind remembered what I was taught: "Look to the point you need to go, and lean to that point. If you are still in trouble, LEAN HARDER!" I dropped down as hard and fast as I could. I skidded into the gravel and slid toward the edge. For a moment I was sure I was going off, but I made the corner, and I brought myself up at the last moment. I had a glimpse of the side of the hill as I brought the bike up, the scattered trees and rocks, terrain Michi and I came within a blink of tumbling through. My body and the scooter made subsequent turns in an automatic rhythm, but my mind and heart were buzzing. I had almost lost it.

About twenty minutes later we were on flat ground in an intersection. There was some discussion between Maggie and Pete about Devon having missed a turn. They gave him directions by phone. He would catch up at the next stop. Pete pulled up beside me, so I lifted my visor and said, "I'm sorry about that back there."

"It's okay. You gave me a good scare, but you did the right thing. It's a tricky turn. It's one of those that has a double apex, so you come up and then you need to go back down again. You did the right thing, you just realized it a bit late."

We were almost to the next stop, the last stop before the part of the trip that would take us to Bixby, where we could pick up the remainder of the riders. Maggie explained this last stretch would be the most difficult. As I walked to the fuel station to use the restroom, Devon put his arm around me. We didn't say anything. In our normal lives I would have gone around the back of the building and started sobbing, but I had to keep my head in the game. We just looked at each other and smiled. If I didn't say anything at all he understood I was in rough shape.

The riders were talking amongst themselves. I heard a couple of them joking about things they had seen along the way, how they had never noticed this one particular farm had horses, or how a house had a flower garden, because they had never driven this route so slowly. I'm sure I spoke to the others, but I have no idea what I might have said. There was a white split rail fence along the edge of the fuel station property. The fence brought a reminder of home and of horses, of childhood, but none of those comforts. I leaned up against it, but I didn't jump up on it like I would have done before I lacked an abdomen. I listened to the riders' chatter. In my state, it sounded more like the adults in the Peanuts cartoons.

The last leg was harder still. I was fatigued. I had to force myself to concentrate on Maggie like a torpedo moving toward its target. I had to keep my body and my mind moving as fast as Michi's engine. I had to maintain control. More curves and alternating inclines.

I felt a sharp, stabbing pain in the upper area of my left hip. I couldn't respond to it. Then it stabbed again, and again. I couldn't stop the bike. There was no place to pull over, no means for me to communicate with Maggie or Pete. I had to continue riding. I knew from experience the pain was one of two things. Either my abdominal flap had herniated, had torn somewhere, which would require another six-month preparation of my body and another twelve-plus-hour surgery if it could even be done, or it was scar tissue breaking up, which was no big deal. It caused flashes of light to cross my vision. I had to ignore them. I had to keep going, keep holding on.

Reconstruction

I'd felt pain like this before, but never to this degree. The first time we had a good scare was about a year after Petrosian had done the reconstruction. We were in the ER when we were informed that he was out of the country. The entire reconstructive surgery department stopped what they were doing and came down to try to read my MRI. They had him on speaker phone, but they still couldn't do it. It was too complicated. Only Dr. Petrosian could make sense of the Frankenstein reconfiguration of mesh, latissimus muscle, wire, and hip-bone which now passes for my abdomen. That trip to the ER and all the others wound up being false alarms, only scar tissue flexing. But the reality I faced in my daily life, and certainly this scooter ride, put me at risk of injury. Maybe I'd finally done it. If I was immobile tomorrow then I'd made a mess of it. If not, it was scar tissue. I wouldn't know until then.

The pain had to become part of the rhythm, an intermittent, unpredictable element of the environment, like rocks hitting my visor. Because the stabbing pains were sharp and random, it was hard to hold my focus on Maggie. I tried to merge my body into the bike—to ride with Michi, ride the corners, ride the pain. But the concentration to hold it all made me weaker. I felt as if there was slack in my sail, and I couldn't catch the wind I needed to fill it.

We rode on. I had no idea how much longer the ride was, or if I would make it to the end. When I rode my typical 150 miles, this was the point I would bellow songs to rally, but I couldn't possibly sing. I began to feel numbness in my hands and arms, and I feared soon my hands would refuse to respond to my commands to brake.

After my body was running on nothing but spirit for the longest fifteen minutes of my life, I saw the general store with an old fuel pump out front. This was the reason for riding to Bixby. We were there. Maggie had explained how the current owners, Bridget and her husband, had emigrated here and purchased this old-fashioned store with a model train which runs along the ceiling. With the exception of adding modern refrigeration for beverages and ice cream, the store had remained unchanged since it opened more than a hundred years ago.

I pulled in and came to a stop. The next thing I saw was Maggie approaching me with her own video camera. "I'm rolling," she said.

What can I say, on camera? Quick, think of something.

"I'm alive," I said, and prayed she wouldn't ask for anything more. Luckily, she shut the camera off. "So, Maggie, is that what one would call a technical ride?" I asked, not wanting to be presumptuous. In my mind, the only technical rides in the US were in California and one portion of Appalachia in Kentucky, but it sure as hell seemed what I just endured had to be a technical ride.[*]

---

[*] "Technical terrain" or a "technical trail" is a region considered to require extensive concentration and experienced technique in order to cross, whether climbing, hiking, biking, etc., where travel is usually difficult or dangerous and may require the use of special equipment.

"Well, yeah. It isn't the most difficult pass in the Ozarks. There are two others which are more difficult."

The OZARKS? Wait a minute! I thought we were doing this "little twisty ride" on the Mark Twain Trail. "Twisty" sounds like a soft-serve ice cream! Besides, the Mark Twain Trail sounds like a leisurely hiking path!

She goes on to tell me, "Yeah, if you take a fall in there, the only way out is by chopper. Several guys have died on the pass we were on, but they were going considerably faster than we were riding today. Bobby," she said, and indicated one of the younger club members, "went off at the spot where your guys were filming."

Thank God I didn't hear any of this before the ride.

People gathered and began to go inside. I gave Devon a wide-eyed look and a tip of my head, so he hung back. As soon as everyone was inside, we walked to the side of the building and I explained, "I don't want anyone to know. I don't want anyone to feel bad, it might turn out to be nothing, but I have severe pain in my upper left hip. I either ripped out my surgery or it is torn scar tissue. I won't know until tomorrow, so I'm gonna try to pretend like nothing is happening. But I'm gonna need Flynn to take the scooter to the hotel even though it is only fifteen miles from here. When everyone is leaving, we will hang back. I will act like I need to get stuff out of the Tahoe or put stuff in. I'll make it work. I'll make something up."

"Of course. My God, Ara that is so scary. I hope you're okay. Do we need to call anyone?"

"No. I've been through this before, just never this intense. I have to wait it out. If I'm in this much pain tomorrow, I'll know I'm in trouble."

We went inside and joined the gang. I had a bit of a sandwich and chatted with the group and a few tourists who were curious about my scooter. As we were getting ready to leave, Bridget, the owner of the General Store, pulled me aside. She had heard about my adventure and was very excited to meet me. She opened a change purse and pulled out tiny sacred objects she had brought with her when she moved to the United States eight years before. She rapidly explained the meaning of each one as she handed them to me and told me she wanted me to have them.

Devon recognized the significance of the moment. There was no time to get the crew and the camera, so he scrambled to get his phone out of his pocket to record the moment. Meanwhile, I was freaking out. We had just met and she was giving me her sacred possessions, like a tiny picture of a saint with a crocheted edge one of her aunts gave her when she left for the States. Even then I knew I wasn't getting all of the stories and felt bad, like I should write all this down. Then here comes a tiny little pig, and another object, and I started to cry. I couldn't believe the magnitude of the gesture, and she was beaming with this huge gigantic smile while she gave me her things.

I told her, "I have a special place in my bike where I will put them. I know they will help to keep me safe. I am so grateful. There is no way I can express what this means to me."

Then came the goodbye photos. I only spent a few days with these people, but I could hardly believe it was over. I was going to do the rest of the ride solo. I stood with Devon and the video crew and said farewell to the Saint Louis Scooter Club. Then, we watched them all ride off.

After a moment, Devon said, "Well, now what?"

Fortunately, my schedule for the next day or so was fairly open. We drove my Tahoe to dinner, then goofed around and chatted for the remainder of the evening in an effort to distract me from the shooting pains in my hip. That night, we went to our respective rooms at a chain hotel the next town over.

I slept hard.

*

The next morning, the shooting pain was still there, but it was less frequent and somewhat less intense, so I decided I was likely in the clear.

Devon had insisted that I call him first thing to give him a status report.

"Glad to hear you're, well, 'okay' isn't really the word, but..."

"Yeah."

"So, what are you going to do?"

"I'm not sure."

Although he acted nonchalant, I suspect Devon knew something was amiss. Being unsure about plans of most any kind was not like me. As soon as we hung up, he came over to my room.

For my next stop, I had originally planned to visit the Laura Ingalls Wilder museum in Iowa, then head east, back under the Ozarks to Toledo, where I would stay with my friends Harry and Carrie. Carrie had begun chemotherapy treatment while I was on the tour, and I wanted to see how she was doing.

At this point I was over being on the road. With only ten days left, I wanted to finish the tour. I figured I could bail on the Laura Ingalls stop, which would have taken me westward and further away from home. If I could get to Toledo sooner, I could hang out there for a few days, get a sense of things, then head home. The only real obstacle between Toledo and me were the Ozarks.

So, I eliminated heading west. That meant I had to decide among three routes to get east, and each presented a problem. The southern route around the mountains was the easiest, but also the slowest, so it would add two or three days to my travel time. The northern route toward St. Louis would be shorter, but would mean taking the highway without Maggie and Pete to babysit me. The fastest and shortest course was directly east.

Through the Ozarks.

That would mean more "twisties."

I rang Maggie to check. The news was mixed. While there would be more twists and turns, she was confident I could handle them, if I wasn't too tired. It was true, I was tired, but I don't think she realized how tired—or how far beyond my comfort zone I'd been the first time.

When I hung up with Maggie, Devon left to grab us some breakfast from the lobby. I spread out the map on the bed to figure out what my options were. When he returned, before he was even through the door, Devon said, "What do you want to do?"

"I don't know. The choices all suck. I'm pretty sure I can't do the mountains. Even if I don't tear up my abdomen, the problem is my hands and arms are so fatigued from the braking, I worry they'll give out a half hour in. Then I'd need to be choppered out. I don't want to be that guy."

"Would you want to stay here at the hotel, recover for a couple days and then try it?"

"No. At this point, I'm agitated. I wouldn't be able to rest. I have to get out of here and get on the road. I want to get to Carrie. I guess this means I want the shorter route. If I braved the freeways and drove up to St. Louis, what would be the nearest town outside the city with a hotel?"

"What about Mount Vernon? It's in southern Illinois. Do you think you could get that far?"

I considered the map. It meant riding the freeway, alone.

Worse, if I couldn't do it, I'd be kind of screwed. There didn't appear to be anything on the map between St. Louis and Mt. Vernon.

But it was flat, and it wasn't supposed to rain. So I figured if I could make it outside St. Louis, and the freeways didn't kill me, that last bit would be the easiest part.

If I was going to navigate expressways in and around a major city, I needed a local's perspective. No map or GPS can tell you which exits to avoid and which exits to take, whether to go through the city or around it. Years in Chicago had taught me that. So, I rang Maggie again. As she gave me the scoop, I wrote the directions down on index cards.

"So what's the plan?" Devon asked once I said goodbye to Maggie again.

"Yeah, I'm gonna go for it. But this is what I need from you guys. While you're on your way back to Chicago, I need you to find a bodyworker willing to meet me at the hotel to give me a massage. I don't know how you're gonna find a person that won't think I want something creepy, but do whatever you need to do, and I will pay whatever they ask."

"Done!"

While I was packing, I gave some of my gear to Devon to take back in the Tahoe. Ideally, I only had a couple more stops at this point, so I figured I didn't need to carry everything I'd needed at the beginning of my adventure.

When we went outside, Brian and Flynn had already loaded all of their equipment in the truck. Brian stepped up and offered to help secure my gear to Michi. I wasn't about to turn down help at that point.

"All set?" he asked.

"Yeah," I replied uncertainly while I stared at the directions Maggie had given me.

"What're those?"

"My directions. I thought maybe I could put them in my pocket and pull them out as I needed them, or I could memorize them or something, but the more I think about it, the more I think it's too complicated to deal with these cards. I might just abandon them and use my nav after all."

"Wait wait," he said, and carefully took the cards from me. He sprinted back to the Tahoe and dug a roll of duct tape out of his bag. "Never leave home without it!" he said, holding the roll aloft.

One by one, Brian taped the cards to the center of Michi's steering column. Once he started working I immediately figured it out. I could check the directions without taking my hands of the grips. Then, when I was finished with the directions on the top card, I could tear it off to reveal the next card, and so on.

"You're awesome!" I said, once he was finished.

"It's what I do," he smiled.

It seemed as though everything had been sorted out, except I still would have to teach myself how to ride on the freeway. So, we bid our farewells and headed off.

I started out cautiously in the slow lane for the first twenty miles, to get used to the speed and the feel of the faster cars passing me. Then I began practicing. I started with small cars when there was a lot of space to maneuver and worked my way up until I could pass a single semi-trailer truck. By the time I hit St. Louis, I was comfortable passing semi-trucks as long as I wasn't on an incline. I still experienced intermittent, stabbing pain in my hip, but it was nothing like it had been on the "twisties," and I made it to Mount Vernon.

After a massage and a good night's sleep, I was ready to head the rest of the way to Toledo. If I could manage a double-mileage day, I could get there by nightfall and collapse at our friends' home. I had no doubt that would fuel me. I rode on the expressways across Illinois, Indiana, and straight through to Ohio. It took me fourteen and a half hours, but the fatigue was manageable, and the hip pain had lessened.

It was exhilarating to arrive at the home of our friends. The last stop before home. Sleeping under a quilt made by Carrie made the bed even more comforting.

The next afternoon, I ran an errand at a local drugstore. On my way to the register I took a shortcut through the toy aisle and out of the corner of my eye I saw a toy snake. This wasn't just any toy snake, but a stuffed cobra about twelve inches high. For a stuffed toy it looked shockingly real. It even had a mechanism such that when you pushed a button at the base, its eyes flickered, the head swayed and bobbed like a real cobra, and it emitted what was probably supposed to pass for a hissing sound. I had a long history of being terrified of snakes. What amazed me was I hadn't had any reaction at all. I stood there, dumbfounded, staring at this lifelike snake. Clearly, something had happened to me. I had to buy it. It felt like a kind of mascot. I couldn't wait to show it to Michael.

Days later, as I rode up my driveway toward the house, Devon and Michael came outside to greet me. The first thing I did was dig the snake out of my scooter. I held the snake with one hand and mimicked it with my other hand. Michael and Devon watched as I activated the scary little stuffed toy. I imitated the snake as I hissed and danced about, bobbing my head back and forth. Michael had a look of horror on his face. Devon laughed.

Michael said, "What is happening? I don't understand! What have you done with my wife?"

Devon chimed in. "That thing is disturbing! What are you doing with a snake? What happened to you?"

I laughed, too, and said, "I don't know, but something definitely happened. I found this and I didn't react to it at all. I don't know what this means for me yet, but I think it's pretty cool."

Home

I was home. My energy was up, and I was ready to move forward.

Devon and I had planned to use footage from the scooter tour to create a documentary. Unfortunately, while I was still on the tour we realized there was no hope of making any drama out of the footage of me alone on the scooter, or even me riding along with someone on another scooter. There was no excitement in watching me scoot along at the speed limit on back roads or highways. I thought this was a loss. While it may not have *looked* like an adventure riding at 35 to 37 miles an hour in the Ozarks on that twistie ride, it certainly *felt* like one.

Eventually it dawned on me—the adventure wasn't visual, it was internal. The way to communicate the experience was with words. As much as I hated to admit it, it was time to return to the book. I finally had more of an ending.

When I'd first returned home from the rehabilitation center, and was so haunted by the delusions I had in the ICU, I began writing them down. I had to do something with them. At the time, as a part of my experiential memory, they still felt more real than the rest of my past. I hoped recording them could somehow lead to the medical profession knowing I wasn't "resting peacefully" while in the medically-induced coma. Maybe it would spark a discussion or inspire them to reassess some of their ICU methods.

Over time, what began as a simple list of delusions grew into a narrative of my experience in the ICU. In 2006, well before the fairy wings, the photography projects, or the scooter tour, I believed I had completed the story. I asked my first editor to assess the manuscript as a book. She believed the manuscript was almost complete, but needed a little development. Though she thought the adjustments were small, her suggestions felt like an enormous amount of work to me. I was still only good for a small part of the day, maybe an hour or two with my brain working in its partial-post-ICU-state. Writing had always been challenging for me, and I wasn't prepared to make that kind of investment.

I abandoned the idea. As my friends will attest, when I drop something, that's it. I'm a forward-propelling machine. The book was dead to me. Michael was devastated. He begged me to give him the book, so he could finish it some time in the future.

Now here I was four years later asking for the manuscript. I knew he would have mixed feelings as he had grown attached to the idea of finishing it himself, but begrudgingly, he gave it back. I opened the large Timberland boot box that had been lying dormant on the floor by his bookshelf. With dread at the enormity of the task ahead of me, I pulled out the 1960's green fabric three-ring binder and the pile of loose papers.

* * *

All of the alone time on the scooter broke the obsessive extrovert in me. I had an expanded capacity for patience and focus. It was now possible to do new activities I couldn't even do before Everything Bad Happened—like origami.

Once, when I was visiting Diane, she found these especially beautiful papers and planned for us to make simple swans together. I felt bad, but I had to take a pass. There was no way I could conjure the focus to follow the instructions to create even a beginner's model. Her heart was in the right place. I suspect she thought of it as a task that didn't require any physicality. But now I wanted to try.

My first attempts were guided by YouTube. Then Julie Hannaford Rundell, the prop master from *We Vow*, sent me a remarkable book called *Origami from Angelfish to Zen*, by Peter Engel. She put a note on it that read, "for inspiration." I was struck by how much tenderness and respect she'd demonstrated with those two words. Even after all these years, the one thing that still brought me to tears was that I never regained my capacity to read.

The first half of the book was dense with theory, but the second half showed how to make beautiful and unique forms, like a reindeer, or a knight on horseback, using an accessible instructional format. I enjoyed the images and put it on the shelf with my art books for later, when I graduated to intermediate models.

About a week later, I had a dream that had a complex origami image in it. Michael makes fun of me because my dreams are often very literal and not actually bizarre myths that need to be interpreted. I had a hunch this might be the case (or perhaps something more), so I went up to my loft to see if I had originally seen the figure in the book from Julie.

I flipped through the book. I didn't find the figure, but I paused at a paragraph with the heading "X and X." It reminded me of the Laurie Anderson song "Let X = X," so I began reading.

I read the first sentence. It ended with a weird word in italics, *iteration*, but I was able to follow along. I kept reading. It was a complex sentence, but I didn't have to go back to the beginning multiple times. I finished the sentence. I understood. I was a little freaked out. Maybe it was a fluke. I read on. A simple sentence. Next paragraph.

There were several more complex sentences in the next paragraph. I never had to double back. My heart began racing. *Oh my God, something must have happened on the scooter tour...* I read another paragraph... I grinned—contained the impulse to jump up and down... still reading, actually reading, containing jumping because that would take my eyes away from the words...

I read one more complex paragraph and then hurriedly took the book down to Michael and said, "I read this," holding the book up to him to show him the page.

He gave me his "Whatever, you-have-a-creative-way-of-interpreting-things" face.

"No, this is fucking real, Michael. I can fucking read, like, no lie!"

"Read to me," he challenged.

"Okay, get this. The heading is 'X and X.'"

"'To manufacture new forms, nature uses a process called iteration. An iterative process (it can also be called a recursive process or a feedback loop) is an efficient mechanism for generating form, creating elaborate structures with a minimum expenditure of energy and information. The results, not surprisingly, are structures that appear self-similar.'"

Michael looked at me blankly. I kept reading.

"'Some of the most beautiful forms I have ever seen are the product of mathematical discoveries less than twenty years old. They are strange and enigmatic shapes known as fractals: Koch snowflakes, Man-del-brot.' Do you know how to say that?"

Michael shrugged.

"I could go on, but I think you get the idea."

"Okay, so you were able to read it, but do you know what it *means?*" he asked.

"Yeah, basically this dude is talking about a process, the iterative process, which is like a repeating process or feedback loop—that occurs in nature and has more recently been proven or been noted to occur in a number of scientific fields. In particular he names these specific mathematical shapes that follow this principle."

"Ara, do you realize what you described is *fractal math?*"

"Yeah, isn't that cool? I can read."

"What the hell happened?"

"I don't know, but I have a guess. I once saw a demonstration of Neuro-Linguistic Programming, where the subjects were people who had reading challenges. They were dyslexic. They would each read a passage aloud, and of course they would struggle and stumble along. The subjects were asked to march with their knees high for about twelve steps and tap their alternating knees with their hands and simultaneously turn their head to the right and left —like this," I demonstrated for him. "Then they would have subjects read a different paragraph and inevitably they would read the next paragraph without struggling. Based on that experience, I wonder if when I was on the scooter and leaning right and left and having to look right and left at every turn, I wonder if I didn't remap my brain."

"Hey, go get the Proust," he enthused.

"No, that's too complicated. I want to enjoy this moment. I don't want to be crushed just yet."

I marked the calendar to remember that most auspicious day. It was October 9th.

*   *   *

As part of my process for revitalizing the memoir project, I was invited to read at a residential community for persons with mental health issues called CooperRiis in North Carolina.

Before the reading, I visited the community's art barn, where I found a young woman in her mid-twenties making a design on the exterior of a shoe box.

The young woman was busily working, but greeted me and quickly began explaining, "I'm making a care package for my friend."

I thought this was interesting, as normally I'd expect a person who was at a residential community to be receiving a care package, not sending one.

"I'm decorating the box to hold some of the artwork I've made here. I've made care packages for other friends, but this friend is the most important because she was there for me in a way other people weren't when my life started falling apart."

I wanted to give her space while she was working at the art table, so I went to the sitting area nearby. There was a cluster of chairs, a couch, and a coffee table with piles of magazines which clearly had been scavenged for projects.

"All of these artworks have meaning to me, but I don't have time to explain. I have to get this done." She was hurriedly gluing images to the outside of the box. Then she proceeded to insert the objects, padding them for safety with colorful tissue paper.

"I'm bipolar," she said.

"Me too." I said.

"Did you just get here?" she asked.

"I'm here to talk about a memoir I'm writing."

"Do you take meds?" she asked.

"I do. They help me a lot. What about you, do you take meds?" I asked tentatively.

"I do, but, they aren't working yet."

"I know it can take a long time to get that worked out. How are you doing today?" I asked.

"I'm pretty fast, today."

"I can see that. What's that like for you?"

"I used to always panic, and then I would get faster. I got into all kinds of trouble. It finally got pretty serious, which is how I ended up here. Now when I'm feeling this way, I have the option to make something. Like right now. There isn't a class happening, but this space is open. I'm over here by myself, dealing with my energy in this way. I'm doing something I can feel good about that is literally constructive."

"That is so cool. Do you think you might be able to take this strategy with you when you leave?"

"Yeah, I told my mom that the other day. It made her cry—in a good way."

Another woman, about thirty-five, was resting on the couch with her leg up. She'd tripped and twisted her knee. She was eager to share her experience as well, but she was calm and relaxed. She described herself as someone who'd been a successful professional, but who'd quite suddenly melted down. Much of her family didn't understand and wanted her to "snap out of it." It made her doubt the veracity of her own reality, and she knew it had slowed the rate at which she'd been able to heal.

While we were setting up for the reading, the center's director, Suzanne, said, "There is a resident away this week for a training, but I wish she was going to be here for your reading. You would maybe find what she is doing interesting, too. She is doing SoulCollage®."

"She is doing, soul—what?"

"SoulCollage®."

There was a lot of sound in the room, and I just couldn't get what she was saying.

"I'm sorry, 'soul,' what?"

"SoulCollage®. They're sort of like tarot cards, but individual personal archetypal cards. They are made by collaging images."

"Oh, 'soul *collage*.'"

"Yeah, SoulCollage®."

Immediately, my mind was whirring. *Oh my God! Individualized personal archetype cards!?*

My reading was in a few minutes, but I wanted to leave and get on the internet to see what this archetype card process was all about.

The reading was engaging. This group in particular was invested in the mental health issues that had impacted me both in the ICU and after. Both the residents and the staff asked fascinating questions, and they were also interested in Michael's experience. During the reading and conversation I forgot about the cards, but the second it was over I remembered and was back to obsessing about it. After dinner, I was able to do a search on the internet and there it was, *Soulcollage.com.*

The web page featured a video of a woman with short grey hair at a small table, on a porch with greenery all around her. She was quietly pasting images on an 8-inch by 5-inch card while piano music played in the background. Then she was standing with a stack of maybe 75 or 100 cards by the porch railing.

"Hello, I'm Seena Frost," she began.

> *I'm here today to tell you about a process I created, which we've named SoulCollage®. It is a process of making individual cards for all the different parts of yourself, and of people you love, and of archetypes that come in to you and to speak to you, and draw you, and even the animals in your chakras.*
>
> *...I love my cards and I'm sure you would love your cards too, because they are creative, fun to make, and anyone can make them, and they are also powerfully transformative. I'll show you how that happens.*

She went on to demonstrate how to make the cards, and I couldn't wait to get home and get started.

At the end of the video, she closed with,

> *You will find you have inner wisdom that comes from these cards. When they speak to you, they come from a place that no one can tell you. A therapist can't tell you what the wisdom is, a book can't tell you, a sermon can't tell you, a lecture can't tell you. Only your own inner wisdom can tell you what these images will tell you. So try it. Get busy and try it. Just find some images and see what grabs you and start cutting.*

I knew I would want to do more than just make cards for myself, so I looked on the website for workshops. There was a seminar to train facilitators in ten days at The Well, in LaGrange Park, Illinois with Audrey Chowdhury. The trainings had a requirement:

The facilitator's training assumes a working knowledge of SoulCollage®, that the person has read *SoulCollage® Evolving* by Seena B. Frost, author and founder of SoulCollage®, listened to two instructional CDs, made cards (at least a few in each suit), and that they want to use it in the work they are already doing or beginning.

I ordered the book and six CDs. They didn't have overnight shipping, so I had to wait.

The package came in five days.

Michael and I were sitting at our front-to-front desks as I opened the package. I started flipping through the book, and I started crying.

"So, it is what you thought it was?"

"Yes."

"I'm sorry."

"Why are you sorry?"

"Because it's been around for fifteen years, and you didn't know about it."

"But the train hasn't left the station. I can still become a facilitator. I can still get on board."

*

I confess I was a little manic when I first started to prepare for the facilitator training. Not an out-of-control manic, but overly excited, and definitely obsessed. I didn't want to stop to eat or to do anything else. I knew I wasn't technically hypomanic because I managed to sleep, but when I woke up I got right back at it. This went on for the few days I had left before the training.

I converted my loft into piles of images. I was making multiple cards at a time until one became close, and then I would zero in and finish it. Once a card was complete, I would put it in a plastic sleeve. It was like framing a painting.

Once I had finished my second card something happened.

I held the first two cards. They told me their names: *Misunderstood* and *Children Are to Be Seen and Not Heard*. I felt this profound acknowledgement. It was in part the subjects of the cards, but it was also the nature of the cards themselves. The images were connecting to me. I was receiving something for the first time. Something which, up until this point, I had been seeking from outside myself... a kind of understanding, a kind of knowing, a deeply penetrating, resonating affirmation. I was giving myself this gift. The gift I had longed for, reached for, grasped for and missed, so many times. It was concrete. I was having this dialogue with myself, in the holding, for the very first time.

*   *   *

My family takes their Lutheranism quite seriously. My great uncle Arnold was the principal and eighth grade teacher at Trinity Lutheran School. This was the school my father and his siblings attended. Julie, my next-youngest sibling, and I also attended this school before my family moved to the next town over when I was in the fourth grade.

My cousin, Herman, obtained a Ph.D. in theology and taught at Concordia University (a Lutheran University) in Seward, Nebraska. Additionally, both of his daughters and one of his granddaughters also became grade school Lutheran teachers.

My Grandfather took immense pride in his Lutheran faith. On Easter Sunday our entire family, meaning my immediate family and my uncle and his children, would all attend his church. He was never happier than on that day with his family all together taking up the first three pews. Last, but certainly not least, my Uncle Danny, my godfather, also went to one of the Concordia Lutheran colleges and went on to be the principal of five different Lutheran grade schools.

In 1975, when I was in fifth grade, my hometown's public high school had a graduating class of only 234 students. Yet this small community supported three Lutheran churches, all of which had parochial schools, kindergarten through eighth grade. Christ Lutheran, the one my sister and I attended, was a Missouri Synod. This subdivision of the Lutheran Church was considered to be the more liberal. The other two churches, St. Paul and Grace Lutheran, were Wisconsin Synod. To an outsider, the issues that divided this religion into various subgroups would be considered subtle, but within the Lutheran community these differing interpretations of the faith and the resulting practices were hotly contested topics.

In the seventies, there was a great debate about whether or not the Boy Scouts should be allowed to have meetings on school property. The debate came about because the Boy Scouts take an oath. The Wisconsin Synod decided not to allow them on their property because they believed one should only take an oath to God, but the more liberal Missouri Synod determined this oath was not breaking any commandment, so the Scouts were allowed on their schools' properties. I remember issues like these being discussed on Sunday afternoons at the card games which my family played at my Grandparents' house, and thinking how fortunate it was we attended the more liberal church.

Another issue that was divided by synod, and impacted me directly, was whether or not girls should be allowed to wear pants to school. The Missouri Synod allowed pants and the Wisconsin Synod did not. We rode the school bus with the Wisconsin kids who went to St. Paul, and I felt so sorry for those girls. In the winter they were allowed to wear snow pants under their dresses, but they had to take them off as soon as they got to school. I thought this was ridiculous.

There were several components to our religious instruction. Each school day began with a Bible verse and a brief inspirational paragraph expounding on a particular theme. Once students reached fourth grade, they became responsible for delivering the devotional. Each was assigned a day in rotation. On Wednesdays we went to chapel for a service attended by all the students

Reconstruction

but was closed to the public. And then of course, there were the weekly Sunday services I attended with my family.

This was a fair amount of religion, and I was into it. It mattered to me. I didn't have the language for it at the time, but I tried to hold the daily devotion, the Wednesday chapel, and Sunday sermon message as not only something to think about, but to try to live by. This also meant I could get righteous when my family or friends didn't demonstrate what I believed we had been taught. As early as kindergarten, I called out racism because I had learned the song, "Red, yellow, black and white/they are precious in his sight/Jesus loves the little children of the world." My behavior only intensified over time.

In my parents' and teachers' defense for what followed, they likely did the best they could to manage a righteous and zealous, undiagnosed bipolar evangelical Lutheran kid. I suspect they did the best they could to manage me while I witnessed to strangers at the grocery store.

I continued to read about religion, not only at school but on my own time as well. Around the time we moved, I found a world religion book at the public library. I was amazed at how the core messages of each of the religions were the same. I thought, if all these different religions came to the same basic conclusion without knowing about each other, this was validation—"proof"—the Bible was "divinely written." I couldn't wait to get to school with the results of my investigation. I was sure my teacher was going to be delighted by my ground-breaking discovery and call the powers-that-be.

He did!

He informed the principal.

The book was confiscated, and I got a very severe talking-to. This didn't dampen my enthusiasm for my religious research, it only made me more careful about sharing my findings.

In fifth grade I began to learn about archeology, I began to think more about the idea that the Bible had been translated multiple times before making its way to English. It intrigued me that there might be different interpretations of a text. I also was impressed by Martin Luther who had the noble idea to make the Bible accessible to the common person by translating it into German. To me, this must have meant the reverse was true, so I became especially excited whenever the minister talked during his sermon about what a Bible verse meant in Hebrew or Greek. I believed it helped me get closer to the original translation.

One Sunday, the minister was explaining 2 Timothy 3:16, which says, "All scripture is given by inspiration." He talked about the Hebrew word *Ruach*, which can mean both "breath" and "spirit." The idea that a root word with two meanings added depth to the verse blew my mind. Prior to this time, I thought I wanted to grow up to be a war correspondent or an archeologist, but now I thought it would be way more interesting to be a minister. I would learn the ancient languages of the Bible and share insights. It would be intellectually compelling and also inspiring.

A few days later, I mentioned this to a teacher, and it was explained to me that the Lutheran Church didn't allow women to be ministers. Jesus had chosen twelve men to be his disciples. They were men, not women. I could be a Lutheran school teacher, but minister—that was out.

Originally, the way I saw it, Martin Luther was a rebellious badass, and that made the Lutherans the coolest of all the Christians. If I was going to be a Christian, I had wanted to be a Lutheran. Now I had a conflict.

Maybe there was another denomination that allowed women to be ministers.

The hunt began. As I looked around, I discovered Harvard Divinity School. Not only did they allow women, their application had more than *thirty* blanks, which included every denomination I had ever heard of, and quite a few I hadn't, including atheist. I was enamored. Now I had a checklist to begin my exploration for a new, more welcoming, religious home.

*

My religious quest led to even greater challenges at the beginning of seventh grade. Our split classroom of seventh and eighth grades began a more rigorous religious study, a two-year preparatory process toward confirmation. In the Lutheran church, confirmation comes at the completion of 8th grade, when the individual is deemed capable of making a conscious and mindful commitment to one's faith, after which one is eligible to participate in communion.

The basis of the instruction is *Luther's Small Catechism*. On the designated Sunday each confirmant makes his or her pronouncement of The Lord's Prayer, the Ten Commandments, the Confession, and the Apostles' Creed. There is also an oral exam where the minister asks each confirmant a single question from the *Catechism*. After this, the confirmant becomes an adult member of the church and takes communion for the first time. I was good to go with everything, except I had technical issues with the Apostles' Creed. Basically, there wasn't much of it I could say in good conscience.

This was serious. Confirmation meant standing up in front of the church and swearing before God, my father—the biological, Lutheran one—and the members of my church. I would have to declare my belief in every word of each of those elements. There wasn't any wiggle room, and I wasn't going to be able to do it with my right hand raised.

I did the only thing I could think of: I asked my Dad if I could go to public school. Whenever we asked our parents if we could do something there might be a debate about, they would confer with one another in private and then come back with the news—a unified front. My Dad tended to say yes to me more than my Mom, so I always went to him first in the hope he would lobby for me. In this case, neither parent was going to say yes. The question was absurd.

I was shaking when I asked. My biggest fear was that my Dad was going to ask me why. Usually, I would have rehearsed my defense. In this case, I had nothing.

But he didn't.

He said no.

It was all over in less than a minute.

*

I didn't see any alternative other than leaving home. I went to live with a couple of different estranged relatives over a span of almost three years. When I returned home, I was required to attend church on Sunday. The issue of confirmation was never brought up. It was awkward since I was the only person over 12 sitting in the pew during communion. I would stand up and sit down at all the designated times, did all the responsive readings and sang the various hymns, but I did not say the Apostles' Creed. I'm sure my Dad noticed, but he never said anything to me.

As the years passed, I searched for a faith wherein I could say their creeds, one where women could be ministers, even if that was no longer my intention. Later, when I became conscious of it, I also sought a faith in which gays were welcome, where they could be married and also ministers. But most importantly, one where I wouldn't have to lie. I spent decades searching. I would find something attractive in every faith, but there would always be a catch.

In 1998, I read an article in the *Utne Reader* entitled, "Should You Design Your Own Religion?" In the article, there was a quote from Thomas Keating, Cistercian (Trappist) priest and monk at St. Benedict's Monastery in Snowmass, Colorado, where he says,

> *The ideal way to develop a practice is to plug into a tradition that has long-range experience, literature, and rituals that support it. When you make a collage of various traditions, you run the risk of digging too many wells in a desert, which might take a lot of time; whereas if you work one well that has a good reputation, where water is to be found, it might be more rewarding in the long term.*

I knew in that moment, my years of seeking had left me with a shallow spiritual feeling. I agreed with his view. I desperately wanted to choose, but still couldn't. So, I decided to write Father Keating, in the hope the act alone of writing the letter might help me process my indecision, help me to settle it. I certainly didn't expect someone who had written so many books and who was quoted in a magazine to write me back.

Ara Lucia Ashburne

Six months later, I received a tiny envelope with a return address from St. Benedict's Monastery. Inside was a small piece of lightweight cardstock. The actual address and phone number were printed below the name of the monastery. I couldn't imagine under what circumstances one could call a monastery.

Then, penned in his hand, was a note to me.

> *3/26/99*
> *Dear Ara,*
>
> *I have a friend who teaches in Chicago. He might be able to help you or direct you to someone. You might also read one of my books to see if you like my approach. We teach a method of Christian meditative practice and have an organization that supports those on this path. There are teachers of the method in Chicago. We also put out a newsletter with schedules of events in various areas of the country. If such information would interest you, please write Contemplative Outreach, 10 Park Place, Suite B, Butler, NJ 07405. The book mentioned above can be obtained at this address as well.*
>
> *My friend's name is Wayne Teasdale, and his phone is 773-288-5555.*
>
> *I hope this note will give you some useful leads.*
> *If not, please write me again.*
>
> Sincerely,
Thomas Keating

I couldn't believe he wrote at all, and I couldn't believe he gave me the phone number of a personal friend. I was even more surprised when I realized this Wayne Teasdale guy was also a monk. I did a little homework and discerned in advance he was on the Board of the Parliament for World Religions. Surely he would be able to help me resolve this no-religion business.

A Life

Brother Teasdale's living space turned out to be in a dorm near a grouping of seminaries on the south side of Chicago. When I knocked on his door, a tall lanky man with wavy hair invited me in. His office was no bigger than an average dorm room, but filled with stacks of papers waist high like little tree stumps all over the room. His desk was covered with more stacks of paper, but had at its center a single blooming white orchid.

He ushered me past his desk, toward a table and chair, and gestured for me to sit. Though the table was tiny, it blocked the entrance to the kitchen. There was barely enough room for him to scoot by. He put on water for tea, placed two mismatched mugs on the table, and sat in the other chair, which was on the other side of the table, lodged in the small kitchen.

With the warmth of a beloved grandfather, he said, "Tell me your story."

He listened attentively as I told him the highlights of the long and relentless search for a religious home that brought me to his door.

He began, "There is a word for you. There are quite a few of you in your generation. You're religious refugees. You left where you came from and you can't go back, but there is nowhere for you to go," he said. His words came over me like a waterfall of deliverance.

I had never heard this term before. Suddenly all of the decades of searching for a spiritual place for my soul to call home had meaning.

I knew it was true. I just didn't want it to be true. There was a degree of panic that started to rise up. How could I live if I were to accept that I wasn't going to find a place—no home—ever?

He continued, "You don't need a religion."

I thought this was funny, coming from a person on the Board of the Parliament for World Religions.

"What you need are two things—a spiritual practice and a community. I have a suggestion for a spiritual practice, something you could do until you find your own, and it might work for a community too. You might want to consider Centering Prayer. Although it comes from the Catholic tradition, anyone from any faith can do it."

He got up and walked in amongst the paper towers. He reached two-thirds of the way down a particular stack and pulled out the edge of one of the pages, then another. "Ah here, yes," he said, "you might want to read this." Then he grabbed the edges of three pages, steadied the pile from the top, and pulled them out.

"I suspect you might like knowing the history and tradition behind the practice." He handed me an academic paper, and I scanned it as he continued to explain.

"There are various groups around the city that get together at different times, if you want to try it out. There should be one that would work for you."

This really does look like neutral Christian ground. I like the direct relationship part of it. This might be a way back to my original faith without having to wrestle with the denominational creeds and issues. But if it is just a simple form of meditation, I've already learned how to do that, then I'm not sure this is gonna help.

He added, "There is something else. You said you are pursuing becoming a therapist. I suspect you would be a good therapist. I don't doubt that, but I think you are truly an artist. You really shouldn't deny that."

My eyes widened. I hadn't said anything about any creative pursuits. Nothing. My heart was racing. *Where did he get that?* I had been accepted into a graduate program at the Art Institute of Chicago two years before, but turned it down because I didn't get the full scholarship I would have needed.

He continued, "I have a video I'd like you to see."

Behind me he had a meditation cushion in front of a tiny television. He dug through a box of videos next to it and pulled one out. He asked me if I had another twenty minutes to watch it and then popped it in. The video was about a Japanese artist who created spiritually inspired landscapes. Teasdale didn't offer any additional commentary. He wanted to plant a seed.

I was stunned. I had been prepared to listen to the Centering Prayer business, even though at this point I was still pretty Christian gun-shy… but that art stuff was going to have to wait until I had an income.

*   *   *

When I got out of the ICU, Michael and I were hit with an astronomical pile of medical bills, way over a million dollars, which of course we had no means of paying. I didn't want to bring a lawsuit because no one had done anything to me on purpose. But the truth was quite a number of things happened that easily qualified as malpractice.

Once I came to terms with the necessity of the lawsuit, I was frustrated to discover the reality of the way the law works. I wanted the lawsuit to be about what I considered to be my significant loss and trauma. As I saw it, my primary loss was my cognition which manifested in struggles with verbal communication and being unable to read. Then, there was the long-lasting emotional trauma in the ICU. Unfortunately, since no neurological and/or cognitive testing prior to my being in the ICU had been done, we had no established baseline. This meant it would only be my word, saying, "This is my experience," which provides no legal grounds for a case. This lawsuit *had* to be about the loss of my abdomen. Although not a trifling matter, that was the least of my worries. It remained true, however, that my life was pretty screwed up. I went in kicking and screaming, but we moved forward.

A complicating consideration was, what we would do if I were to be injured? This was a real and ever-present concern. Even if we were to win our case, Dr. Petrosian wasn't sure he would be able to duplicate the surgery, which would also be incredibly costly. My medications were expensive, a couple of thousand dollars each month. Our ongoing financial medical concerns had us terrified.

As a result, back in 2003 we began the arduous process to emigrate to Canada. It took three years, but in the end, we prevailed. We had a shiny hologram inserted into each of our passports, and we were given a deadline by which we had to cross the border. Three weeks before the deadline, an event happened which would not only change the direction of our lives forever, but would also change our understanding of who Michael was as a person.

*

Six years after the ICU, the lawsuit was settled. The truth was, we wouldn't have to work. That wasn't our plan—we still wanted to make a contribution. We were excited. This enabled us to choose work without concern about whether or not it paid well or at all. We would be able to use the resources to augment our salaries. So, we began making plans to build a home.

We sought out the leading green architecture firm in Montreal. They created a plan for a home, a stunning physical manifestation of who each of us was and how we lived together.

The home was designed for a wooded lot about 45 minutes from Montreal. The north face of the house, all along the kitchen, dining and living rooms, would be glass. These rooms would be on the ground floor along with the master bedroom. There were to be studio spaces for both of us. We planned to die in this house, so we didn't want any stairs to the main rooms. Additionally, four rooms—three upstairs and one downstairs—were going to be available for other artists or writers to do residencies with us… all of us hidden away in the woods, living, working, and making stuff.

In that third week before crossing the border, we had a conference call with the architects about the house. They gave us final numbers regarding the construction costs.

It turned out that the architects were way off. It was going to cost two to three times what they had originally estimated. We couldn't do it. Michael was devastated, and he melted down. I don't mean "melted down" as in, he was yelling and shouting and pacing about, or slumped down on the couch with a beer and didn't want to talk to me. I mean he basically became catatonic, in a ball on the floor. I had seen him like this a few times before, although when it happened previously, he had been sitting up and rocking.

This time he did not move.

I had talked him through meltdowns before, even though I had never seen one this intense, so intuitively I knew what I needed to do. I spoke calmly.

"Honey, I'm gonna take care of this. I promise. This is a big one. I know you're freaked out right now, and you don't see a way out of this. It's going to take me a few days, but I promise I'll figure this out. I'm going to have to leave, so I can go talk to my brother John. I'm going to need to get you upstairs to the bedroom. I will be back in a few hours. I'm going to put Calder beside you. You'll be safe."

I didn't know what I was going to do. John was in the process of building his own house at the time, so I figured he would have compassion for our situation, and maybe be able to help me figure out our options.

Within a few days, Michael came out of his state and was ready to talk. I offered my proposal of building in southwest Michigan where I grew up.

He was adamantly against it. "No way, you would kill yourself for lack of cultural stimulation."

I protested, "I'm resourceful. I can deal. Besides, it's only a couple hours from Chicago."

We went back and forth for several hours, but in the end he agreed, with one condition.

"I don't want this decision to destroy us. You have to promise me if you are getting the least bit crazy, you will get yourself on a plane and go somewhere."

"Of course," I agreed, thinking that was an easy enough arrangement.

*

It would be another year before we understood what that day with Michael in a ball on the floor meant. Eventually, there came a coalescence of clues.

Another year of our accumulated stresses and frustrations, and we had another one of our daily arguments. These were heated fights that would go on for several hours (in the end, we usually realized we were fighting over semantics). They were exhausting for both of us. This time was different. Michael had had it. He wanted to go to couple's therapy again.

I was tired of couple's therapy. In my view, it only gave us little moments of insight, but never solved the core problem. I pitched for accepting the problem and learning to live with it.

He asserted, "We are better than this."

I was pissed, because it wasn't an assertion I could argue. We went back to therapy.

This time we found the perfect therapist for us in Gwen Hurd.[*] I will never forget the moment, about ten minutes into the first session, when Michael and I gave each other a look that said, "Yep, she's the one!"

The first clue came during my analysis of our relationship. We had different types of conflicts. In some cases, one of us only needed additional information in order to happily accommodate the other. Sometimes we had to simply agree to compromise. Much of the time, we clashed over Michael's rules. He had numerous procedures or preferences for a vast range of things. In these areas he was unyielding. I would agree to comply or not, but this didn't seem tenable for the long run. I couldn't understand the disparity between how easily he could adjust in some circumstances and how impossible he was in others.

I posed the question to Gwen, "What if Michael doesn't change? What if we just accept that?"

This was a turning point for her. She believed in our relationship as profoundly as we did, but now she was looking at the problem from a new vantage point.

---

[*] Technically, Ms. Hurd is a Licensed Clinical Social Worker.

The second revelation came while Michael explained his experience when I would return after I had been out of town for a few days. It was a miserable transition for him to negotiate, going from near-total isolation to what felt to him to be an abrupt re-entry upon my return. The problem was lessened when we had dinner out before heading home. This procedure reminded Michael of a dog training technique we learned: when bringing new visitors over for the first time, having them meet the dog outside beforehand can make the dog less territorial inside the house. When he noted the way these methods mirrored one another, he recalled a story he had heard about an autistic woman who got along better with cows than people. He wondered if there might be a correlation between that woman's situation and his struggle.

"Maybe I'm autistic?" he said flippantly.

Together we three began to assess the data and it started to take shape. Eventually, Michael and I set up an appointment with his psychiatrist and received an official diagnosis.

Michael had Asperger's Syndrome.

Now everything that was mysterious had a name and began to make sense. Now we could both strategize. In Michael's case, knowing he was on the autism spectrum changed his perception of himself in the world. Now I needed to change how I communicated with him.

My biggest adjustment was designing my communication to accommodate his difficulty with conceptual ideas. Persons on the autism spectrum are often able to see the trees, but not the forest. Before, during a misunderstanding, when I offered a metaphorical example to explain an abstract concept and he didn't get it, I would offer another. He would then accuse me of changing my story just to "win the fight" (this would always end with me in tears). Now I understood why.

Going forward, I would stop sharing these kinds of stories and experiences unless they were monumental or critical to our relationship. I would also choose my battles more carefully. If he got lost as I explained something, I could decide, "Is this going to be worth the trouble?" Basically, I had to become more selective in my communication. I could share quick and easy tidbits or the really important stuff. The stuff in the middle I had to save for someone else. This is just one example of the kinds of adjustments we both made. There were many others.

This knowledge came very late in our marriage. We were 14 years in before we learned the basic rules of communication that fundamentally changed how we related to one another. But it bettered our relationship, and we became more loving and respectful of one another.

* * *

By the early fall of 2008, construction had begun on the house. Early one morning, I received a call from our financial advisor explaining there was trouble. I had been watching the stock market. He was concerned about what I was going to hear in the media, and he wanted to reassure me. I explained that I understood his obligation to make these calls, but we weren't the type of clients who were going to over-react to market fluctuations, even if they were dramatic. In the weeks and days that followed, it became increasingly clear—the market was plummeting hard and fast. Before we started construction, I did my homework. We could lose a third of all we had and still be financially stable.

A few weeks later, we were out of town at a large hardware store, trying to locate an obscure piece of plumbing we needed for a salvaged sink. CNN was on a television behind the counter. I saw the scroll on the bottom of the screen that showed how much further the stock market had dropped that day. I knew from those numbers that we were sunk. Since it wasn't "official," I waited to tell Michael.

A few days later, I'd just driven up to the construction site with beverages for the carpenters when I got the call.

We'd lost *half*.

I sat there, stunned, watching the carpenters pound nails into two-by-fours. There was no way to turn back the clock and unbuild the house. There was no way to sell a house that was in the process of being framed. I had to figure out a way to save it. Michael needed that house. We spent three years designing a home that was to be his haven, a fortress to protect us both. Although it is said that each autistic person is unique, there are some common traits. It's safe to say that coping readily with sudden, radical change is not known to be one of them.

Michael needed the house not just to provide shelter for him, me, and the animals, but to order and protect his possessions. Michael is attached to his things. It isn't just the old adage about a boy and his toys. It has to do with what is described of people with Asperger's as having a "Special Interest." This is an intense interest in a broad subject or a narrowly-focused topic. Some are lifelong, some are short-term. It's not uncommon for individuals to have multiple special interests throughout their lifetimes, too. Maybe you have come across the guy or gal who has studied and loved trains or dinosaurs and knows everything there is to know about them or some sub-genre of them. Michael is one such case, which is complicated by his inability to let things go.

It all began with his superhero figures. He played with them as a child and referred to them as his dolls. These were played with aggressively, and his mother repaired them over and over. They were loved beyond love. Additionally, there were comics: *Amazing Spider-Man, Uncanny X-Men,* and *Incredible*

Hulk. These are ones that everyone knows, but there were many other, lesser-known and "underground" titles as well.

In his high school and college days it was alternative music. He had his favorite bands that he followed and proceeded to collect all of their albums and singles and remixes. Then it was on to the side projects that each of the bands' members pursued, and these all evolved over time. His knowledge in this area made total sense to his friends and other people who were really devoted to the scene, but the database he kept in his brain and the size of his music collection would astound the casual listener.

Now these were the special interests that could be easily pointed out, but that isn't the only stuff that he kept. By nature Michael is a conserver. Very little gets thrown away in our house. Recycling is a complex and full-scale operation of which I, on even my best day, am only capable of complying with at about the 75% mark. If an item still works or can be repaired, then it is declared "perfectly good" and retained (even if it is never actually repaired). He has stated with pride that, to this day, he still owns—and can wear!—three pair of underwear he has had since *high school.*

Originally, the architects designed the house with several rooms as multi-use. He couldn't do it. He needed an Aspie house. Each room a single function. That is what was being built in Michigan. If he were to lose the house, we would lose the first thing that could give his life the structure he so desperately wanted. If we moved into something smaller, he would likely have to shed his possessions, his memories, his life. All I could think about was that ball on the floor that was Michael before he had a house. Now it was a matter of making sure he would be able to keep the ground under his feet.

* * *

When I returned from the rehabilitation hospital in 2001, my private practice and my graduate program were not a life I could return to, but I couldn't wrap my mind around a new career. My brain was unable to follow a three-step recipe, and my body couldn't stand long enough to make it through a simple shopping trip. These limitations meant even the minimal rigors of a retail job or the basic cognition for a customer service job were impossible. I was at a complete loss. I attempted to sort and resort the options like a never ending video game, but I kept failing. I finally sought help.

My plan had always been to follow my graduate degree with coaching training, so it seemed logical to bring on a coach to help me solve this seemingly impossible puzzle. As I saw it there were a bazillion different coaching programs and the majority fell into two different formats. The first is what I would call the "Woo-Woo." This approach was made up of prancing unicorns, dancing light, and the magic that heals all. The other approach was just the opposite: programs that often attracted business people and were focused on goals and achievement.

I was looking for someone who would have a balanced approach, one that believed both being *and* action were of value. Based on my investigation, there were only two coaching models that did this well: Coaches U and Coaches Training Institute (CTI). I limited my search for a coach to someone trained in one of those two models. More importantly, I needed someone rock-solid strong, someone who would hold my situation with sensitivity but wouldn't be overwhelmed by the drama of it. I didn't want someone who was going to feel sorry for me. I knew I was going to have to fight my way out of this, and if I was getting in my own way I needed to be called out.

I narrowed my search down to Elizabeth McAloon. Not only did we connect, she got the spiritual without the unicorns, the compassion without the goo. She possessed a no-bullshit clarity I loved. Quick, smart, and savvy, she even had a word for clients with convincing justifications for their actions —"slippery." I wasn't going to get away with anything.

Together we would sleuth out a solution.

*

More than a decade later, it was time for me to train as a coach.

My original selection criteria were affirmed at my first training. I decided to follow in Elizabeth McAloon's footsteps and train with Coaches Training Institute. When I assessed my thirty colleagues in the room, I knew I had made the right choice.

The basic training took approximately a year to complete. Afterward, I chose to go on to the next level, which was certification. This is a chance to raise one's game and learn the ethics of the industry and how to use the model to develop one's own personal style as a coach, to truly become a professional.

Although I was interested in receiving the industry stamp of approval, I intended to do double-duty during the already-grueling certification process. I planned to amp up my coaching from a few clients to a full-time, thriving practice that would bail us out of our financial woes and save the house. I knew this sounded a bit crazy, since most people don't start thinking about the kind of coaching they want to do until their certification is over. If my coaching practice was going to be the Hail Mary pass, I estimated I had a year, maybe eighteen months, to get my income up to the level an average executive coach usually earns. I'd read about three different people who accomplished this through marketing alone.

It seemed extremely challenging, but not impossible.

I'd done challenging before.

A few months in and the numbers were not progressing at the incline I'd anticipated. I was frustrated, because I knew the work was out there, and I had data to back it up. According to a 2012 Global Coaching Study by the International Coaching Federation, coaching was still on a steady rise. More than 60% of coaches had experienced an increase in clients the previous year. I just needed to distinguish myself from all the other coaches. I had to assert what was unique about *me*. What would I bring to the table? What would I deliver to my clients? I needed my niche. But with each passing month, my panic about the not-niche-knowing escalated.

I called Diane. She offered to hold my hand through the process of creating a business plan. It was an education, an MBA-ultra-lite. Diane was a generous, patient, resourceful, and clever guide. She *coached* me through it. When we finally arrived at the marketing component of the business plan, there were lots of unanswered questions. There seemed to be a wide age range of potential customers and three or four possible scenarios wherein a customer might seek out a coach. She tried one trick after another supporting me to get at "it." The problem was, she couldn't go into my psyche and undo whatever was stuck.

I signed up for a tele-course in authentic marketing, designed to help coaches figure out who their core clients were. Since I was so stuck, I couldn't do any of the homework in the course either.

Finally, I reached out to Sheryl Kosovski, a business and financial coach who helps creative entrepreneurs take control of their finances. I thought if anyone could help me crack this nut, it would be her. I asked her if she would be willing to hand-hold me through the tele-course materials. She was willing, but wanted to see if she could help me without them.

She did, in fact, abandon the materials. First, she asked me questions about my finances in order to understand my goals and situation. Then, she asked me about my previous projects. Why wasn't I considering doing coaching related to the arts?

"Blech, I don't want to do that," I said reflexively. "Besides, you and I both know that in general, artists aren't able to pay what I need to charge for my services."

Sheryl looked at me with raised eyebrows.

I felt like I was backed into a corner. I knew all the talk. *"Do what you love, blah blah, the cream rises to the top, blah blah, you can succeed at anything if… blah blah."*

I knew the reality of all of these things. I just didn't want to swim upstream anymore. I was too tired.

She ignored my resistance and persisted. "What aspect of the creative experience do you get into? What about it is of interest to you?"

I laughed. For a moment I forgot we were talking about business, and I answered her, "Well, everyone makes fun of me about this, because I really love process. The example I give is that if someone said to me, you have to choose: you can watch the 'behind the scenes,' making-of for a film, or you can watch the actual movie, I would always choose the 'behind the scenes.' I am endlessly enthralled by the artistic process."

She was smiling, "Well, that is really interesting because there isn't someone capitalizing on that right now."

Sheryl rattled off a list of professionals. One was helping artists market themselves to museums. Another was helping them make more money selling their work. There were others.

She made the point, "There are people making money and not making money in every field. This is true of doctors, lawyers, artists, and architects. Your income is not defined by your profession."

I knew she was right.

Sheryl had ripped the door off my resistance. We talked for an hour about what it would mean to do creativity coaching. There were other creativity coaches. I wouldn't be the first. I'd have to stake my claim, to analyze and articulate my own creative process. Where would I mark out my territory?

I left that meeting surprised that I had turned the corner. I was giddy about coaching creatives to find their true authentic voice. This was something I had the education, experience, and know-how to do. There was no obstacle. I just needed to articulate the creative process as I saw it: the pathway to one's authentic creative vision.

It took me another month or so, but I came up with a universally applicable six-step methodology. I called it The Spiral Process. Whether a person was making a simple creative choice or a more involved one, The Spiral Process is the journey one goes through over and over throughout making any creative work.

*

Meanwhile, Michael was also going through a stressful life transition. Everything Bad had happened to him, too. It had all started when his parents died, then he had testicular cancer. At the point when I was finally moving toward the other side of Everything Bad That Happened, he found himself beyond fatigued and unable to climb out. His diagnosis of being on the autism spectrum provided understanding and allowed for a few strategies, but it didn't make life easier. After more than a decade of supporting me, he was struggling to find a new direction, a new purpose. He wanted to matter, not in a famous rock star kind of way, but to have a legacy, to make a difference. He needed something of his own.

Although YouTube had been around for several years, by then it had become an undeniable component of our culture. Pop stars' careers were built from the foundations of their YouTube channels. Even the venerable *Tonight Show* had a channel with over five million subscribers. YouTube had changed the landscape of media, and things were going to keep changing. Though we were late-comers, Michael and I had begun following a number of channels and celebrity "YouTubers." While I was pursuing my certification he became obsessed with a select few. He tracked their social media accounts—Facebook, Instagram, Twitter and Tumblr—so as not to miss any "breaking news." There were rabbit holes within the rabbit holes.

I proposed he start his own channel. I figured if he invested any amount of time in any sort of creative endeavor, it would lead *somewhere*. Despite his initial resistance to my suggestion, he eventually agreed. Dubbed *Mr Snayl's Wild Ride,* it began as a chronicle of his search for a life that mattered. Over time it morphed into a platform for him to talk about issues of importance to people on the autism spectrum in a way that could be understood by the general public.

It was an uphill climb. Coming up with topics, writing the scripts, shooting, editing, and promoting each episode demanded all he had. Building an audience proved to be a challenge, but there were people who responded, for whom it made a difference. It was a modest start, but at the time, it was something that was his. Who knew where it might take him.

*

Working with my creativity clients hammered home that I needed to get back to work making my own art. I just didn't know what I wanted to make next. I discovered this amazing book, entitled *Draw It with Your Eyes Closed: The Art of the Art Assignment.* The book contained a series of graduate-level art assignments—some impossible, some inspiring, almost all fascinating. I used tabs to mark passages of note. In this thin little book of only 128 pages, I had two tabs sticking out the bottom, three out the sides, and eleven sticking out the top.

Reading it, I had to face the truth. I had pursued photography because I believed I could never draw or paint. This wasn't a new insight. I'd said it out loud many times before, but now I needed to do something about it. I needed to explore creativity in a raw, unfettered way. I needed to start over and see where it would lead.

My explorations with that book and another, *Drawing Projects: An Exploration of the Language of Drawing* by Mick Maslen and Jack Southern, got me over the initial hump of my drawing terrors and on to thinking about what my next artworks might look like.

*   *   *

Finally, Brother Teasdale's seed had sprouted. My work life and personal life were coming together.

When I recalled my experience at the SoulCollage® facilitator training, it now had an added layer of meaning. The facilitator's training was three days long. At the time, I arrogantly thought that from my counseling training, reading the book, and listening to the CDs, I already knew enough to be a facilitator. Regardless, I was excited to experience the process with my newly discovered community.

When I arrived, there was a circle of thirteen chairs, for twelve participants and the instructor. Somehow that seemed perfect and oddly humorous to me, like the twelve disciples. Except, of course, these were all women.

As a way of introducing ourselves, the trainer, Audrey, asked us to choose the card from our deck that brought us to the training. I thought about all I had done since first hearing of SoulCollage® what was then a mere ten days prior. And I thought about what I had accomplished to arrive at the training: an intensive SoulCollage® education, and I had created the 31 cards that began my personal deck.

I chose to share my Mission Control card. The most prominent image on this card was a young business woman. She was surrounded by scores of engineers in short-sleeved dress shirts, like from a 1950's NASA control center. The back wall was covered in sticky notes, and a rocket soared over all of their heads as if it were about to fly right off of the card.

Though I had arrived prepared to throw off the shackles of being a spiritual refugee and ready to celebrate the bond I felt with these women, I suddenly felt vulnerable and exposed—shy, even. I thought back to my first two cards and wondered how many people initially made cards that represented their core psychological issues.

Over the course of the training, I learned much and gained many valuable insights. In the final session, I did a consultation with three cards. I was able to see just how far I'd come.

> *I am the one whose life was decimated*
> *I am the one whose life is reconstructed*

And it has become just that: a life, reconstructed. Put together from scattered fragments of pain and loss, carefully collected, carried all through those bleak years leading away from the ICU, and finally gathered together, reassembled, first this way and then that, through trial and error, into a slowly-emerging patchwork of interlocking pieces.

First a body... then a life.

These interlocking pieces become an image made from broken fragments, like a stained glass window, an image of my self and my world shining with color and light.

> *I am the one whose life will never be the same.*

...but whose new life has meaning.

I see now, how desperately my spirit wanted to create. How those fairy wings and my niece Olivia's innocent, passionate belief—they woke something in me. A life force, decimated by torture and a fatigue I could barely climb out of, rekindled.

Finding a spiritual practice gave me the center, the courage, and the resonance with my own truth to make what became the evolutionary steps of my new life: from gallery owner to artist, from therapist to creativity coach, from the one who wrestled throughout her life with not being heard to the one who wrote this book, telling her story.

I am the one who survived.

...and even more beautiful than that:

I am the one who is finally living.

How This Book Came to Be

(contains spoilers)

Wendy introduced the concept to Michael, Devon and I, that men and women like to hear stories differently. Men want to know the end of the story first. Then, they are willing or able to tolerate hearing how one got there. In contrast, women like to hear the story from the beginning, the long evolution of how things happen. What follows is most definitely the "Girl's Version," as it were, of How This Book Came to Be.

My initial reason for writing this was to speak out about my ordeal in the ICU. I wanted people, especially the medical community, to know how much trauma I experienced. I hoped to provoke a larger discussion about ICU practices and procedures and the kind of support a person might need to help them process any trauma after a stay in the ICU.

Additionally, I had no avenue for restitution or closure regarding the mental and emotional cost of what I went through. The way malpractice law works, our only grounds for a case were the loss of my abdominal wall, of ability to earn income, things along those lines—not for any so-called "intangibles." Not to say that the loss of various physical capabilities hasn't impacted my life dramatically, but compared to the psychological pounding I took, there's no comparison. Left with little recourse, I was driven to put the story on paper.

Unfortunately, at that point in my life, my writing ability was pretty poor. This isn't humility talking. I never learned the skills, and it doesn't come naturally to me. My strength is as a visual artist. I can create visually or art direct for days on end and never tire of the experience. Any time I had important correspondence to send, I would have Michael review and edit it first, so I wouldn't look like a complete idiot. Writing and I are the family members that have learned to get along.

When I began writing down the delusions, I knew I would have to hire an editor to help give shape to these initial forays. My first editor was Jan Allegretti. She was a tender guide. Jan responded to my early drafts and gently helped me clarify my jumbled, misshapen sentences. With her guidance I began weaving the hallucination vignettes together with my memory of what happened in the ICU.

I continued to plug along. Over time, my collection of vignettes grew, and soon began to resemble a memoir. Much of my trouble with writing stems from the fact that I am an extrovert and creating a memoir is solitary. In the hope of combating my isolation, I joined a writer's group in 2004. Though it wasn't to my taste, I eventually formed my own group with two other former members: Deborah Steinkopf and Jim Picard.

I introduced them to a modified version of Proprioceptive Writing,* a journaling technique I had learned in grad school. We did this at the start of each of our meetings, then we would each read whatever we had worked on during the week and offer each other loose feedback. Each of us was developing his or her own work, so it was a perfect fit at the time, and I am grateful to Deborah and Jim for helping bridge that very difficult gap.

In autumn of 2005, I was granted a three-week residency at the Ragdale Foundation. It was an incredible gift. The mojo from the other writers (and two visual artists), all focusing in other rooms right there at the same time, felt like a community. We convened for dinner and discussed the day's efforts and other musings. I was amazed at how overheard bits of random conversation could inspire solutions to whatever writing problem I was working on that day.

It was there I was finally able to work on the three most technically challenging delusion vignettes: the one in the Worthington sweet shop, the Gore/Bush election, and the one on the island in the Pacific with the combination air traffic/radio show.

A residency is such a precious thing. One leaves their life behind, packs up their things and goes away to work. Ragdale was so beautiful, with both sculpted and wild grounds to walk in, and an amazing chef made dinner for us every evening. The mix of wonderment from the meadow, the energy of the people, and my magical room—with its little round window and the door at the foot of my bed leading up to a cupola—gave me both a spaciousness and a focus I couldn't get in my daily life.

It was at Ragdale when I figured out a technique which became critical for getting unstuck during my creative process. At first I used it while writing, but eventually came to use it with any creative endeavor. The solution was simply

---

* A self-guided writing practice. Trichter Metcalf, L., & Simon, T. (2002). *Writing the Mind Alive: The Proprioceptive Method for Finding Your Authentic Voice*. New York, NY: Ballantine Books.

to dance. This helped me break through creative blocks, and I learned it could be used as a general problem-solving technique to get me out of my head and free my body. I definitely attribute discovery of this important technique to the Ragdale magic.

Later I returned to Ragdale to attend a StoryStudio Chicago workshop hosted there. Once again, I luxuriated in the Ragdale culture and the mojo of its buildings and grounds, this time coupled with the guidance of one of StoryStudio's writing instructors. This was when my voice as a writer became clear to me.

By spring 2006, I figured I had finished the book. At the time, the book comprised the ICU experience and a bit about moving to Canada—what now makes up chapters six and seven. Though I had been out of touch with Jan Allegretti for a couple years, we reconnected and I asked her to reassess this new version. Fortunately, she agreed. What she had described as "minor adjustments" sounded to me like major changes and an overwhelming amount of work. I wanted to be done with the project, so after I got off the phone with Jan, I called it quits. I was so sick of all the "efforting"—sick of writing. I wanted to move on to other creative endeavors, something more in line with my interests and experience. Something visual, perhaps. Despite how I reacted to her review at the time, her support and encouragement of me as a writer, and her care in particular to my development of the ICU content was crucial. While many said I had a story worth telling, Jan assured me what I wrote was worth *reading*, for which I can never thank her enough.

When Devon and I returned from the scooter tour in 2010, I didn't immediately hop back into working on the book. We experimented with a number of concepts that might make use of the footage we'd spent so much time, money and effort to collect (at one point, Elizabeth and I were hard at work on a concept for a potential television series). None of those panned out. Once I realized I had an ending for the book, I had to reacquaint myself with what I had written all over again before I integrated my journey back to life. The whole process took several months.

When that task was finally completed, I needed an objective assessment of this new version. I asked Devon, a fiction and screenplay writer, to take a look at it. He thought I had something, but believed the story needed to start before the ICU, so the reader would have some idea why I was there. I had the idea to use Kelli's emails as a way to introduce the reader to Michael and me and the series of events that put me in the ICU.

He was also concerned readers wouldn't be able to follow what was happening once I was in the ICU. In the draft he read, that section was only narrated via my delusions and conversations I'd overheard. It was his idea to include the medical records as a way of showing the reader what was happening to me without completely breaking the established narrative viewpoint. Devon always sees story structure with a very keen eye, so I've learned to trust him. I'm incredibly thankful to Devon for his insight and suggestions, because without them the book wouldn't have its current form.

To execute his brilliant idea, I had to go through about eight feet of disorganized medical records to determine which would be relevant to the story. My friend Jamie Murphy, a massage therapist and nurse, spent three weeks with me going through every single paper record (my time in the hospital was before the switch to computerized records). We went over the data again and again and again, because I was convinced the integrity of the memoir depended on us not screwing this up. I don't know how we could have accomplished this part of the process without her help.

Michael and I went over the notes with painstaking care. He matched up all the brand names for drugs with their generic names, as some had been used interchangeably in the records. He created a kind of guidebook for us to use—a glossary of terms, initialisms, and so on. We also abridged the surgical reports, careful to avoid inadvertently changing information. Next, I tracked down the emails Wendy sent out. We owe a debt of gratitude to the archives of Michael Madill and Jenn Meyer, because thanks to them, we were able to assemble a complete set. The final task was mine alone: to interlace the timelines of the medical data, delusions and Wendy's emails into a single, cohesive narrative someone else could follow.

Once all of this new material was assembled and sequenced, I asked Michael to do what I thought would be a quick technical edit of the book for continuity, spelling, and so on. I believe Michael is a brilliant writer, and with his eye for minute detail, I figured it would be a fairly simple task. He was shocked when he read the passages containing the delusions—not because he hadn't heard the stories before, but precisely because he *had*. He remarked that the written versions of those scenes contained little other than dialogue, and none of the lush, precise, descriptive detail from when I had told him the stories before. (See? I told you I wasn't very good at this.)

Thus, we began a new stage. Michael would ask me questions about the content and I would answer. He would transcribe what I said verbatim, then go back and fix the structure, grammar, and style, and substitute or add words when necessary to clarify meaning. Then he would have me check it out to make sure the prose rang true to me. We did this for about four hours at a stretch, line by line, for several days. Once I caught on to his "formula" for fleshing out a scene, around the time he developed a sense of my "voice," we moved on to the next stage. We sat typing, side by side, each at our own laptop. I added detail where it was lacking and Michael shaped and restructured my language to better say what I intended. During this process, he was truly teaching me how to write. In my view, that was when this went from being *my* book to *our* book.

Once we were finished, I knew two people I could trust to appraise the manuscript and say whether or not it held up as a book. One of them was Michael Madill, and the other was a colleague of mine from graduate school, Janet Bridgland. Since I was pretty sure that my audience would largely be women about my age, I chose Janet to make the final assessment. She gave it a pretty strong affirmation in general, but had some concerns about the content toward the end.

While we were printing the manuscript to send to Janet, we realized we had an even bigger problem. We had created a beast. It was 750 pages! Since the standard length for memoirs is between 300 and 350 pages, this meant we had to cut the book in half. This was in 2012, and I still planned to contact an agent/publisher. That meant adhering to accepted "rules" as best we could in hope of securing a publishing deal. At that same time, though, I was completing my training to become a certified coach. I couldn't do both, so I had to temporarily set the book aside… for another 18 months.

When I picked it back up again, Michael wasn't available to oversee the trimming required to cut the book in half. I invited Elizabeth Cross to the project. She did a test run of one chapter and though the changes she made could be said to be small, they were profound. Elizabeth is a close friend, but first and foremost, a poet. We had worked together previously on various word-based projects, and she served as the Guardian of the Narrative for both *Tala & Louison* and *We Vow*. As Michael saw it, she was just continuing in that role. Working creatively with Elizabeth had always been as much a spiritual experience as it was creative.

We were in a challenging situation. This surgical work wasn't as simple as removing a single chapter or cutting out every other sentence. The majority of the book had to be unraveled and woven back together. Taking out content required tidying up the story threads and holes left behind, which was effectively putting content back in. Each excision was the proverbial two steps forward, one step backward. Periodically we would encounter structural problems and Elizabeth would request Devon's input. He always had a solution—eventually—which Liz described as the cavalry riding in. While his recommendations were sound and brought relief, they took considerable effort to enact.

Things were moving along well and the end was in sight when we hit another snag. Elizabeth had to bow out rather suddenly to attend to some personal matters. Picking up where Liz and I had stopped, mid-reravel, would be no easy task.

Once the final two chapters were reconfigured, I still needed to cut another 150 pages. I did the rewrites and Michael had to do a final editing pass while he did the typesetting.

We were nearing the end. Though we took extreme care with the medical records, so many hands had touched the book, I wanted to ensure nothing had happened along the way. I hired a medical consultant, Danielle Friedman, as a proofer. She was thorough and caught some typos, but most importantly she intercepted a drug substitution error. This was a critical aspect of the story, so I couldn't be more grateful she caught that! She also wrote several passages to help us "translate" the more complex medical language in notes and reports, so readers wouldn't miss important points that might otherwise have been buried.

Once the chopping, reweaving and rewriting were finished, we needed one last set of fresh eyes to ensure we hadn't lost cohesion or consistency. We reached out to dear friend Amanda Leat. I've always said she is THE single most creative person I have ever known. If you gave her a bag of garbage she could transform it into the most glittering and magical work of art you ever laid eyes upon. In this instance I didn't need magic, just clarity. She agreed and brought the exact amount of conceptual and targeted detail needed that allowed us to put the book forth with confidence.

No book is truly complete without a cover, of course. The cover is still the most important deciding factor for more than half of book buyers. I wanted an illustrator who could convey both the dark and light parts of the story, and was thrilled to find exactly that in Alan Pollack. He began his career as a sci-fi/fantasy illustrator and later moved on to more surreal and conceptual imagery. I absolutely love and am honored by what Alan brought to the story.

Because in the end I decided to self-publish, I looked to Monica Crowe. I had worked with her on my coaching website (*Soulnavigation.org*) and other public relations projects, but for this her support would be critical. Without her contributions there wasn't a chance the book would reach anyone who didn't already know me. I am thankful for her tireless dedication to seeing my book through to completion and beyond.

Jim Picard was the single most significant supporter of this book, second only to Michael. Not only did he advocate loudest and most persistently for its completion, he took on a huge and significant support role the entire time I wrote the second half of the book. He was my writing cyber-studio-mate. He held my fears, my frustrations and all my rants about how much I truly hated writing, and he held my hand during every twist and turn this book has taken. He did it through the ether, all via email and not in real time. Quite honestly there is no way in hell I, being the person that I am, could have borne the weight of the loneliness it took to bring this book into existence without him.

We created a routine: before I would begin to write for the day, I composed an email and dumped all of my concerns and anxieties and issues about whatever the book needed that day, and sent it to him. Sometimes I followed that with my hybrid version of the proprioceptive writing before I got to work, or sometimes I just dove in without any other spiritual support.

Often he would write and send something supportive, which I wouldn't see until the end of the day. Not only were his affirmations to me lovely, inspirational writing by themselves, but often the words were exactly what I needed to hear. Whatever he wrote fit perfectly with what I went through that day, as if he composed the message in response to my struggle. Whenever I took a break or was in some wild, inverted tailspin, Jim's emails were waiting for me. His words were there to affirm a solid landing—he was in the wings, truly on my wing, my book-conjuring wingman.

It's notable that Jim has had, for many years now, considerable health issues of his own. The missives he wrote to me were often from bed. Much like the very early days of my own recovery, the energy he gathered to write a response to one of my emails might be all he had for that day, making his support for me that much more valuable and sacred.

I am also grateful to the early supporters when I had only written a few delusions and a couple of ICU scenes… barely a notion of what the book would become. Some of these brave individuals invited me to do readings in their homes. The first were Amanda Kaleta-Kott and Jeff Kott. It was at their home I realized there truly was an audience for the story beyond my family and close friends, those personally invested in what happened to me. The second was Mary Longe, in whose home I met the women of Marsha Foley's Excellent Book Group. They were extremely enthusiastic and it seemed as if they were not just trying to be nice, but responding to the content, which was encouraging. When the book was more fully formed, Denise Tackett and her writer's group at the Box Factory in St. Joseph welcomed me for another reading.

In 2011 I had the opportunity to read at CooperRiis Healing Community, a residential community for people whose lives have been impeded by mental or emotional illness. I can't say enough about my experience there. What they do at that facility is absolutely remarkable, and the conversations I had with both staff and residents were nothing less than mind blowing.

While writing chapters nine and ten I received consult from a number of Nerdfighters and a couple librarians. My biggest thank-you goes to Dan McCurdy, who verified my Bible history, but these additional Nerdfighters all pitched in with theological data and/or insights when I was writing chapter nine: Joseph Taber, Travis Darling, Karen Mares, Brenda Jacobson Noland, Jim Kline, Nic Holas Martinez, Maggie Vosburg Mansueto, Anthony Mansueto, Megan Bennett, and Claudia Schaffner, Yih Jian Sung, Catherine J. Hardin, Moriah Phares, Clark Shelley Callahan, librarian Eric Blum at the Lincoln Township Library, and Melody McMahon at Catholic Theological Seminary Chicago Library assisted with information about Brother Teasdale.

Even though I have worked hard to make this list inclusive, I am certain I have forgotten someone; this was not intentional, but an oversight. Many people helped bring this book into being and it took fourteen years to make it happen. My intention with this longer acknowledgement is to show that it really can take a village to create a thing like a book (at least in my case), or a play, or an album… so I want to encourage anyone who has even the slightest inkling toward any creative endeavor, but feels daunted—to just *begin*. You don't have to go it alone. You don't know whose help you might need until you hit various problems, and when you hit those problems, you can go ferreting about for the kind of support you need.

I have immeasurable gratitude for all of these people. Thank you for your gifts of time and love and support and energy and effort, all of which have allowed me, in turn, to give this book to the world.